JUN   2005

UNTOLD GOLD

UNTOLD GOLD

THE STORIES BEHIND ELVIS'S #1 HITS

ACE COLLINS

CHICAGO
REVIEW
PRESS

An A Cappella Book

Library of Congress Cataloging-in-Publication Data

Collins, Ace.

  Untold gold : the stories behind Elvis Presley's #1 hits / Ace Collins.—1st ed.

    p. cm.

  Includes index.

  ISBN 1-55652-565-6

  1. Presley, Elvis, 1935-1977—Criticism and interpretation. 2. Rock

music—History and criticism. I. Title.

  ML420.P96C64 2005

  782.42166'092—dc22   2004030468

Cover and interior design: Scott Rattray, Rattray Design

Cover image: © 1956 Bettmann/Corbis

Page iv image: Robert W. Kelley, © Time & Life Pictures

First edition

Published by Chicago Review Press, Incorporated

814 North Franklin Street

Chicago, Illinois 60610

ISBN 1-55652-565-6

Printed in the United States of America

5 4 3 2 1

To my Aunt Joy Wood, who first introduced me to
Elvis's music as she babysat me on Shell's Hill
in Salem, Arkansas

Contents

Acknowledgments

Without the help of these individuals, this book would not have been completed:

Heather Axton
Mark Axton
Ken Beck
Kathy Collins
Mac Davis
Mark James
Rheda Jones
Baker Knight
Jerry Leiber
Dennis Linde
Louise Mandrell
Layng Martine, Jr.
Madeleine Morel
Randy Poe
Don Reid
Abby Schroeder
Mike Stoller
Judi Turner
George David Weiss

Introduction

From 1956 until his death in 1977, Elvis Presley lived in a surreal world. The isolation in which he spent his days and nights was due in part to his incredible fame, but the cocoon that was Elvis's life was reinforced by the management style of Colonel Tom Parker. Parker controlled every facet of Elvis's career (and took 50 percent of every dollar he earned), and very early in Elvis's career he pushed out of the real world—and kept the real world away from the singer. The private Elvis, the one the public never saw, had little more freedom than an animal in a game preserve. He was safe, but he was hardly able to roam free. Elvis Presley was, in the words of one of his last #1 hits, "caught in a trap," and he could not get out.

For a brief time in the mid-1950s, at the very beginning of his career, Elvis seemed to live a fairly normal life (by celebrity standards). He performed on television, was interviewed by the press, ate meals in restaurants, and even mingled with fans. Although Parker, and Elvis's own fame, soon put an end to those aspects of his life, Hollywood offered the entertainer a chance to grow, develop, and stretch his creative wings in motion pictures. Yet by 1961, the Colonel had decided to end Elvis's dreams of becoming a fine actor. Instead, the manager opted to showcase the singer in films that were nothing more than a little scenery, a bit of dialogue, and a parade of girls, all there just to spotlight a dozen largely forgettable songs. At that point, the only creative outlet left open to Elvis was his music—and ultimately, it would be only in the studio that Elvis's passions, interests, directions, dreams, and real talent would be showcased.

Even as far back as 1954, at Sun Records, Elvis was his own producer. In the studio there were no restraints; Elvis was free to express himself as he chose. Free to be who he wanted to be. It was Elvis who decided on the vocal inflections, the style, and the drive of each song. He listened to the demo recordings, in most cases he picked the material, he put his own spin on each session, and it was his energy that brought each recording to life.

Over the course of twenty-three years, Elvis Presley recorded material that had been created by some of the greatest rock, pop, R&B, and country songwriters in the world, almost all of whom marveled at the singer's ability to bring their work to life. This book reveals the thirty-four stories of thirty-four of Elvis's #1 hits. The men who wrote these songs were inspired by a host of different images and situations.

This book is truly a labor of love. The effort that was required to gather the information found in these pages was at times consuming, but incredibly rewarding. The hundreds of hours spent interviewing, researching, digging for new sources, trying to track down writers, thumbing through dusty books, and looking at thousands of pages of old charts—not to mention listening to the recordings—included many periods of great joy.

The songwriters (some of whom were in poor health at the time of their interviews) who generously gave their time to tell their stories brought great insights into the world of Elvis Presley. I hope that some of those insights found their way onto these pages. I cannot thank these men and women enough for not only sharing their tales of these songs, but, in many cases, sending the original demos of their records to help enhance my knowledge of each song's roots as well.

When it comes to charts, *Billboard* magazine is the bible of the music world. In one form or another, the magazine has been ranking hits since 1890. In the 1940s *Billboard* split the pop country listings into two separate charts. Later, adult contemporary, R&B, gospel, and rock would join the original playlist. All of these charts were used in compiling the #1 hits featured in this book. But *Billboard* was not the only source of chart information. *Cash Box* magazine charts were employed by many radio stations, as were the lists of *Radio and Records*. In Britain the BBC had its own pop charts. All of these lists, as well as some random jukebox play charts, were consulted during various stages of this project.

These charts, which track the sales of songs and the frequency with which they are played on the radio, provide the means of determining which song is #1 in the chart's category each week. In the music world, chart position defines success. With more than a billion records sold, Elvis is the most successful artist in the history of music. No other artist has even come close.

It would take a dictionary-sized book to cover all of Elvis Presley's #1 songs. More than eighty of Elvis's singles have hit the top of charts in one corner of the globe or another. As a result, some choices and cuts had to be made for these pages. This book includes all the *Billboard* #1 hits in the genres of pop, R&B, country, easy-listening, and Christmas Singles. The songs that hit #1 in the United Kingdom and that came very close to hitting #1 in the United States are here as well. A *Cash Box* magazine #1 hit, "Burning Love," only made it to #2 on the *Billboard* charts, but is included because it remains one of the best of the post-1950s rock 'n' roll songs. When they merit inclusion, important extended-play chart toppers are included, as are special-merit inspirational singles. The stories behind the songs that defined Elvis in America and shaped his worldwide appeal can all be found in this book.

While the story of why each #1 tune was written is fascinating in its own right, there is more to this book than just those tidbits. Elvis was the face of rock 'n' roll. His voice was the most important and influential musical voice of the last century. Carefree moments filled with stuffed animals and young love, times of worship and prayer, and days of lost loves and broken hearts—as well as periods in which the world was caught up in war, distrust, and social upheaval—can all be found in the Elvis Presley jukebox. Elvis sang about these elements of life, and he probably did it better than anyone ever has. Therefore, each song in this book reflects a moment in time, a piece of the fabric of history, a commentary on where the world was and what was making it tick. For this reason, these songs are as much a glimpse into America's biography as they are Elvis's autobiography.

I think these stories will help us understand why Elvis Presley's songs still mean so much to so many. The tales of some of the greatest songs ever recorded, from Elvis's first #1 hit, "I Forgot to Remember to Forget," to his last (to date), "A Little Less Conversation," frame a new image of Elvis Presley. It is in these songs that the instincts, energy, direction, and evolution of the world's most renowned personality are most pointedly revealed.

UNTOLD GOLD

I FORGOT TO REMEMBER TO FORGET

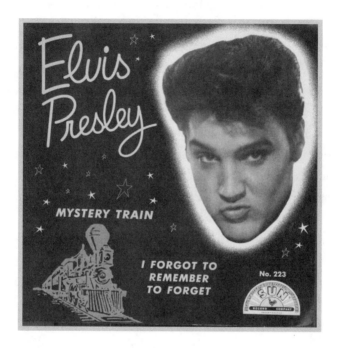

Elvis Presley probably never would have made much of an impact in the world of music if his parents had not moved from Tupelo, Mississippi, to Memphis. The river port city was a musical melting pot teeming with men and women singing the blues, country, and gospel music. In bars and churches, on street corners and in parks, at fairs and even political rallies, music was literally everywhere. It is no exaggeration to say that during the late 1940s and early 1950s, Memphis was like no other place in

America—a nonconformist center of musical creativity where originality was encouraged, treasured, and embraced.

One of those who fostered this spirit was Sam Phillips. A high school dropout, in 1942, the nineteen-year-old Alabama native found work as a disc jockey in Muscle Shoals, Alabama. He stayed there until 1946, when he moved to WREC radio station in Memphis. In the optimistic days after World War II, this white country boy became enamored of all forms of African American music. In a world defined by the lines that separated the races, Phillips mingled as comfortably in the black neighborhoods as he did on the white side of town, where he lived. Phillips was not a musician, but he sensed that the unique riffs he heard in dives and on street corners along Beale Street had the potential to gain an audience beyond Memphis. What this music needed was exposure, and he believed he was the man who could bring these inspired sounds to the world.

In 1950 Phillips opened the Memphis Recording Service at 706 Union Avenue. Within a few months he was producing records for the likes of B. B. King, Ike Turner, and Bobby "Blue" Bland. From these beginnings in R&B, Phillips opened his doors to country and gospel artists, and he created his own label, Sun Records. Though it did not appear that Sun would ever rise high enough on the entertainment horizon to make national waves, Phillips's company quickly emerged as a powerful regional recording label.

The ambitious Phillips could have made a solid, middle-class living with his business, but he wanted more. While he loved black music, he recognized that segregation would severely dampen his efforts to take it beyond the few stations and stores that dabbled in what was then called "race" music. He informed his studio manager, Marion Keisker, that what Sun needed was a "white man who sounded black." The record executive was convinced that there had to be someone out there who could bridge the racial gap. But his long hours of auditioning a host of talented singers revealed no white singer who, in Phillips's opinion, could successfully perform black music.

It was Keisker, not Phillips, who finally found such a singer. In 1954 Elvis Presley walked into the Memphis Recording offices. He was not looking for a musical career; instead, he simply wanted to make a record as a gift for his mother. Elvis's recordings of "My Happiness" and "That's When Your Heartaches Begin" would mark the beginning of a remarkable career, yet it would take a series of recordings and six singles before Elvis emerged as a viable act. Iron-ically, the song that put Sun Records on the national map and that first took the future "King of Rock 'n' Roll" to the top of the charts was a country music song. It would also be the only major Elvis Presley hit produced by the man who discovered him.

Stanley Kesler, a steel guitar player, first met Elvis in the Sun Records studio. At that time he had no idea that he would play an important role in the young singer's career, much less help initiate the explosive birth of a musical form that would dramatically alter the entire entertainment world. Yet, without Kesler, Elvis Presley might have remained a regional act, and rock 'n' roll might have become little more than an urban fad.

In 1954 Kesler was freelancing as a session steel guitar player at so many of Sam Phillips's Sun recording sessions that his mail was often delivered to the studio. During this period there didn't seem to be a country-song recording session that Kesler didn't par-ticipate in. But when Phillips shifted the studio's focus to R&B, Kesler's studio time suddenly diminished. There was rarely a need for a steel guitar in R&B sessions. Kesler's income was drying up.

Sensing he needed to adapt to survive, Kesler "evolved" into a stand-up bass player. This allowed the musician to work not only Sun's country gigs, but on its blues sessions too. Yet, even with these new gigs, Kesler realized that session work was never going to make him any real money. To enlarge his bank account, he needed to develop other talents.

"Besides switching to bass," Kesler explained, "I started writing songs. I thought that if I could write the kind of things Sam was looking for, I could really cash in on this new music Sam was recording."

For a late 1954 Elvis recording session, Kesler offered Phillips a snappy country/blues-style number that he had written with another local musician. Sam listened to "I'm Left, You're Right, She's Gone," then passed it along to Elvis to record. As it turned out, Kesler had done more than break into the songwriting business with the song; he had helped create a formula that Phillips would use to promote his newest act, and he had provided the vehicle that put Elvis on the *Billboard* charts for the very first time.

In the mid 1950s, there weren't enough blues stations across the South to generate many record sales. There were also no radio stations that played music aimed strictly at teenagers. In order to generate buzz at record outlets, Phillips needed to produce records that would be played on country music stations.

With this in mind, Phillips made sure that all of Elvis's Sun singles featured a hard-driving, rockabilly song, with a softer, more "country music" cut on the B side. In this way, the few stations that played black, or "race," music could spin the rocker, and the other tune could find a home with the stations that leaned toward Hank Snow and Eddy Arnold. Phillips continued to employ his formula of pairing an R&B song with a country tune until he sold Elvis's contract to RCA Victor.

By the middle of 1955, the "Hillbilly Cat," as Elvis was now being called, was pulling down eighteen dollars a week doing a couple of songs each Saturday night on *Louisiana Hayride*. Thanks largely to the R&B singles he recorded for Sun, Elvis was the fabled venue's top draw with teens. But when Elvis performed at small clubs and fairs, it was the older country fans who turned out to hear the music they'd caught on their rural stations. Because of Phillips's formula, two distinctive types of Elvis fans emerged—as well as two unique Elvis Presleys, neither of which was really known outside the South. In his first year with Elvis, Phillips didn't produce a single record that hit any major playlists. That all changed when Kesler's new song, "I'm Left, You're Right, She's Gone," which was coupled with "Baby, Let's Play House," won over country radio stations. The Sun single peaked at #3 on the *Billboard* charts.

The label needed a strong follow-up to this Top 10 hit, and Phillips again turned to Kesler. But there was a problem: the session player hadn't written anything new. With Elvis due to record again in midsummer, the pressure was on and the clock was ticking. Kesler found himself unable to write anything that had the "feel" that Phillips wanted. He'd all but given up trying to create a new song for Elvis—then the songwriter walked out of the studio and onto Union Avenue, where he overheard a conversation that would change the world of music forever.

"One man was complaining to the other about the other man failing to make an appointment," Kesler laughs. "The second man apologized by saying, 'I just forgot to remember.'

"At that time I was on the kick of catchy titles. When I began to think about that phrase, it just expanded into 'I forgot to remember to forget her.' From there I just started working on it, and it all fell together."

Kesler needed to make a demo tape to present the new composition to Phillips and Elvis. He sought out a local singer, Charlie Feathers, to help him turn his song into a polished product. A few days later, Phillips heard the song and approved it. Elvis liked it, too.

Though Phillips had originally planned to market Elvis as a white blues singer, the success of Elvis's Top 10 country hit persuaded Phillips to consider making Elvis "the next Hank Williams" instead. It made sense: the late country music legend had scored with teens as well as with traditional country audiences, and Elvis was already doing the same.

To build on his recent success on the country charts, as well as on his popularity in the *Louisiana Hayride*, Elvis began to tour with Hank Snow. As strange as this union now seems, at the time Elvis seemed to fit pretty well with the likes of Johnny Horton, Marty Robbins, and other young Nashville-based stars.

Elvis had always loved country music, and he would continue to sing country songs for the rest of his life. He would probably have been very happy dressing in rhinestones and working the Grand Ole Opry, and it's likely that in the 1950s he would have been perfectly satisfied to follow in the footsteps of the three great Hanks—Snow, Williams, and Thompson. For these reasons, Kesler's newest song seemed perfect for the hot new rural star. What neither Elvis nor the writer realized, however, was that "I Forgot to Remember to Forget" was also one of the best commercial songs written in this era.

In modern terms, "I Forgot to Remember to Forget" is a formula song. It has a very catchy lead line that allows folks to easily remember the song's name—making radio station call-in requests a breeze. In terms of vocals, it's not not a demanding tune—almost anyone can sing—or sing along to—it. In addition, the lyrics that anchor the chorus can be remembered after hearing the song only a few times. Finally, and maybe most important, the tune is infectious.

Elvis recorded Kesler's song in July 1955. In the sparse confines of Sun's small studio, Elvis, guitarist Scotty Moore, and stand-up bass player Bill Black put together an arrangement that seemed like a cross between a Marty Robbins rockabilly number and Hank Williams's classic rendition of "Lovesick Blues." While, in terms of lyrics, "I Forgot to Remember to Forget" is truly a country song, with its weepy tale of broken hearts and lost love, thanks to Elvis's style of attack on the chorus, his voice playfully echoing off a stairwell located at the back of the studio, the final cut had all the earmarks of a up-tempo pop/blues standard. It was a unique sound and style that no one had ever heard. In truth, Elvis had just invented it.

In August 1955, "I Forgot to Remember to Forget" was released as the country side of Elvis's sixth Sun single. The flip side was a blues standard that had been recorded in February of that year. Today everyone remembers that blues number—"Mystery Train." In the 1970s, Elvis opened hundreds of concerts with this tune. But "Mystery Train" never became a big hit. In fact, the main reason it garnered radio time was because of the popularity of Kesler's country composition.

"I Forgot to Remember to Forget" landed on the country charts in early September 1955, where it steadily climbed throughout the fall and winter. Just as the song was about to ascend to the top of the charts, things dramatically changed for Elvis, Sam Phillips, and Sun Studio.

With his second major hit record, Elvis had become a hot property. First Atlantic Records, then RCA Victor visited Sun and offered to purchase the singer's contract. Steve Sholes and RCA Victor won the bidding contest with an offer of thirty-five thousand dollars. The deal was closed just before Elvis knocked the Webb Pierce–Red Sovine duet "Why, Baby, Why" off the top of the country music charts. As he moved to his new label, Elvis's "I Forgot to Remember to Forget" held the top spot for two weeks ("Mystery Train" rose no higher than #11, and it stayed on playlists for only a month). "I Forgot to Remember to Forget" was knocked out of the #1 spot by Elvis's first RCA Victor release, "Heartbreak Hotel," a song that would rule the country chart for seventeen weeks. The Hillbilly Cat would reign as the new country king for twenty-two straight weeks before being replaced by another Sun act—Carl Perkins and his "Blue Suede Shoes."

Though rarely played today on most radio stations, "I Forgot to Remember to Forget" assured the world that no one would ever forget Elvis. This song's first five weeks at #1 marked the beginning of a slew of #1 songs from a man who would become the greatest hit maker of all time. Yet it also marked the end of the singer's most uncomplicated and, perhaps, purest work as an artist. While RCA Victor's session musicians, equipment, and production facilities were far better than those of Sun Studio, the youthful and simple enthusiasm that drove Elvis's six singles at the bare-bones Memphis recording facility would never again be captured. The innocent sounds of the raw Elvis reached their peak on his first and only #1 record for Sun.

It is all but forgotten now that not only did Elvis score his first #1 record on the country charts, but also that *all* of Elvis's early rock 'n' roll releases made the country playlists. In 1956 alone, Elvis ruled the top of the country charts for thirty-four weeks. As he had done with "I Forgot to Remember to Forget," it was usually his own new single that knocked his existing #1 hit off the top of the charts.

Within the space of a few short months, Elvis had left Sun, joined RCA Victor, landed on national television, and signed a movie contract. Nevertheless, he never forgot Memphis—or Stan Kesler. Over the course of his career the King would cut "Playing for Keeps," "Thrill of Your Love," and "If I'm a Fool (for Loving You)," all songs penned by the old Sun Studio steel guitar and bass player.

"I think the thing that surprises me most," Kesler explains, considering Elvis's unfathomable career, "[is that] of all the hit songs he had and of all the records he cut, 'I Forgot to Remember to Forget' stayed on the charts longer than any other."

Elvis's cut of Kesler's song rode the *Billboard* country playlists for an incredible thirty-nine weeks. The Elvis tune that had the next longest ride would be "Hound Dog," at twenty-eight weeks on the Top 100 chart, followed closely by the song that would grace the flip side of that hit: "Don't Be Cruel," which stayed on the chart for twenty-seven weeks. While those latter cuts may have helped to immortalize Elvis as the "King of Rock 'n' Roll," it was "I Forgot to Remember to Forget" that set in motion a career that would land Elvis in not only the Rock and Roll Hall of Fame, but the Country Music Hall of Fame, as well. Thanks to "I Forgot to Remember" no one would ever forget Elvis Presley.

HEARTBREAK HOTEL

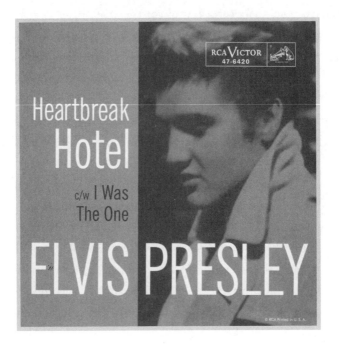

Heartbreak
Hotel
c/w I Was
The One
ELVIS PRESLEY

RCA VICTOR
47-6420

here is really not just one story behind "Heartbreak Hotel"; in truth, there are two. Each of the songwriters, Tommy Durden and Mae Axton, has his own version of how the song was written and who was the principle force behind the composition. Which story is right? We may never know, but what cannot be debated is what the song meant to the career of a then–*Louisiana Hayride* star and regional personality named Elvis Presley. It put him on the show business map—and it altered pop culture forever.

Before there could be a "Heartbreak Hotel," two things had to fall into place. The first was that an almost directionless Elvis had to be brought under the wing of a solid manager. Country music star Hank Snow wanted to promote Elvis. The singer had seen the way crowds responded to Elvis, and Snow fully understood that there was money to be made with the kid. Imagine the different direction the Hillbilly Cat's career might have taken if Hank had called the shots. Yet Snow lost out to Colonel Tom Parker, a fast-talking Dutch import whose legal status in the United States was questionable at best. It would be Parker, a former carnival hawker and manager of Eddy Arnold, who would transform Elvis from a regional rockabilly star into a national sensation. This strange professional marriage would also prove to be one of the most lopsided in entertainment history. At a time when most managers claimed between 10 and 15 percent of the take, Parker pulled down half of everything Elvis made from day one of their partnership.

With Parker in control, however, things began to happen. The manager realized that Sun Records, while rich in talent with the likes of Johnny Cash, Carl Perkins, Roy Orbison, and Jerry Lee Lewis in the stable, was cash poor. Seeing an opportunity to move his act to a bigger company with greater potential, Parker convinced several large record labels of the marketing potential of his "Hillbilly Cat," thus beginning a bidding war for the hot country-music talent. RCA Victor won with a bid of, by most accounts, as little as $35,000, plus a $5,000 bonus to Elvis and the Colonel. In the process, the company also purchased the rights to the master tapes of all the recordings Elvis had completed his original label's Memphis studio. With management in place and with a major label signed on, all Elvis needed now was a nationwide hit song.

RCA Victor was one of the largest players not just in country music, but in the entertainment world. Immediately upon signing Elvis, they put out the word in Nashville, New York, and Los

Angeles that they had a new male talent, and that they needed
original compositions that would appeal to young, postwar audiences that were listening to radio in ever-growing numbers. Using
the Elvis records that Sun had already released as guides, some of
the most established writers in the country began to pen possible
Elvis cuts. But, ultimately, it was not a professional songwriting
team that delivered the first mainstream #1 record for Elvis.
Instead, it was two almost unknowns, working with a new publishing house, who would complete the song that would start a
music revolution.

Mae Axton was a Florida schoolteacher who dabbled as both
a music promoter and an advertising copywriter in her spare time.
She had seen Elvis perform in a concert that also featured Hank
Snow and the Carter Sisters and she had sensed his raw talent and
his magnetic stage presence. Probably because of her time spent in
high school classrooms, she also knew that there was a new musical genre ready to explode in the 1950s and that kids were looking for a leader for this movement. The young people of the era
didn't want a Frank Sinatra or a Dean Martin; they yearned for
someone new and hip.

When her friend Tom Parker obtained the rights to manage
Elvis, Mae truly believed that the singer was going to quickly go
from a fifty-dollar-a-night regional act to a national sensation.
Axton envisioned Elvis being the musical icon that she believed
would lead the youth revolution. When RCA Victor signed Elvis,
Mae sensed that she could be a part of this revolution, too. What
she needed was the right song.

As a promoter, Axton knew all of the regional country acts, as
well as many of the national artists. She was familiar with folks
who were pretenders and with those who had real talent. One of

the locals, Tommy Durden, was not only a pretty fair singer, but he was a solid songwriter, too. It was probably no accident that, at about the time Elvis began to make some waves, Durden was invited over to the Axtons' for a brainstorming session.

Durden and Axton got together in 1955 at Axton's home. Axton would later write in her book, *Country Singers As I Know 'Em,* "Tommy came over and showed me a story in the paper about a man who had rid himself of his identity, written a one-line sentence, 'I walk a lonely street,' and then killed himself." Axton said that the idea for the song originated from that line. More than five decades later, what can be established as fact is that Durden had been so haunted by the newspaper story of the nameless man who had jumped out of a hotel window to his death that he had started to pen a song about the tragedy. It is at this point—with the song in a raw form—that the story behind Elvis's first pop hit takes two different roads.

In later years Durden claimed that he had already written "Heartbreak Hotel" when he came to visit Mae Axton, and that he had even performed it at his local shows. He told friends and family that he had brought the song and the newspaper story to Axton to help him find a major act to cut it. Axton claimed that Tommy had only written a few lines of the song, hit a creative wall, and asked her to help him finish it. Axton remembered that she had introduced the name for the hotel, "Heartbreak," thus developing the catchy title that took the song from an unfinished idea to completed product.

In retrospect, it is likely that both stories contain a great deal of the truth. Durden had probably written at least a part of the song before contacting Axton. He even might have performed what he had written in some of his shows. But without Axton's help, he probably would have never polished the idea nor gotten the song to Colonel Tom Parker. Certainly, without Axton, the song would never have never gotten to Elvis.

Ironically, the unproved Elvis was not even given the first crack at recording "Heartbreak Hotel."

Axton felt that the song was perfect for the Wilburn Brothers, an already established country music act, and she used her contacts to get "Heartbreak Hotel" into the hands of the Hardy, Arkansas, musical duo and Grand Ole Opry stars. Doyle and Teddy Wilburn heard the "Heartbreak Hotel" demo, which had been cut, not by the song's cowriter, Tommy Durden, but by a singer named Glen Reeves. The brothers were not impressed, and they passed on the offer to record what they viewed as a strange and almost morbid number. Even though the Wilburn Brothers believed that "Heartbreak Hotel" had little commercial value in country music, Axton still felt the song had mass appeal, and she continued to promote the song.

Buddy Killen, who would become one of the best-known and most influential music publishers and producers in Nashville, was, in 1955, simply a country music bass player looking for new songs for his fledgling Tree Publishing Company. Axton knew Killen, and she gave him a copy of the new song. Buddy liked "Heartbreak Hotel" enough to obtain the publishing rights to the song, in a deal that was based on little more than a handshake. Little did he realize then that Axton had brought him the "root" that would allow Tree Publishing Company to grow into a music-publishing giant.

With a demo made and a publisher for the song secured, Axton felt it was time to take the song directly to Elvis. She called the Colonel and found out that Elvis was going to be in Nashville for the annual country music disc jockey convention. Working through Parker, Axton arranged to meet with the singer in his hotel room. Elvis listened to the demo, then (allegedly) said, "Hot darn, Mae, play it again." Without hesitation, Axton put the needle back at the beginning of the record and played it again. Before she left the room, the innocent and unproved talent had learned all the words to the still-unknown song.

Axton knew, however, that Elvis's fondness for the song was not enough to ensure that it would become the singer's first RCA Victor release. In fact, if it had not been for Colonel Parker seeing a way to make some cash on the side, "Heartbreak Hotel" might not have been cut at all. The powers at RCA Victor were not impressed with the Durden/Axton cut. They didn't think it had the same feel as the songs that Elvis had scored with at Sun Records. They wanted something with a more upbeat sound than "Heartbreak Hotel," something that captured the rockabilly flavor that had excited the crowds at the *Louisiana Hayride*. But Axton knew that if the Colonel smelled cash, he would move mountains to get the money into his pocket. She used this to her advantage and set in motion a plan that would enable her and Durden to secure "Heartbreak Hotel" as Elvis's first national pop hit.

The songs that RCA Victor had brought to Elvis for recording consideration had been penned by men and women who were tied to firm publishing contracts. Most of these folks were experienced writers who had already composed hits for some of the top artists in the business. Axton and Durden were not well connected, and neither was Buddy Killen. The three badly needed a break. With Axton's business savvy pushing the way, Colonel Parker cut a deal with the trio. The writers and Killen would share their publishing rights with Elvis and his new publishing company. Since Parker owned 50 percent of both Elvis and the company, he stood to make a great deal of money from the song if "Heartbreak Hotel" was released as the first Elvis single with RCA Victor. Despite RCA Victor's lack of enthusiasm for the song, Parker insisted that the company release it as Elvis's initial record. Little did RCA Victor realize that giving in to the Colonel on "Heartbreak Hotel" would set a precedent that would assure Parker a part of the songwriters' royalties earned for "Heartbreak Hotel" for decades to come.

Elvis recorded "Heartbreak Hotel" on January 10, 1956, at RCA Studio B in Nashville. For his first session at the new label, he used his own band—Scotty Moore on guitar, Bill Black on bass, and D. J. Fontana on drums—as the musical foundation of the song. Added to the trio were Chet Atkins on lead guitar and Floyd Cramer on piano. Coming into the studio that cold winter day to sing backup vocals were gospel music performers Ben and Brock Speer and Gordon Stoker. Bob Ferris was behind the board, mixing the performances.

"Heartbreak Hotel" was cut several times, with several different musical riffs and styles. As was usually the case, the original lyrics were slightly altered in various cuts. By take number seven—the version that was ultimately released—the line "so lonely they pray to die," which had been penned by Axton and Durden, had been replaced with "so lonely they could die." Elvis recorded "Heartbreak Hotel" using neither a rockabilly nor a country style. The singer reverted back to pure blues, and it could be heard in his tone and pacing. His voice sounded mournful, his pain was obvious, and his loss could be felt in the words. The band's simple instrumentation highlighted these feelings. The recording is very much like something that would have been done at Sun Studio, with the exception of that studio's built-in echo effects. When everyone was satisfied with the playback of "Heartbreak Hotel," the group moved on to record other songs picked for the session.

Even after hearing the final cut, the executives at RCA Victor did not like the song. To their ears, it didn't sound at all like the songs that Elvis had recorded for Sun Records. There was no echo effect, the beat was all wrong, and the final product didn't seem suited for either a country or a pop playlist. As they shipped "Heartbreak Hotel" in late January, some at RCA Victor questioned whether Elvis was worth even a fraction of what they had invested in him. As time would prove, they had nothing to fear.

The Colonel had arranged for Elvis to appear on Tommy and Jimmy Dorsey's CBS-TV's prime-time *Stage Show* on January 27. That night, Elvis sang "Heartbreak Hotel" in front of a live audience for the first time. It was an electric moment. The performance drew so much mail that the Dorseys would bring Elvis back five more times, and on three of those occasions the singer would perform "Heartbreak Hotel." These performances helped to cement television as a major player in the entertainment world, not only as a way to market a hit record, but as a way to quickly introduce a local or regional act to a national audience.

The *Stage Show* appearances triggered thousands of requests for the new song, both in record stores and on radio stations. It also opened the door for Elvis to make an even more important TV show appearance, this time with Milton Berle. On April 3, 1956, Elvis sang "Heartbreak Hotel" for Uncle Miltie—and a viewing audience that comprised more than 25 percent of the American population. Thanks in no small part to Berle's power and Elvis's charisma, "Heartbreak Hotel" jumped to #1 on *Billboard's* pop charts two weeks later. The single would hold that position for eight straight weeks. On the country side of the charts, the Elvis tune would more than double that mark, controlling the top spot for seventeen weeks.

The song, inspired by a hopeless man's suicide note and penned by a schoolteacher and a forgotten country music wannabe, launched Elvis Presley as a mainstream force in American entertainment. Yet, even as "Heartbreak Hotel" topped the charts, in many people's eyes the singer was nothing more than a flash in the pan. Show business history was filled with artists who had scored a major hit and dropped out of sight, and recording a single #1 song for RCA Victor was not enough to establish this Hillbilly Cat as a major player in the entertainment world. He would have to follow up "Heartbreak Hotel" with something even better to make a lasting impression. Elvis's next #1 hit would not have the necessary impact to accomplish that, but it would prove to be one of Elvis's most dynamic efforts.

I WANT YOU, I NEED YOU, I LOVE YOU

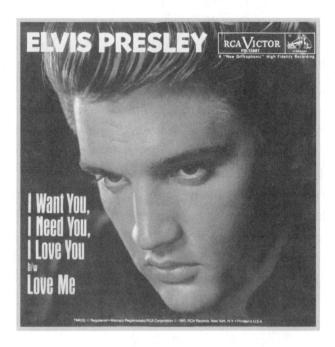

B y the spring of 1956 the incredible impact of "Heartbreak Hotel" and of Elvis's first LP, *Elvis Presley*, had made Elvis one of the most talked-about personalities in the United States. Before the extended-play 45 RPM of "Heartbreak Hotel," complete with extra cuts, was released in March, it had sold more than 350,000 copies on prerelease orders alone. The single would become the first EP ever to sell more than one million copies.

RCA Victor became so caught up in a wave of "Elvismania" that it jumped back into the marketplace with a host of new singles even before "Heartbreak Hotel" hit the top spot on the charts. Because of these releases, Presley was on the air seemingly around the clock in every part of the United States and most of the free world. To the horror of many conservative adults, Elvis seemed to be everywhere.

In addition to "Heartbreak Hotel," Elvis had "I Was the One," "Blue Suede Shoes," "My Baby Left Me," and "I Want You, I Need You, I Love You," all in the Top 20 at the same time. Yet, because "Heartbreak Hotel" was so strong on playlists and in the market-place, it was all but impossible for Elvis, or anyone else, to bump the song from its #1 position on the charts with another record. The only Elvis song that was able to break his initial release's stran-glehold on the top spot was "I Want You, I Need You, I Love You."

Legend has it that the demo of the song had been uncovered by Steve Sholes and given to Elvis for review, along with scores of other similar demos. The songs were being previewed by the pro-ducer and the singer for an early April recording session that, it was hoped, would produce a strong follow-up to "Heartbreak Hotel." And this time, RCA Victor wanted a record that it believed in, not just one from which Colonel Tom Parker could make some side money by licensing rights to it through Elvis Presley Music (a divi-sion of Hill and Range Music Company). Ultimately, however, that would happen, too.

"I Want You, I Need You, I Love You," a pretty, standard love ballad, was written by Ira Kosloff and Maurice Mysels. Elvis liked the song the moment he heard it. Though "I Want You, I Need You, I Love You" would be the songwriting pair's biggest hit, Kosloff also penned songs for the likes of Frank Sinatra, Connie Smith, and Jerry Lee Lewis, and he contributed music for stage shows. His hits include "Break the Chain," "The Day the Sun Forgot to

Shine," and "Forbidden Love." In truth, however, the writer's greatest impact, though rarely noticed by the general public, was in jazz: some of his music can still be heard in Chicago and New York jazz clubs.

The main story behind "I Want You, I Need You, I Love You" centers not around the song nor its writers, however, but the events that led up to the recording session and the fact that RCA Victor felt a need to release a single that seemed radically different from the music that was generating such incredible excitement in Elvis's live shows.

Just five months before, Elvis's performances in the small venues of the South and the Southwest had gone all but unnoticed by both the media and the cultural establishment. Now, with a nationwide hit record, Elvis's live shows were eliciting a great deal of negative publicity for the performer. His "vulgar" movements, executed while performing almost frantic versions of old R&B standards, had preachers, PTA groups, and conservative politicians in an uproar. Because of this, the singer—who claimed that his hip swinging was "involuntary" and that it was just the music getting inside him and causing him to respond—was making more enemies than friends in the adult world. While kids were flocking to his shows, their parents and other community leaders were meeting to try to figure a way to ban the new sensation. Worst of all for RCA Victor, many residents of the singer's native South considered the music that Elvis performed "race" music. A large number of concerned citizen groups believed that the singer from Memphis was opening the door for blacks in a white world, thus starting the integration of society though the "vulgar" sounds of the blues. Elvis's music was not "civilized," they argued, and it was leading to lowering cultural standards among middle-class teens. Many claimed that watching Elvis in concert led those who attended the shows into a world filled with sex and booze. Even as he established a national presence, Elvis became a lightning rod for all that was wrong within society.

Colonel Parker and Elvis both claimed to be shocked by these views, but they did not feel moved to have the singer stop shaking his hips, singing R&B standards such as "Ready Teddy" and "Tutti Frutti," or wearing clothes that fit in far better on Beale Street than in places like Waco, Texas. The ducktail and sideburns stayed intact as well. Yet, while the manager and the singer rode through the criticism showing little concern and no thought of changing course, RCA Victor seemed intent on toning Elvis down. Rather than promote a wild rocker who shook up the charts and generated passion in the kids who were flocking to Elvis's shows, the label focused on pitching the singer's love ballads. "I Want You, I Need You, I Love You," was probably the best of the lot that they had chosen for Elvis's consideration.

RCA Victor checked Elvis's busy road schedule and booked him into its Nashville studios on April 10—Easter Sunday. To the devoutly religious Elvis, recording on such an important Christian holiday seemed almost sacrilegious. He felt that he should be in church. In addition, Elvis and his band were scheduled to perform a late show in Texas the night before the recording session. They would have to charter an airplane to make the session. The singer was leery of air travel, especially in small planes. As the group packed into the small, prop-driven plane and headed for Nashville, Elvis was not a happy man.

About halfway through the late-night/early morning trip, the charter plane developed engine trouble. Several times the plane dipped close to the ground. Dripping with sweat, Elvis prayed for deliverance. He vowed he would never fly again if he could just survive this experience. Friends said later that, even though he had signed a contract to make three movies for Paramount Pictures just four days earlier, Elvis considered giving up entertainment altogether as the plane's trouble continued. Finally, the sputtering engine restarted, began to run smoothly, and took the weary musicians to Music City. The landing was uneventful, but Elvis was still visibly shaken as he entered the studio and shook hands with Steve Sholes.

Exhausted, traumatized, and even unsure of his ability to sing, Elvis was inclined to ask for the day off. The recording session was probably saved by the presence of Ben and Brock Speer, as well as the Jordanaires' Gordon Stoker. These men, legends in gospel music and longtime spiritual icons for Elvis and his family, served as anchors for the shaken singer. After warming up with the singers on some gospel standards, Elvis felt steady enough to give himself over to the work that Sholes had laid out for him.

The first song scheduled for the day was "I Want You, I Need You, I Love You." After a few run-throughs to get the performers familiar with the song, the producer switched on the tape recorder and the session began in earnest. Perhaps because of the almost tragic flight, Elvis had problems. He fumbled with the words and the phrasing, several times even reversing the order of "I Want You, I Need You, I Love You," singing instead "I Need You, I Want You, I Love You." Each time he made a mistake, the ever-polite singer apologized to everyone present, then tried again.

Elvis sang this song as if it would be his last recording. His voice seemed to be pleading, and he became not just the singer but the subject as well. Although the song is not as smooth as his later ballads would be, and the youth of his voice was evident, Elvis drew out the words of "I Want You, I Need You, I Love You," to emphasize emotions, not vocal skill. As a result, the song has a pulse like a heart monitor—listeners can actually feel the fear of loss in every word.

It took almost twenty takes to come up with one that Sholes thought was worthy of considering for a single. Sensing that Elvis was simply not up to the task of recording any more quality material, the producer cut the session short and sent everyone home. A pile of songs that were supposed to be a part of the session were forgotten.

After the session, Sholes listened again to the multiple takes of the song. He wasn't encouraged. Various cuts had potential, but none hit him as being a complete-enough performance to merit release. The real problem facing the producer was time. Elvis was so busy with his tour dates that it might be months before he'd be able to rerecord "I Want You, I Need You, I Love You" (in fact, it would be three months before Elvis found time to record anything). RCA Victor was not going to wait that long for a new record, and the producer had to do something to make this session workable. Using a tactic that had rarely before been successful, given the recording techniques of the time, Sholes began to play with various parts of different takes. Using a cut-and-splice method, the producer took parts of the fourteenth and seventeenth tracks and combined them into a product he liked. His splicing work was so precise that the recording seemed seamless to even the most professional critic. No one at RCA Victor could tell the recording had not been generated from a single take. "I Want You, I Need You, I Love You" was sent to the pressing plant and issued as Elvis's next single.

The song was shipped in late May 1956. On June 5, three days after it had entered the Top 40 playlists of all the major record publications, Elvis sang the song live on Milton Berle's television show. His performance sparked such great interest that the single quickly gained momentum, and by July 14 it was the most frequently played record on the country charts, knocking Ray Price's "Crazy Arms" out of first place. Two weeks later, "I Want You, I Need You, I Love You" displaced Gogi Grant's "The Wayward Wind" as the #1 song on the pop charts. It was Grant's single that had knocked "Heartbreak Hotel" out of the #1 spot.

Today, the Maurice Mysels and Ira Kosloff love ballad is tagged as a classic love song. Certainly the gut-wrenching emotion evident in Elvis's performance has to be considered one of the rock 'n' roll king's greatest recording efforts, and the work of producer Steve Sholes, in making two different cuts into a single hit, was masterful. But this #1 hit is considered just a footnote in the history of Elvis Presley. Because "Heartbreak Hotel" had ruled the charts for two months, the mere seven days that "I Want You, I Need You, I Love You" spent atop *Billboard's* pop list seemed to indicate that the power of Elvis was waning. Maybe, as many critics had predicted, the singer was a flash in the pan, a momentary fad. To cement his place in the music world, Elvis had to score a hit that would shake the establishment as much as his performances shook up audiences. To do that, RCA Victor had to have the guts to turn him loose and give him a number that embraced the real spirit of rock 'n' roll. Three months after the recording session that produced "I Want You, I Need You, I Love You," the label would do just that.

HOUND DOG

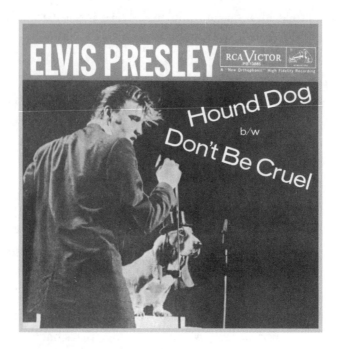

Until the middle of 1956, radio audiences had not really been exposed to the raw Elvis—the one whose live performances had spawned numerous protests by religious and social groups around the country. Elvis's cover of Carl Perkins's "Blue Suede Shoes" was a solid rocker, and it had landed at #20 on the pop charts in the late spring, but that was a rather innocent number compared to some of the songs that Elvis was pounding out onstage. The singer might have been setting off a storm of protest in some communities because of the songs and gyrations that he performed at his concerts, but RCA Victor had yet to release an Elvis number that unleashed, on vinyl, the tornado-like energy that could be seen in the entertainer's live performances. The Elvis songs the label had put out so far were good tunes, but they weren't very hot. Whether or not this was intentional on the part of RCA Victor is unknown. But it seemed that if Elvis was going to introduce a hot, rocking song to his studio work, he'd have to find that song himself.

On April 23 Elvis made his debut at the New Frontier Hotel in Las Vegas. The hotel was initially excited about the entertainment phenomenon's potential. This enthusiasm would quickly die. Elvis didn't draw much of an audience, and those who did come to see him were not impressed with his performance. The middle-aged men and women who paid the bills for Sin City were simply not interested in the man the teens thought was the hippest person in the world. Elvis's monthlong engagement was cut in half, and even that was too much for Elvis. Yet, in spite of humbling reviews and, at best, polite crowds who reacted to his songs with deafening silence, something positive did come out of Elvis's time in Las Vegas. That something came to light when the singer and his friends took some time off to catch another group's act.

Freddie Bell and the Bellboys, a group with Philadelphia roots, was one of the main acts at the Sands. A white R&B and pop band, the group had won a strong legion of Vegas fans with solid musical performances and tongue-in-cheek humor. They understood the demographics of the local crowd, and they played to it. When they sang a song that was considered more "teen-oriented," they usually put a comical slant on it, making it appealing to their older audiences. That was how they attacked the former #1 R&B hit "Hound Dog." Elvis, who saw the group's show several nights in a row, laughed hysterically each time Bell sang the song. In fact, Elvis was so impressed with the group's performance of that one standard that he added the blues number to his own shows. Far from being the frenetic, hard-driving song that he eventually would record, Elvis's early live renditions of "Hound Dog" usually moved pretty slowly, with an almost burlesque feel. Many who heard it during his shows at the New Frontier Hotel thought that it was an original tune. Neither Elvis nor his audience realized that this "Dog" had a rich, if not long, history and that it had been penned by the men who would become the Rogers and Hart of youth music.

A writer once said, "If Elvis Presley was the King of Rock 'n' Roll, then Jerry Leiber and Mike Stoller were certainly two of the most important powers behind the throne." This songwriting duo would produce not only some of Elvis's greatest singles, but many of the finest rock 'n' roll standards ever recorded, as well. In the 1950s and 1960s, Leiber and Stoller were the musical voice of America's youth, and in their work they covered every possible range of teen emotion and activity.

Both men were born on the East Coast in 1933, but grew up in Los Angeles. Introduced by a mutual school friend, Leiber and Stoller soon discovered they shared a passion for boogie-woogie and blues. Living in a musical world that was heavily influenced by African American culture, the two Jewish teens began to write songs together. By the time they were nineteen, their work had been noted by R&B performers such as Jimmy Witherspoon, Little Esther, Bull Moose Jackson, and Ray Charles, and the pair was already making money penning hits.

In 1952 the two were asked to create a new song for an emerging talent named Willie Mae "Big Mama" Thornton. Born on December 11, 1926, this daughter of a black minister grew up singing in church. As a young adult in the 1940s, she gained a degree of fame in African American clubs in Houston, Texas. But it was an appearance at Harlem's Apollo Theater, in which the tall, lanky woman sang the Dominoes' hit "Have Mercy Baby," that made her a genuine R&B star. Peacock-Duke Records signed Big Mama, and one of the label's executives, Don Robey, contacted Leiber and Stoller for fresh material for their new artist. After listening to some of Thornton's live performances, the songwriting team settled on a idea that seemed to be the theme of a great deal of the singer's material—ridiculing slothful men. The inspiration for the title of Leiber's and Stoller's song came from a common term given to a worthless person during this era: "a dog." To really emphasize how shiftless Big Mama's man was, the duo took the idea a step further and made him a flea-covered, mangy "Hound Dog," a critter so valueless that all it did was beg, scratch, and sleep.

Thornton's cut of the Leiber and Stoller composition was recorded in Los Angeles in August 1952. It immediately took off on the R&B charts, hitting #1 in late 1953. During this era, a top-selling R&B hit did not generate a great deal more than pocket change in royalties—the song's writers were not going to be moving to a better side of town thanks to Big Mama. But they loved her cut and, as it would be proven three years later, their "Dog" would soon provide them a solid return on their investment.

It was the original Thornton version of the song that Freddie Bell spoofed in Las Vegas. The fact that Elvis used Bell's lyrics, which had been inserted into the original lyrics to bring laughs, seems to verify that Elvis was not familiar with Big Mama's version. If he had been, he probably would not have sung, "You ain't never caught a rabbit and you ain't no friend of mine." That line was pure Bell. As country folks pointed out when they first heard Bell's version, a hound dog was not supposed to catch a rabbit, just track and point it out. The "Hound Dog" that Thornton sang about was so worthless it didn't hunt at all; it just hung around her door.

With the exception of "I Want You, I Need You, I Love You," Elvis had not recorded any new material since his first RCA Victor sessions in January. When he walked into his first studio session in New York City on July 2, 1956, he had no plans to record "Hound Dog"; he wanted to cut some of the original songs whose demos he had been listening to between shows. But Steve Sholes had different ideas—he wanted to start the session with the Leiber-Stoller number.

Initially Elvis balked at the idea. Yes, he admitted to the producer, the song had received a dramatic response during his live performances, and the singer had also performed his version of the number on both Milton Berle's and Steve Allen's television shows. On the latter's program, Elvis had even sung "Hound Dog" to a live basset hound wearing a bow tie. Needless to say, the singer did not consider that one of his better moments. Perhaps because of that, Elvis thought of the tune as nothing more than a novelty song (which, in truth, it is), but Sholes insisted that "Hound Dog" was now so identified with Elvis that fans would demand a record of the concert standard. The producer insisted that they cut the "Dog," and Elvis finally gave in.

Both Elvis's band and the Jordanaires—Gordon Stoker, Hoyt Hawkins, Neal Matthews, and Hugh Jarrett—were in the RCA studios that summer day. The Jordanaires would become a staple of not just Elvis's recordings over the next decade, but of those of Ricky Nelson, Pasty Cline, Eddy Arnold, and hundreds of others. Though they are now largely forgotten, the Jordanaires appeared on more records than any other artists in the history of the recording industry.

Shorty Long had been hired to play piano on the session, but he was running late that morning. Fortunately, in addition to being a solid vocalist, Stoker could also play the keyboard. Not wanting to wait for Long to arrive, Sholes asked Stoker to sit down at the ivories on the first day of the recording session. Then Sholes sat back and gave control of the recording session to Elvis.

Elvis may not have wanted to record "Hound Dog," but he had a definite idea about how he wanted the finished product to sound. Though he usually slowed it down and treated it like a blues number in concert, in the studio Elvis wanted the song to come off as fast and dynamic. As he sang his up-tempo version for the studio musicians and backup vocalists, he began to beat his hands, in a machine-gun manner, against the body of his guitar—and anything else he could find. Then, to emphasize to drummer Fontana what he wanted, he had the Jordanaires clap out the rhythm with him. It would take the percussionist thirty-one takes to get it just like Elvis wanted, and even on the final version, the quartet's clapping can still be heard setting the pace.

Steve Sholes loved the final result of the session. But what impressed him more than the perfect final take was the focus and determination that Elvis had exhibited as he toiled to get the number just right. The producer usually worked with artists who simply recorded a song a time or two and said, "That will do." When Elvis took over this session, it was obvious that the singer would settle for nothing less than perfection. With its rapid beat and dynamic pacing, the song was a real rocker. Because of this, "Hound Dog" probably had more to do with making Elvis the "King of Rock 'n' Roll" than anything he recorded before or after.

"Hound Dog" was shipped on July 13, 1956. It was one side of what would become a huge double-sided hit. The single remained on the pop charts for twenty-eight weeks, eleven of them at #1. It also held the top spot on the R&B chart for six weeks, and it ruled the country charts for ten, thus becoming one of the first records in history to earn the #1 spot on all the major playlists simultaneously. With this accomplishment, the song easily eclipsed "Heartbreak Hotel" as the biggest Elvis release and seemed to assure the world that the singer was something more than a flash in the pan.

What "Hound Dog" meant to Elvis is easy to ascertain, but what did this version of the song mean to its writers? After all, Leiber and Stoller were already well established in R&B and pop music circles. They had previously penned scores of hits. Yet, as Stoller remembers, Elvis's decision to record the song was such big news to his partner that it all but overshadowed an actual life-and-death situation.

"I was sitting in a lifeboat with sixty or seventy other people somewhere in the Atlantic," Stoller recalls. "I was relieved to be away from the sinking *Andrea Doria*, the beautiful Italian liner I had been on for the past eight days, which now had a large, gaping hole in its side and was going down fast. The lifeboat had a broken rudder and couldn't be steered. I wondered what would happen to me next. Fifteen hours later I stepped on the dock in New York and was greeted by Jerry Leiber."

What was the first thing Leiber told the damp, cold, and traumatized Stoller? "Elvis has cut 'Hound Dog,' and it is going to be his next single!"

DON'T BE CRUEL

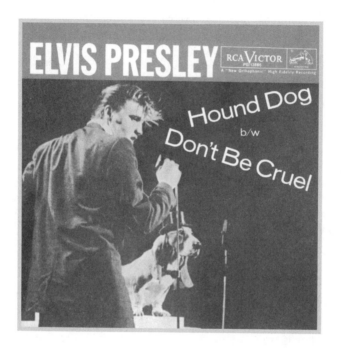

B y the time of the July 2, 1956, New York City recording session, the nation was in the grip of Elvismania. Elvis's records dominated the airwaves and flew up the charts. Elvis had a movie deal, played to sold-out houses at increasingly larger and more prestigious venues, and was giving television programs their best ratings in history. With the exception of his failed efforts in Las Vegas, he had suffered no setbacks. Elvis was on top of the world. Colonel Tom Parker had also turned the singer into a franchise that seemed on the verge of challenging Disney in both variety and numbers of products. Elvis lipstick, scrapbooks, notebooks, pictures, postcards, record players, combs, and a host of other cheap items were selling like hotcakes at five-and-dime stores. But everyone, from Elvis to Parker to RCA Victor, knew that fame could be fleeting. Thanks to to his "overnight" success, the pressure to produce hits was now greater than it had been at either of the singer's first two RCA Victor recording sessions. The label believed that singles that raced up the charts were the only sure way to keep Elvis in the public eye. If the records fell flat, their latest star would quickly fade away.

In the months before the summer New York City recording session, RCA Victor had received a room full of demos from songwriters all over the planet, all of whom believed that they had penned the perfect song for the next Elvis single. Many of these writers were well known and had decades-long track records. They had written for the greatest names in the music world, and they'd won scores of awards. Unfortunately, being an established professional in the music world actually worked against most of the songwriters, as the Colonel was looking for a piece of the publishing action. It was one of the less-recognized writers, a then-obscure, Brooklyn-born African American, who would next use an Elvis hit as the foundation for a body of work that would include some of the greatest songs of the rock era.

When Otis Blackwell was inducted into the Songwriters Hall of Fame in 1991, it was written, "Blackwell is without question one of the select songwriters whose songs literally helped redefine America's popular music." Time continues to prove this assessment. Before his death in 2002 the writer had composed more than one thousand songs and generated two hundred million dollars in record sales. But before Blackwell would ride the elevator to the music penthouse, he'd endure more than a decade of very tough times.

In the late 1940s, Blackwell worked as a presser in a tailor shop. He wrote songs during his breaks. In the evenings he auditioned the numbers at small New York City clubs. Blackwell had dreams of becoming an R&B or jazz artist. He finally got a chance to pursue his goal when he recorded his own "Daddy Rolling Stone" for a tiny Brooklyn label. But the song went nowhere, as did Blackwell's performing career. Though he was blessed with obvious vocal talent, it appeared that he would never be given the break needed to make it in the racially divided entertainment world of the immediate post–World War II era.

By the mid-1950s, Otis Blackwell was praying for a hit and pitching his compositions to anyone who would listen. On Christmas Eve 1955, he stood outside New York City's Brill Building, bitterly cold, hungry, and so poor that he had no hat to put on his head, and the soles of his shoes contained huge holes. Through the falling snow, Otis recognized a passerby as the arranger for R&B artist Screamin' Jay Hawkins. He approached Leroy Kirkland and informed the man that he was trying to sell some tunes to get some Christmas money. Feeling sorry for Blackwell, Kirkland listened to a couple of Otis's efforts. Impressed, Kirkland immediately took Blackwell to Shalimar Music and introduced the writer to Al Stanton. Stanton also liked what he heard, and Blackwell was promised that one of his songs would be recorded during the next Screamin' Jay recording session. The writer also received a publishing contract and an advance, as well as a spot to call his own in his new publisher's suite of offices. For Blackwell, it was not only a merry Christmas, but a sign of great things to come in the new year, as well.

Blackwell took every advantage of his big break. He impressed the folks at Shalimar with his hard work and his talent. He literally churned out songs on a daily basis, many of which were aimed directly at the new, younger, white pop music listeners who had embraced cleaned-up spin-offs of R&B songs. With Blackwell's teen tunes, Shalimar's song pluggers had ready products for a new hot market, a commodity that most New York music publishers could not supply. Best of all, Blackwell could sing, and he recorded demos of his own songs, thereby cutting out the middleman and saving a great deal of time between the writing and pitching parts of the process.

In addition to saving Shalimar time and money, Blackwell's ability to both write and record demos of his songs gave him the opportunity to stamp his ideas of arrangement and pacing into each of his songs. Much more so than demos of songs whose writers did not cut their own material, Blackwell's demos directly reflected the way he thought his songs should sound. Ultimately, it was Blackwell's phrasing, arrangements, and style that would intrigue Elvis, even more so than the writer's actual words and music. As a result, it can be argued that Otis Blackwell influenced Elvis's sound and style as much as did any other man in the world.

Blackwell had written one particular tune that echoed the upbeat feeling of Elvis's Sun releases "Mystery Train" and "I'm Left, You're Right, She's Gone." The melody had, for lack of a better description, a "casual bounce." And while it did not possess the driving pace that Elvis had employed when cutting "Hound Dog," it was definitely a rocker. It was a masterful tune, but it was the song's lyrics that were almost magical.

As he almost always did, Blackwell wrote the lyrics with a rock 'n' roll audience in mind. The teens who were buying Elvis's records and attending his shows, as well as those of Carl Perkins, Bill Haley and the Comets, Sonny James, and other early rock artists, usually lived each day as if it were their last. To many of these young people, each new crush, heartbreak, and moment of joy took on an unrealistic importance that set their emotions on a nonstop roller-coaster ride. When a teen was treated badly by a love interest, it was as if that teen's heartache was the biggest problem facing the world that day. "How could this happen?" they would ask each other. "How can someone I treated so well be so mean and cruel?" These were two of the most-heard questions posed by millions of kids each day. Blackwell transformed this lament into lyrics and music, and he cut a demo of the song, in which he sang and played the piano, while a friend beat out the song's percussion on a box.

Blackwell's understanding of teenage psychology and the way that teens maximized each of life's small emotional dramas inspired a song that he felt was perfect, not only for Elvis, but for the millions who now hung on his every musical word, as well. Blackwell believed that "Don't Be Cruel" was a song that the teens, both boys and girls, would not just listen to, but would *relate to*, as well. That is, if he could convince Elvis to record it.

Being in the right place at the right time helps to ensure any success. In that regard, Blackwell was fortunate: one of the personalities who haunted Shalimar's offices, Aaron "Goldie" Goldmark, had a solid contact with Elvis's producer, Steve Sholes. Goldmark delivered the demo to Sholes at RCA Victor.

Had Blackwell's demo been shipped directly to Elvis, it probably would have never been cut. Elvis was so busy during this period that he didn't have the opportunity to listen to every demo that was forwarded to him. Sholes had a great deal more time, and he loved the song the moment he heard it, weeks before the summer recording session of "Hound Dog." But, for unknown reasons, the producer didn't spring "Don't Be Cruel" on Elvis until the singer had finished cutting "Hound Dog." Then, during a "take ten" break, Sholes asked his singer to listen to the Blackwell demo. As Sholes had figured, Elvis wanted to cut the song even before it had finished playing. Elvis's initial and genuine affection for this number never faded—"Don't Be Cruel" remained one of the entertainer's favorite songs for the rest of his life.

While Elvis, acting as his own producer, had completely changed the style and pacing of "Hound Dog," he made virtually no alterations to the Blackwell submission. Instead, he copied Blackwell word for word and note for note. The vocal inflections, the rhythm and the timing—all mimicked what the songwriter had done on the demo. Nevertheless, it took twenty-eight hard and exhausting takes before Elvis felt that they had gotten the song right.

Playing on this long, difficult session were the Elvis regulars: Scotty Moore was doing the lead guitar work; Bill Black was on bass; and, though he had missed the session on "Hound Dog" earlier in the day, Shorty Long had arrived at the studio in time to play the keyboard on this song. As would be the case with most of Elvis's future hits, the Jordanaires supplied the elementary vocal backing. Although D. J. Fontana was listed on the record as the "drummer," Fontana didn't actually play the skins on this recording. Instead, the beat that is heard throughout the song was created by a mallet striking a leather-covered guitar. A secondary "drumbeat," which can also be heard on the recording, was something of an accidental element—it's the sound of Elvis slapping the back of his own guitar to create the pacing he felt the song had to possess.

Sholes wanted this new cut to be on the flip side of the pressing of "Hound Dog." In truth, he saw "Hound Dog" as the B side of the record, and "Don't Be Cruel" as the side that would generate the most play. But the Blackwell number still had to pass muster with the Colonel to make the grade. Parker liked the song and thought it had great commercial possibilities—but he was not about to allow it to be released as a single if the publisher and writer didn't give up half of the song rights. This time the manager not only obtained 50 percent of the take for his publishing company, but he even won the right to list Elvis as the cowriter of "Don't Be Cruel."

It's likely that Elvis did not understand enough about the music business to realize how much this deal would cost Shalimar and Blackwell in cash, but he did know that he didn't like having his name on something that he had no hand in writing. Though he did not fight his manager on the issue, Elvis remained uncomfortable with that aspect of the deal for the rest of his life. Whenever anyone asked about it, he freely admitted that he had had no part in writing the song, thus deflecting all praise for the work to Blackwell. Still, because of Parker's deal, even to this day many people believe that Elvis helped to compose this rock 'n' roll masterpiece.

With the publishing deal quickly secured, "Don't Be Cruel" was slapped onto the opposite side of the "Hound Dog" single. Yet the question of which song was the biggest hit remains today.

As soon as they received the record in mid-July, Pop, R&B, and country radio stations played both sides. The number of requests for the songs that were received by the DJs were about equal, varying only a bit by region. Juke box spins were almost exactly equal, as well. Hence, from the first week of the release of the 45, RCA Victor had a double-sided hit. This twin success was extremely rare then, and it is unheard of now.

Shipped on July 13, 1956, "Hound Dog"/"Don't Be Cruel" hit #1 on the Billboard chart less than two months later, on September 5. The double-sided single earned a gold record award—and a second, third, fourth, and fifth gold record award, all in the same week. The release would knock the Platters' "My Prayer" off the top spot in pop music, and it dethroned Elvis's old Sun Records colleague Johnny Cash and his "I Walk the Line" on the country chart. "Don't Be Cruel" was credited as holding the #1 spot on *Billboard's* pop singles chart for eleven weeks, on the country playlists for ten weeks, and the R&B chart for one week. The song was a triple-chart hit. In truth, though "Hound Dog" would garner a great deal more publicity, "Don't Be Cruel" is a far superior song, and it would not only set the tone for the Elvis hits that would follow, but it would also help the singer to develop the musical style that he would use in recordings and onstage for the rest of his life.

With a monster double-hit record now under his belt, Elvis Presley was so hot that Ed Sullivan broke his vow that he would never book the singer onto his show. On September 9, 1956, Elvis sang both "Don't Be Cruel" and "Hound Dog" on *The Ed Sullivan Show*. The performance earned Sullivan his highest rating ever. During Elvis's appearance on the show, it was announced that the singer was making a movie with Hollywood actress Debra Paget. The combination of a double-sided hit and the exposure that he received on *The Ed Sullivan Show* changed the entertainer's life. In the space of just three-quarters of a year, Elvis Presley had gone from regional act to international sensation.

A few months after he recorded "Don't Be Cruel," Elvis stopped by Sun Studio in Memphis. Carl Perkins was there, finishing his recording of "Matchbox." Also on hand that day were Johnny Cash and Jerry Lee Lewis. As the four friends sat around a piano, swapping stories and singing gospel standards and some of the latest pop hits, a reporter took a picture of this "million-dollar quartet." Sensing the historical importance of the moment, producer Sam Phillips also switched on a tape recorder.

As the reunion heated up and the group shared more and more tales, Elvis related a recent experience he'd had during a vacation in Las Vegas. There, the singer had seen a band called Derrick and the Dominoes. Elvis said that he'd enjoyed the black R&B group so much that he'd seen them four nights in a row. His fondest memory of the shows was the way in which the Dominoes had spoofed Elvis during their slow, deliberate version of "Don't Be Cruel." Elvis thought the group nailed the song, and he wished that he had recorded it their way instead of in the upbeat, casual manner he had used in the studio. To emphasize just how brilliant the Dominoes' version of the huge hit had been, Elvis picked up his guitar and played "Don't Be Cruel" in their style, using their phrasing patterns and inflections. This moment in rock 'n' roll history is special because it gives great insight into Elvis's musical influences and taste, as well as into his unspoiled nature and modesty at this time. But, in this case, the singer's assessment of his own recording was dead wrong.

Through the years, scores of critics have chimed in to state that "Don't Be Cruel" is perhaps not only the best Elvis recording effort ever, but one of the most perfect sessions in the history of rock 'n' roll music. This is made more ironic because of how few people were involved in the production and that the song was a last-minute addition to the July 2 session. Yet even in the well-arranged world of music, lightning has a way of striking without warning. The lightning is still striking each time someone plays "Don't Be Cruel."

LOVE ME TENDER

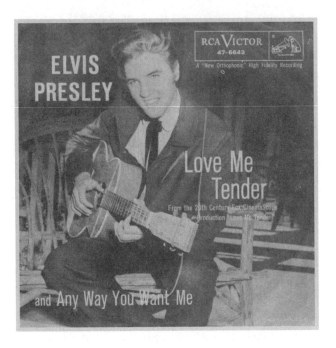

As "Hound Dog" and "Don't Be Cruel" climbed the charts of all three of *Billboard's* major playlists, Elvis arrived in Hollywood to begin work on his first motion picture, *The Reno Brothers*. Pulling out all the stops to ensure that Elvis's first screen vehicle would be a success, Twentieth Century Fox assigned the role of producer to award-winning veteran David Weisbart, who had produced *Rebel Without a Cause*. In addition, the studio cast stars Richard Egan, James Drury, Neville Brand, and Debra Paget to fill out the lineup for this black-and-white Western.

The actors, who'd been assigned by the studio to guide Elvis through the movie, were probably not aware that their own roles would be all but lost in the national spotlight that seemed to follow the singer's every move. Elvis, in the role of Clint, the youngest of the Reno Brothers, was himself really a part of the supporting cast—Egan and Paget were the stars—but few in the media seemed to notice that. Every blurb about the movie that came out over the airwaves or in the press seemed to lead with the singer's name.

Ironically, Elvis had not been the studio's first choice for the role. The part had originally been intended for Robert Wagner. But Elvis had performed so well in his April screen test that the studio powers opted to place the movie newcomer in the flick instead of the proven commodity. As the box office would prove, it was not a mistake.

Looking back on Elvis's career, many today wonder why the initial movie choice for the singer was a period piece. It would seem that a flick set in the moment would have been a better way to spotlight the singer's talent and to appeal to his fans. It is easy to forget that the hottest genre on television and at the box office during the 1950s was Westerns. That, coupled with the fact that Elvis's sideburns were already the right length for a period picture, the marriage of this particular movie and its most talked-about star seemed a natural.

In the film, Elvis plays the only Reno brother who stayed home, while his siblings went to fight in the Civil War for the Confederate army. Supposedly, the brothers are killed in battle, and Clint then marries his older brother's girlfriend. Of course, all of the brothers are alive, and when they return home a love triangle is born. The first part of the movie focuses on how the family struggles to adapt. But when Richard Egan's character, Vance, is involved in a train robbery, the family splits and the action takes over. In the end, it is Elvis's character, Clint, who is killed, and his death brings the Renos back together again. The movie is no *High Noon* or *Stagecoach*, but its plot was pretty typical of Westerns of the period. Elvis was thrilled with the script.

Had Wagner stayed in the role that Elvis ultimately took, it is likely that two things would not have occurred. The first is that the film's name would not have been changed from *The Reno Brothers* to *Love Me Tender*. The second is that the studio probably wouldn't have had four songs written and inserted into the film's story line. To accomplish the task of creating songs for the adventure story, Twentieth Century Fox turned to a veteran Hollywood tunesmith.

Born in Nebraska in 1909, Ken Darby had had a long and successful career in music and film. By the time he received the assignment of writing and directing the music for *The Reno Brothers*, Darby was not just a songwriter—he was a dynamic choral director, conductor, arranger, singer, and author. He originated the King's Men male vocal quartet in 1929, and he later led and arranged music for the Ken Darby Singers. His band backed Bing Crosby on "White Christmas," the biggest-selling record of all time. Darby also led the way as a writer for scores of other major hits for other major artists, including "If You Please," "Riders in the Sky," "Far Away Places," and "Anniversary Song."

Before World War II and his association with the Crosby parade of hits, Darby did some of the orchestral and vocal arrangements for *The Wizard of Oz*. In various capacities—music supervisor, musical associate, arranger, or choral, vocal, or musical director—he participated in a long string of hit films, including *State Fair*, *Song of the South*, *Rancho Notorious*, and *The Robe*. Elvis had to have been both impressed and intimidated by Darby's track record. The feeling was probably not mutual.

Though he never said so publicly, working with rock 'n' roll's new king was not a job for which the sophisticated musician would have lobbied. After all, he had just finished *The King and I* for which he would win an Academy Award. He also had a list of prestigious work lined up. In a very real sense, his assignment to *The Reno Brothers* had to be considered a step down for the music man.

After reading the script, Darby penned four very simple numbers and dropped them into the movie at appropriate spots, such as a family gathering on the porch and a local county fair. Two of the songs, "Poor Boy" and "Let Me," have a real rockabilly feel, and it's obvious that they were tailor-made for Elvis's rock 'n' roll fans. Certainly they have little connection to anything remotely tied to the Old West. A third entry, "We're Gonna Move," has a certain gospel-folk feel that at least seems to echo the time and setting of the film. With those three numbers for the body of the movie in place, Darby drew from history to create the movie's theme, or title song.

"Love Me Tender" was based on the old American folk song "Aura Lee," which had been written in the days just before the Civil War, about the same time in which the movie was set. W. W. Fosdick and George R. Poulton are credited with creating the song. While *Aura Lee* had strong Southern ties, the West Point class of 1865 actually rewrote the words, called it "Army Blue," and used it as their class song. The tune was so well known, it was in most school songbooks. For the movie, Darby added his own new lyrics to the tune. The lyrics are very simple, very direct, and in a style that would have probably pleased fans of Bing Crosby as much as fans of Elvis Presley.

After completing the four songs, the composer reserved a date to record them. As per Darby's plans, this session would be much different than those that Elvis had experienced at Sun and RCA Victor. For starters, Darby would not allow Steve Sholes or any of Elvis's usual musicians to work on this gig. The writer/arranger did not feel that Elvis's band had the talent to deliver the final product he needed for the movie. Instead, he sent out invitations to several Los Angeles session players: Vito Mumolo for the guitar work; Mike "Myer" Rugin for bass; Richard Cornell for drums; Luther Rountree for banjo; and Dom Frontieri for one of the most unlikely instruments ever used on an Elvis recording—an accordion. Backup vocals were provided by Red Robinson, John Dodson, and Chuck Prescott. The engineers were Bob Mayer and Ren Runyon. Elvis was ordered to join these men in the studio on August 24, 1956.

The recording session was held on Fox Stage 1 in Hollywood. Rather than booking the kind of small, intimate studio that Elvis was used to, Darby put him on a huge Twentieth Century Fox soundstage. With no opportunity to influence the direction of the session—no chance to demand a new rhythm or to do any rearranging—and without his familiar musicians at his side, Elvis may have reverted into the shy shell that he had displayed during his days as a high school student at Humes High in Memphis. Also, because of his mother's teaching to always be respectful of elders, the singer may have naturally deferred to Darby's wishes without questioning whether the music met his own needs and wishes. In reality, Elvis had not wanted to sing at all in any of his movies, wishing instead to hone and show off his acting skills. The addition of these four songs to the film must have deeply disappointed him. Perhaps for one or all of these reasons, the recording session lacked the energy of earlier Elvis sessions. In the final recording, Elvis's voice is steady, the pacing is slow, and the song has a homey feeling to it. The production values are so simple, in fact, that it almost sounds like a demo record. Darby had transformed the entertainer into a man who was simply singing into a microphone, instead of a whirlwind of dynamic energy, as he had been under the direction of Sholes. Nevertheless, Twentieth Century Fox was pleased with the results. With the studio happy and the work of the session behind him, so was Elvis.

The best known of the songs cut that day is the tune "Love Me Tender." The producer and others at Twentieth Century Fox believed the number was so strong that they renamed the movie after the Darby tune. Evidently, however, the songwriter was still not as impressed with Elvis, or with the four songs, as the studio heads were. Rather than claim the songs as his own, he assigned credit for them to his wife, Vera Watson. Though Watson had nothing to do with composing "Love Me Tender," "Let Me," "Poor Boy," or "We're Gonna Move," her name appeared on the final version of the single as a writer.

Colonel Parker had already made the deal that he and Elvis would get half of the publishing rights and royalties to any songs that were used in the film. Elvis's manager had also demanded, and was given, the right to add Elvis's name as cowriter of all four of the songs. Darby's and Parker's deceptions represented one of the few instances in history in which a song's real writer claimed no ownership of a monster hit, making "Love Me Tender" one of the most unusual songs ever.

The executives at RCA Victor knew a good thing when they heard it. They loved "Love Me Tender," and they were ecstatic that the movie's title had changed to highlight the song. They also realized that Twentieth Century Fox would be spending big bucks publicizing its first Elvis flick. RCA Victor therefore opted to release "Love Me Tender" as Elvis's next single. Elvis previewed the number on *The Ed Sullivan Show* on September 9, 1956. With fans crazy to see Elvis on the silver screen and the fact that this was a ballad in the traditional style of a Bing Crosby or a Dean Martin, the label received more than a million orders for "Love Me Tender" before it was even released. This time, orders were coming in from almost every demographic and age group. For the first time, Elvis's appeal seemed universal.

RCA Victor listened to all of the Twentieth Century Fox session work and chose the second take of the movie's theme as the single release. (The movie cut would actually reveal an extra verse at the film's conclusion that was not included in the single released by the label.) It was shipped on September 28, 1956. By November 3, "Love Me Tender" pushed the double-sided single "Hound Dog"/"Don't Be Cruel" to the #2 spot on *Billboard*'s pop chart, marking the first time in history that a singer had knocked himself out of the #1 position. The movie's title tune held the top spot for five weeks and stayed on the chart a total of 23 weeks. "Love Me Tender" also reached the #3 spot on *Billboard*'s country singles chart, and the #4 spot on its R&B singles chart. It was a strong hit, yet the movie did even better.

Love Me Tender opened in New York City on November 16, 1956. Over the next twenty-four-hour period Twentieth Century Fox sent distributed prints of the film to 550 theaters nationwide. Though Elvis's acting skills received very mediocre reviews, the studio's entire production and publicity costs were recouped in just three days. Incredibly, although it was only in theaters for six weeks of the year, *Love Me Tender* would become the second-highest-grossing film of 1956. There was no doubt about it: Elvis was a draw at the box office.

From its writing to its recording, "Love Me Tender" is hardly an inspired song. In the tradition of Hollywood show tunes, it was simply written to fit a script and to flesh out a plot. But this single set the pattern that would be used in over thirty Elvis features over the next decade. Within that mix are a few inspired classics, but for the most part, the movie songs served as little more than filler. Sadly, within a few years, Elvis movies would devolve as well. Though they fattened the Colonel's and Elvis's bank accounts, both the majority of the songs used in Elvis's movies and the majority of the movies themselves represented a tremendous waste of Elvis's talent.

In the space of just over eight months, Elvis ruled the top spot on the pop charts for twenty-five weeks. Thanks to the success of the Sun single "I Forgot to Remember to Forget," the total number of weeks at the top of the country chart was twenty-eight. No artist had ever before so dominated the playlist, and most people believed it would never happen again.

PEACE IN THE VALLEY

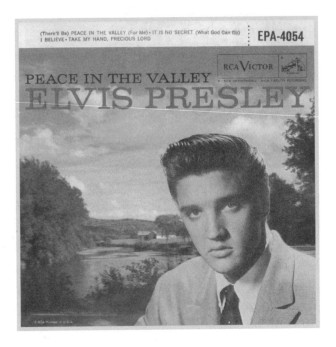

By early 1957, Elvis was the biggest sensation in the entertainment business. He controlled the record charts, dominated the show business magazines, and created huge TV ratings for the likes of Steve Allen and the Dorsey Brothers. Though he had once vowed never to book the singer for his show, by September 1956 even Ed Sullivan had caved in to the hurricane that was Elvis. Laying out the largest fee ever paid to a single performer, the CBS network host brought Elvis into New York for six appearances on Ed's top-rated program.

Elvis's hip-shaking performances on *The Ed Sullivan Show* sent teenage girls into a frenzy, but they created more bad publicity for the man that *Time* magazine had just called "the Pelvis." After receiving thousands of protest letters regarding his upcoming third appearance on Sullivan's television show in January 1957, CBS announced that it had opted to censor Elvis's act by showing him only from the waist up. Yet this did little to appease the millions of parents, clergymen, and government officials who were up in arms over the singer. From the pulpit, from the halls of Congress, and from living rooms around the nation, thousands demanded that Elvis be banned from television and radio. The fact that RCA Victor had a tremendous amount of money invested in Elvis, and that Paramount had him under a long-term motion picture contract, meant that parties on both sides of this issue were very nervous. But on a cold Sunday evening in New York, Elvis took matters into his own hands and, with one song, all but silenced his most ardent critics.

What most outside of Elvis's family and friends did not know was that Elvis had grown up listening to and singing gospel music. Many of his stage moves were inspired by evangelists and gospel singers. His vocal style carried distinct phrasing that echoed that of Jake Hess of the famed Statesmen Quartet. Elvis was a regular at Saturday gospel singings and at the annual gospel quartet conventions, and he knew more sacred songs than he did pop standards. In his early teens, his dream had been to join a Southern gospel quartet. Before he signed with Sun Records, he had even tried out for an opening with the Blackwood Brothers Quartet. J. D. Sumner, the group's bass singer at that time, later remembered that Elvis's tryout had failed because Elvis wanted to sing all four parts, not just the lead. Yet to Elvis, gospel music was more than just a type of music that he liked. It was a passion that was a part of his fiber, and it was deeply rooted in his soul.

When in trouble as a child, Elvis had sought comfort in gospel music. While others prayed, he sang about God. Now, with millions railing against him as a symbol of the nation's moral decay, the singer naturally reached in that same direction again. He chose to perform "Peace in the Valley" during his third appearance on *The Ed Sullivan Show.*

Elvis had long been a fan of the song's composer, Rev. Thomas A. Dorsey. As a child, the singer had been known to frequent both black and white gospel singings and, though it has never been verified, Elvis might well have even heard the songwriter and choirmaster perform the song. What is known for sure is that Elvis had heard country music legend and radio star Red Foley's 1951 recording of "Peace in the Valley" on many occasions—the gospel standard had been a pop hit. Even so, Elvis's version of the song, as he performed it on Sullivan's show, would have a much greater impact on audiences. Backed by the Jordanaires, Elvis's sincere performance of "Peace in the Valley," from its first note to its last, caused an entire nation to take a second look at the singing sensation.

Though Elvis probably chose "Peace in the Valley" simply because he liked it, the story behind this gospel standard and its composer is one that probably would have deeply impressed the young man from Memphis. In many ways, the musical roots and experiences of Rev. Thomas A. Dorsey—known as "the Father of Gospel Music"—were very similar to those of this new musical king.

Born on July 1, 1899, the son of a preacher, Thomas A. Dorsey never had an easy life. As a child growing up in one of the poorest areas in Georgia, Dorsey had a host of friends and family who remembered living not as free people, but as slaves. As his poor white neighbors had done with Elvis, these African American men and women shared with young Dorsey the fact that music, especially spiritual music, helped them make it through times when their lives were literally not their own. Songs like "Roll Jordan Roll," "Swing Low, Sweet Chariot," "Go Tell It on the Mountain," and "Walk Through the Valley" gave them hope during hopeless moments, and faith when they had nothing on this Earth to lean on. It was music that fed their souls when nothing else could. Music ultimately sustained their very lives. Like Elvis, young Dorsey was shaped by his musical foundation. As Dorsey grew to understand the power of music not to just sustain people through bad times, but to inspire them to move forward, his future unfolded before him.

Dorsey first took piano lessons at the age of eleven. His time spent on the well-worn church keyboard would be the second key to setting into motion a life that would ultimately and radically change the structure of gospel music in both black and white America. The little boy with all the musical talent would even sound a charge for civil rights and integration through his work, an integration that really began in the music business and saw its first victories in jazz and rock 'n' roll. Yet before Dorsey could redirect his soulful sounds of inspiration to challenge the minds in Washington, D.C., and around the nation, he first had to make a radical change in his own life.

Dorsey was a teenager when his family moved to Chicago. It was in this atmosphere—the Northern "home of the blues"—that the young man blossomed into an innovative jazz musician. He attended the Chicago College of Composition and Arranging, and he became an agent for Paramount Records. He also began to write jazz numbers, and he even worked in some independent recording sessions. Yet he made his biggest mark on the Windy City not as a

composer and businessman, but—under the name Georgia Tom—
a honky-tonk piano player for Al Capone's houses of prostitution
and speakeasies. "Tight Like That" was not just Dorsey's first best-
selling record; it also described a great deal of his life as a blues
musician. He ran in wild crowds and was a part of the Windy City's
hippest group. He was a cool cat long before Elvis had been labeled
"the Hillbilly Cat."

For reasons he didn't fully understand, Dorsey returned to his
roots in the late 1920s. Even while he was making waves and
seemed to have a bright future as a club entertainer, he began to
attend church again. He even started to use his musical talents for
worship services. Ultimately, though he would suffer great financial
hardship, he left the nightclubs to become the first independent
publisher of black gospel music. The Dorsey Publishing House
released its first song in 1932. Sadly, the Depression stifled almost
all employment opportunities that had been open to blacks, and
neither churches nor their parishioners had money to spare to purchase a new song. Dorsey's timing could not have been worse.

"I borrowed five dollars," he later told a reporter when remem-
bering his early days in publishing, "and sent out five hundred
copies of my song, 'If You See My Savior,' to churches throughout
the country. It was three years before I got a single order. I felt like
going back to the blues." At the time, it seemed that whenever
Dorsey wasn't playing the blues, he was living them.

Yet the songwriter/publisher stuck it out it in the face of rejections and financial disasters. He continued to write and publish
his own and other black composers' gospel music. Finally, at the
darkest point in his life, after the death of his wife and new baby,
he wrote "Precious Lord, Take My Hand." The success of this song
made Dorsey the central figure in African American gospel music

circles. Beyond writing and publishing, he expanded his power and influence by founding and presiding over the National Convention of Gospel Choirs and Choruses. Through this organization he taught his songs to hundreds of thousands of church singers, including some, such as Mahalia Jackson, who would later become famous. With Dorsey taking the lead, black gospel music became one of the most important and visible African American contributions to the United States during the Depression. By the end of the decade, the composer was so much in demand for personal appearances that he was rarely ever home.

In 1939, while on a train headed to another appearance before thousands at a convention, Dorsey picked up a newspaper and began to read about rumors of war in Europe. After studying the article for some time, he came to the realization that Germany's Hitler would push and push until England and other nations would have to answer with force. Dorsey was overcome with a sense of dread. He got up to stretch his legs. As he walked, he began to hum the old spiritual "Walk Through the Valley of Peace." Finally he quit singing and pacing and found a seat next to a window.

The news of potential war contrasted sharply with the beautiful pastoral scenes that Dorsey viewed as the train rolled down the tracks. It would be this stark contrast, along with the music he had learned from former slaves, that would inspire him to write one of the most popular black spirituals of World War II, and one of the most powerful anthems of Christian peace ever penned.

"It was just before Hitler sent his war chariots into Western Europe," Dorsey recalls, years later. "I was on a train going through southern Indiana on the way to Cincinnati, and the country seemed to be upset about this coming war that he was about to bring on. I passed through a valley on the train. Horses, cows, sheep, they were running through the valley, and up the hill there I could see where the water was falling from. Everything seemed so peaceful with all the animals down there grazing together. It made me wonder, what's the matter with humanity? What's the matter with mankind? Why couldn't man live in peace like the animals down there? So out of that came 'Peace in the Valley.'"

Dorsey's "Peace in the Valley" was certainly inspired by the scene he saw from the train window, but it's also likely that the writer drew on the stories he'd heard from former slaves, too. There can be little doubt that the image of people being forced to do things they didn't want to do—such as work in a field for nothing, as they had in the days before the Civil War, or die in battle, a fearful possibility that was facing millions now, had to contribute to the songwriter's urgent desire to write this specific song. Ultimately, Dorsey would not turn the concept of peace loose until the work had been completed. Upon its publication a few months later, Dorsey admitted that he hoped his new song would somehow help keep America out of the European conflict, which may explain his rush to complete the song and get it on the market. While "Peace in the Valley" did not accomplish that lofty goal, it did pave the way for something just as important.

The lyrics that Dorsey penned on the train to Cincinnati resonate with the same kind of feeling as those of "Precious Lord Take My Hand" and other earlier gospel contributions by Dorsey, but this song's music did not come from the same "black blues" source as had the songwriter's other well-known works. The melody and pacing of "Peace in the Valley" really have a "white country" feel. Even Dorsey could not explain why he had chosen to compose this number with an almost hillbilly/folk score. He would tell others that this was just the way the Lord gave it to him. Yet ultimately the song's tune was probably the reason that "Peace in the Valley" was quickly adopted not by just the black churches, which already looked upon Dorsey as the greatest African American songwriter in the country, but in thousands of rural Southern white churches that had all but ignored black religious music in the past. By focusing on the common concerns of black and white people, and by employing a musical style that was influenced by both cultures' musical heritages, Dorsey brought together black and white voices at a time when the United States was all but separated along racial lines. As had been the case with Dorsey, it was this combining of black and white music that would later make Elvis Presley a star.

By late 1941 the United States had no choice but to enter the worldwide conflict, and "Peace in the Valley" became a gospel music standard that, ironically, went to war with thousands of black and white men. This song about peace was sung everywhere that Americans fought. It was requested for battlefield funerals, and it was a staple at quickly set-up battlefield worship services. As the bloodletting grew worse, the song of peace became even more important to Christian Americans. Soon, the song that had been written as a tool for spreading the gospel was embraced even by Americans of other faiths, who saw Dorsey's "Peace in the Valley" as the picture of the way life in America should be.

As a product of poverty, and as the son of a man who had spent time in prison, Elvis would have strongly identified with Dorsey's own experiences. The singer was a man who also saw no color in his dealing with musicians and songwriters. In his powerful rendition of the song on Ed Sullivan's stage, the Elvis Presley who loved gospel music, honored his parents, and was unashamed of his humble roots came out in every word of "Peace in the Valley." With the help of a two-minute-long gospel standard, Elvis redefined his image and won over a host of new adult fans.

As it turned out, one performance of the song was simply not enough for America. By the end of the following week, RCA Victor had received thousands of letters demanding a recorded version of "Peace in the Valley." Bowing to fan pressure and sensing a new market for Elvis's music, the company decided to put the singer back in the studio for a gospel session. Elvis was given an opportunity to choose the music for this new release. In addition to "Peace in the Valley"; the singer picked another Dorsey classic, "Take My Hand, Precious Lord"; a Stuart Hamlin hit, "It Is No Secret"; and "I Believe," a pop standard taken from a Broadway musical. In Los Angeles, on January 19, 1957, backed by the Jordanaires and his regular band and using elementary arrangements like those employed in rural black churches across the South, Elvis finally got to live his dream of being a gospel singer. Elvis sang this song as if he were singing in church. The arrangement and the quartet's backup vocals, especially that of a driving bass line, frame Elvis's sincere voice. The star's tone reflects the meaning of the words, which range from rather shallow and plaintive when referring to human fraility to strong and deep when showcasing the power of the Lord. Ultimately, this was not only gospel in its purest form—it was also a song that embraced the freedom of African American gospel.

Though some thought was given to adding six to eight other sacred standards at a later time to make a full album, RCA Victor executives ultimately opted to simply release these four songs as an extended-play (EP) 45 record. The "Peace in the Valley" EP was shipped to record outlets in early 1957 and immediately created a sensation. The "mini-album" flew off shelves. In less than two months it not only topped the EP lists, but its sales earned it a spot as the largest selling extended-play 45 of all time, as well. Yet the bestseller and Elvis's performance of "Peace in the Valley" on *The Ed Sullivan Show* did more than simply change the public's viewpoint of Elvis and make RCA Victor a great deal of money. It paved the way for a new musical genre.

Before "Peace in the Valley," gospel music was a small segment of the music market, and it was never aimed at teenagers. Elvis's EP changed that. Impressed with what Elvis had done, Ricky Nelson would soon sing a gospel song on his family's ABC-TV show— Baker Knight's "Gospel Train," an original sacred standard written with both adults and teens in mind. Teen interest in "Peace in the Valley" and "Gospel Train" helped pave the way for the development of contemporary Christian music. When Elvis sang "Peace in the Valley," the performance changed not only his reputation, but music history, too, opening the door for Amy Grant and a host of others in Christian music.

TOO MUCH

If not for Guy Mitchell's cover of the Marty Robbins country hit "Singing the Blues," Elvis could have scored another #1 hit in December 1956, and he would probably have begun the new year at the top spot as well. Mitchell's more-than-two-month rule of *Billboard's* list kept the Elvis ballad "Love Me" stuck at #2 for five weeks. Elvis would have to wait until the second month of 1957 before he would again vault to the top of the pop chart. The song that would take him there was almost too much for the radio stations to handle, much less play.

"Too Much" was not penned with Elvis in mind. In fact, in the early 1950s, when Lee Rosenberg and Bernard Weinman wrote the musical ode to a decidedly one-sided love affair, mainstream audiences were simply not ready for it. For starters, though the lyrics seem mild by today's standards, they were viewed as being too suggestive for anything outside of a blues or R&B venue. This was a number that oozed a blatant kind of sexuality that mainstream white audiences—the people who watched *The Adventures of Ozzie and Harriet*—would not accept on their radios, records players, televisions, or in their homes. Remember, this was an era when even married couples still slept in separate twin beds in almost all Hollywood films and television series. Before Elvis came into the picture, "Too Much" was just that: too much!

The song was first recorded in 1954 by Bernard Hardison for the Republic label. As was expected, this initial version of "Too Much" went nowhere. That same year a female artist, Judy Tremaine, cut the song, and the record was shipped out to radio stations on the Signature label. It also fell flat. Two years later, Frankie Castro (who is not to be confused with the modern-day Elvis impersonator of the same name), another R&B–type singer, recorded the song for Mercury. Again, the song didn't touch the charts. It was not a bad song from a musical standpoint; it was just too hot to garner play on pop stations in the pre–rock 'n' roll era.

The probable reason that "Too Much" did not earn very much notice or airplay had to do more with the song's message than with its driving beat. Unlike Elvis's hit "Don't Be Cruel," which may have hinted at the same kind of relationship but which had an innocent feel to its message, "Too Much" was raw and very direct. Unlike other numbers that hinted at hanky-panky, "Too Much" actually left no doubt that there was action taking place. Worst of all, this was not a song of mutual love; instead, one lover was being used, then tossed away like garbage. As a result, mainstream recording artists had stayed away from the song altogether, and "Too Much" was certainly not a song that either RCA Victor or Colonel Tom Parker would have been eager to place in a recording session. Because it had generated no chart time, Elvis would not have heard it while listening to his radio or to a jukebox. So how did it end up in a late summer 1956 recording session? As unlikely as it sounds, it started with a train trip.

Thanks in part to having almost been the victim of a charter plane crash one Easter Sunday, Elvis did not like to fly. Whenever possible, he used trains to get to his destinations. He not only felt safer in trains, but the trips gave him time to relax, visit with his friends, and listen to some of the many demos that RCA Victor producer Steve Sholes passed his way. But even coast-to-coast train rides did not provide Elvis enough time to listen to all of the demos that were given to him. One cut, "Don't Forbid Me," sat in the "to do" stack for months before Elvis finally got around to listening to it. He loved the song, smelled "hit" written all over it, and even sensed how he would arrange it—only to find out that Pat Boone had already recorded it. The man in the white shoes would score a #1 hit with it, too. "Too Much" might have been lost as well if it had been in the demo stack, but it wasn't. Elvis found this future hit in the palm of his hand.

Lee Rosenberg was hungry for a hit. He and his songwriting partner had never charted with any of their tunes. Like the rest of America, they knew who Elvis was, and they were well aware that a recording of one of their songs by the singer would have a lasting impact on their careers. Upon hearing that Elvis was leaving Nashville via a train headed for Los Angeles and a Hollywood soundstage, Rosenberg got to the depot early and kept an eye out for the singer. The story goes that, after spotting Elvis, Rosenberg approached the rock 'n' roll star, politely introduced himself, and handed Elvis the Bernard Hardison recording of "Too Much." The writer must have realized that it was a long shot that Elvis would even listen to the cut, and that the record would probably find its way into a trash can before it was spun on a turntable. But it was the only chance Rosenberg had, so he took the gamble.

Elvis had promised Rosenberg that he would listen to the record. He kept his word, too. Even before he sorted through the stack of material from RCA Victor, he put the Hardison 45 on the portable record player he used to screen his demos. The rocker liked "Too Much" enough to file it away for an upcoming session in Los Angeles. Yet even with Elvis's stamp of approval, this song was still a long way from being a release, much less a hit.

RCA Victor had set up a session on September 2 at the Radio Recorders studio in Hollywood. The location was dictated by Elvis's filming schedule for his first movie. Unlike the Darby-orchestrated Los Angeles session for the *Love Me Tender* sound-track, this session would use the same formula and most of the same players that had created hits in Nashville and New York. It would also see Elvis pushed back into the forefront of deciding how the numbers would be cut.

Of course Steve Sholes oversaw the recording session, and Thorne Nogar, a well-known and highly respected industry figure with a solid track record, was assigned as engineer. Joining Elvis in the studio on this mild California day were Scotty Moore, on guitar as always, D. J. Fontana on drums, and Bill Black, playing his now almost legendary bass licks. The Jordanaires were there for the background vocals, and, as he had for the recording of "Hound Dog," the quartet's Gordon Stoker had volunteered to sit in at the piano.

One of the songs scheduled to be cut that day was "Playing for Keeps." This pleading ballad captured an Elvis who sounded much as he had in the Sam Phillips's sessions at Sun. The final cut of "Playing for Keeps" was simple and direct, honest and seemingly heartfelt. This recording represented what Steve Sholes had been looking for in the very early RCA Victor efforts.

"Playing for Keeps" had a country feel, which made it the perfect flip side to the rocking song that Elvis would record next—"Too Much." This kind of pairing harkened back to the Sun method of double selling Elvis by including on his 45s one song that was deemed proper for the rural stations, and another that was based in R&B and that would appeal to pop radio stations. RCA Victor had used this same marketing ploy with the previous Elvis hit, "Love Me," placing the old country standard "When My Blue Moon Turns to Gold" on the B side.

Recorded in the same session that produced "Playing for Keeps" and "Too Much" was "Paralyzed," another Otis Blackwell tune. The song might have been even better than "Don't Be Cruel," but it was never pushed as a single for fear that radio stations and listeners would take offense at the casual use of the term for a crippled or handicapped person in a bouncy love song. The fact that this hot number was not considered radio material seems to prove that political correctness did not begin in the 1990s. It was alive and well even when Ike was in the White House. Yet somehow this fear of offending folks did not stop RCA Victor from releasing "Too Much," which, in its original version, pushed the envelope far more than did "Paralyzed."

The band and singers learned the Rosenberg–Weinman song by listening to the old Hardison record. Vocally, Elvis's work on the song was very similar to Hardison's, but a few subtle changes created a final product that seemed far less bold and sexual than the initial cut. For starters, Elvis took out a "mama's little baby" bridge that oozed double entendre. Not only would this make the song sound a bit more innocent, but it would also reduce the finished song's length to two minutes and thirty-six seconds. A single that was longer than three minutes had a difficult time finding airplay; it was common practice to stick to a two-and-a-half-minute cut as the standard for songs.

The second bit of genius that gave the final take an almost comic flair was the work of the Jordanaires. The bass vocal, performed by Hugh Jarrett, repeated an "uh-oh" after each of the song's lyrical accusations of mistreatment. There was a playful quality to "Too Much" that reminded many of the easygoing pacing first created in "Don't Be Cruel." This not only made the number more commercial, it made it more acceptable, too. Yet, even though these two steps transformed "Too Much" into a much better song than the one featured on the initial Hardison cut, it was Scotty Moore's guitar work that probably ultimately transformed it into a hit.

Elvis drove his playing partner to create a lead guitar solo that stretched the limits of Scotty's playing ability. Time and time again, Moore was forced to record a series of walking guitar licks that Elvis demanded be tight and precise. Because of these complicated riffs, as well as the complexity of the seemingly simple background vocals, there were no perfect cuts of "Too Much" completed during the session. As he had been forced to do with "I Want You, I Need You, I Love You," Sholes had to splice together several different takes to get a final product that the producer felt was worthy of issuing as a single. At that point, the Colonel once again came into the picture.

The song's writers had no track record in the music business, and they needed a hit to establish their careers. When Parker called on Rosenberg and Weinman, the two were more than happy to give up part of the rights to the song in exchange for the chance to have an Elvis single. In this case, Elvis was not added to the song as a writer, though it can be argued that the singer had reworked this tune far more than he had "Don't Be Cruel" or any song from the "Love Me Tender" session, in which he did get writing credits. It is not stretching the truth in this case to conclude that, without Elvis's refining touches on his version of "Too Much," the song might not have become a hit.

"Too Much" was shipped the week of Elvis's twenty-second birthday, in 1957. On January 6, Elvis sang the song on *The Ed Sullivan Show*. In this most famous of his television appearances, Elvis was shown only from the waist up to prevent the public from seeing his liquid hips. It would be Elvis's last appearance on Sullivan's show. In addition to singing six of his current and past singles, Elvis sang the gospel classic "Peace in the Valley." With these performances, the singer waved farewell to the medium that had introduced him to the world. Except for a single appearance in 1960 with Frank Sinatra, Elvis would avoid the small screen until his famed "1968 Comeback Special."

A month after its release date, "Too Much" knocked Marty Robbins's "Singing the Blues" out of the top spot on the pop charts. Beginning February 9 and continuing for three weeks, the single ruled the *Billboard* playlist. In March, "Too Much" was finally replaced by movie star Tab Hunter's cover cut of the Sonny James country hit "Young Love." Ironically, it was James and the original "Young Love" that kept Elvis's latest single from reaching #1 on the country chart.

Lee Rosenberg had waited at a train station hoping that, by giving "Too Much" to Elvis, he'd not only land himself and his partner a hit single, but he'd also jump-start their careers. The depot meeting did produce a hit, but the team never again scored with Elvis. They also never had another tune that dominated the pop charts, and the duo dropped out of the national spotlight. The same could not be said of the singer who cut "Too Much." Elvis returned to Hollywood to work on a new film—one that would produce another #1 record while reviving a nation's craving for teddy bears.

ALL SHOOK UP

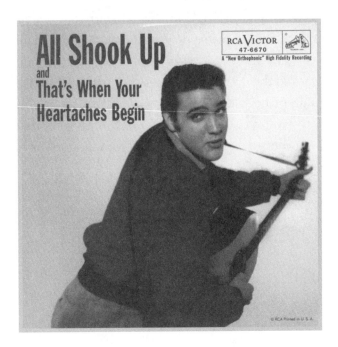

On Christmas Eve, 1956, Otis Blackwell sold six songs to Shalimar Music for an advance against royalties of one hundred and fifty dollars. That amount doesn't sound like much today, but to a man who was close to starving to death, it was like finding a gold mine. Certainly that is just what the New York City music publisher found in the songwriter, as well. Before his death, Blackwell would become a member of numerous songwriting halls of fame and the winner of hundreds of awards. He'd pen compositions that would help define an era, and he'd generate 185 million dollars in record sales—a figure that is still climbing today. Those who recorded his songs include five decades of the "who's who" of the entertainment world, and Blackwell's songs are still being recorded today. Over the course of his life he would become a legend, but in the fall of 1956, Blackwell was still just known as the guy who wrote "Don't Be Cruel" for Elvis.

Though Elvis never met Blackwell, he must have felt that he knew the songwriter well just from hearing his demos. Without a doubt, Elvis thought that Blackwell was one of the greatest tune-smiths in the business, and he shared that belief with many people. Whenever the singer received a new demo record from Blackwell, that demo almost always found its way to the turntable ahead of every other demo in the stack. In Elvis's heart, he and Blackwell were somehow connected. For those who knew both men, this con-nection was obvious in the way Elvis moved, sang, and even talked.

After "Don't Be Cruel," Elvis had immediately cut Blackwell's "Paralyzed." The latter was a great song and a favorite of fans who discovered it on the 1956 *Elvis* EP, and it was one that the singer loved to perform. But the song was never released as a true single. This was due to RCA Victor's conviction that some handicapped individuals might take offense at the number's lighthearted use of the term often utilized to describe the results of a horrific injury. In the song, the term is used as a way of portraying a man's frozen condition whenever he is around the woman he loves. Most likely few people at the time connected the two, or, if they did, allowed that connection to concern them. But because of the use of the word "paralyzed," few today have heard this incredibly well-writ-ten and beautifully performed tune. In order to produce another Elvis hit, as well as some much needed cash for his bank account, Blackwell was forced to go back to the drawing board.

To say that Blackwell was a prolific tunesmith is a vast under-statement. The writer could find an idea almost anywhere, and he seemed able to reshape it into a pop song in a matter of minutes. He often joked, "I can write a song about anything." He did just that over one thousand times.

A number of those at Shalimar often challenged Blackwell's claim. Aaron "Goldie" Goldmark constantly brought in off-the-wall ideas, saying, "Otis, see if you can write a song about this." Invariably, Blackwell always come up with something. Often the results were commercial, such as the huge Jerry Lee Lewis hit, "Great Balls of Fire." The best known of the challenge efforts would become the second #1 hit penned by Blackwell for Elvis in 1957.

On a warm fall day, Goldmark purchased a nickel Pepsi-Cola from a vending machine. Before he could pop off the top, he dropped the bottle onto the floor. Now he faced a dilemma. With the dark liquid in an explosive state, Goldie knew that if he opened it, he'd spray half the drink all over the office, and probably also onto his white shirt. Instead of consuming the beverage, he walked over to Blackwell's desk, set the soft drink in front of the songwriter, and said, "You say you can write about anything. Well, write about this." With that he turned and left Blackwell with the fizzing bottle of pop.

Blackwell studied the Pepsi-Cola for a moment. He probably thought about the product's slogan, "Twice as Much for a Nickel." He might even have pictured the company's spokesperson, movie star Joan Crawford, hawking Pepsi-Cola on TV. Finally he picked up the bottle. Shaking it, he watched the fizz redevelop. Though no one witnessed it, he must have grinned then, because he immediately set the bottle back on his desk and picked up a pen. He wrote the new song so quickly that the drink was still cold by the time he finished the number.

After completing "Goldie's Pepsi-Cola song," Otis asked everyone at Shalimar to stop what they were doing and take a place around the company's piano. Smiling, the songwriter sat down and began to pound the ivories while singing his new lyrics. Not only had Blackwell just triumphed in what had to be the first-ever "Pepsi Challenge," but it took only one performance of the song for everyone at Shalimar to agree that the writer had written a rock 'n' roll hit. Blackwell sensed that, with a title like "All Shook Up," he had done more than that; he had penned a classic for the king of the genre. It is therefore ironic that Elvis was not the initial artist to cut the new song. Instead, two separate singers, David Hill and Vicki Young, each put his or her stamp on "All Shook Up" first. Neither effort earned a place on radio playlists, however, and the song was still an unknown when it found its way into Elvis's hands.

RCA Victor and Elvis were both filled with expectations even before they'd heard a copy of the latest Otis Blackwell demo. When they finally got to listen to "All Shook Up," Elvis loved it, Steve Sholes thought it was a hit, and even the Colonel gave it a thumbs up. Parker hammered out the usual publishing arrangements, and the song was scheduled for the singer's very next recording session. After all, Sholes laughed, what could be a more perfect marriage than a song called "All Shook Up" and a singer who couldn't stop shaking when he sang?

On January 19, 1957, the same day he recorded the gospel standards for the bestselling EP release in the history of music, "Peace in the Valley," Elvis recorded the new Blackwell cut. At Radio Recorders studio in Los Angeles, Elvis rejoined the familiar group of performers who had worked on the earlier L.A. session that had produced "Too Much."

Few people knew then, and many don't realize today, that Elvis did not read music. He learned a song by listening to its demo over and over again, not by looking at a sheet filled with lyrics and music notes. Because of this, Elvis was often heavily influenced by the style that was employed on the demo recordings. It was only natural that he learned to sing "All Shook Up" with all of Blackwell's singing nuances intact. It is also not surprising that, along with the songwriter's casual approach to the song, most of those nuances found their way into the final recordings. In fact, Blackwell's interpretation, attitude, vocal inflections, and pronunciation are all evident in the Elvis cut. Yet even Blackwell must have wondered about the steady thumping that made it onto the released recording.

Those who listen closely to the final version of "All Shook Up" often pick out what sounds like the beat of a drum badly in need of a new skin or head. In fact, the sound was a result of Elvis slapping the back of his guitar to keep the song at the pace he wanted. In a couple of places the band pauses to allow Elvis's vocals to carry the number, and the slap is the only instrumental sound heard on the recording. Another interesting fact about this well-known hit is that the "All Shook Up" grunt, which is used repeatedly, and enthusiastically, by everyone who covers the song, is actually heard just once in the single, right before the final "I'm all shook up."

Elvis did not drive his group as hard in this session has he had in others. This was a fun session. Elvis didn't attack this song; he played with it. His vocal work embraced this playful attitude, and the final result is a song that does not have the drive of a typical rock standard, but that has more of a laid-back blues feel coupled to a rockabilly beat instead. It only took ten takes to get a solid version of the two-minute song. Elvis and the band then moved on to record the weepy balled "That's When Your Heartaches Begin," and the A and B sides of the singer's next record were complete. Just a little more than two months later, on March 22, the single was shipped. Again, as had been the case with "Don't Be Cruel" and "Paralyzed," Elvis was credited as being one of the song's writers.

Three weeks after its release, on April 13, "All Shook Up" knocked Perry Como's non-rocking "Round and Round" out of the #1 spot on the pop charts. Elvis's latest single ruled the *Billboard* chart for eight weeks, blocking a number of great songs, including the classic "Little Darlin'" by the Diamonds, from reaching the top spot. More remarkably, considering its meteoric three-week rise to the top of the charts, the single remained in the Top 40 for twenty-two weeks, and Top 100 for thirty. On most pop radio stations, "All Shook Up" stayed in heavy song rotation for the remainder of the year, and *Billboard* named it the bestselling and most-played record of 1957. It was the second year in a row that Elvis had accomplished this feat.

Over on the Country Juke Box chart, "All Shook Up" claimed the #1 position for a single week. The record ruled the R&B playlists for a solid month. Across the pond, it held the top spot in the British charts for seven weeks. "All Shook Up" was one of only a handful of records that would rule all of these charts at the very same time.

Elvis's new single did more than just generate sales; it infected American culture. "All Shook Up" became a catchall phrase used to describe anyone who was too nervous to do something. A student would get "all shook up" and fail a test. A lovesick boy would be "too shook up" to ask a girl out. A basketball player would get too caught up in the pressure of a key moment in the game and miss a shot, and fans would say, "Boy, did you see him? He was all shook up," or "We shook him up, didn't we?" Eventually this catch-phrase was shortened to just "shook," and five decades later it is still a part of American language.

Some critics believe that "All Shook Up," as well as Rick Nelson's "Stood Up, Brokenhearted Again," did more to capture the innocence, awkwardness, and daily pain of youth than any other songs in the history of music. That opinion can be argued, and surely, hundreds of other numbers could be picked to fill this role. But what can't be debated is that, in "All Shook Up," Otis Blackwell said more about the emotions of a lovesick teen in just two minutes than most writers could pack into a hundred-thousand-word novel. That is the real genius of "All Shook Up"—the same mark of genius that Blackwell would bring to hundreds of compositions.

TEDDY BEAR

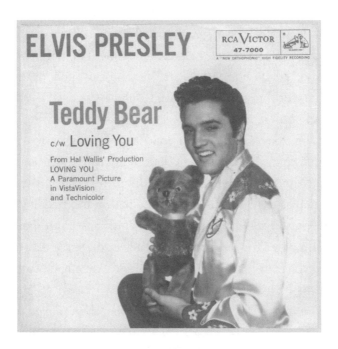

With his second chart topper of 1957, Elvis Presley made history and influenced culture by inserting a new expression into the English language. While "All Shook Up" affected the way Americans spoke, the next Elvis hit would make cash registers ring from coast to coast as it jump-started a renewed affection for a lovable toy. And this time, for a change, Colonel Tom Parker could not claim a piece of the action.

The inspirational foundation for Elvis's third #1 song of 1957 predates the singer's birth by more than three decades and centers around a pardon given by the president of the United States to a resident of the singer's home state of Mississippi. On November

15, 1902, avid sportsman and the U.S. chief executive Theodore
Roosevelt was on a hunt with some friends in the woods of Mississippi. The hunting party had split up and one segment of men
tracked a lean black bear, getting close enough to lasso the unfor-
tunate critter. By the time the president caught up with this group,
the bear had been tied to a tree and its captors waited for the leader
of the free world to record the kill. Roosevelt refused to shoot the
exhausted animal, and instead ordered that it be set free.

The next day, Clifford Barryman, an editorial cartoonist with
the *Washington Post*, created a comic rendering of the event. His
paper ran the humorous display on its front page. Other papers
picked it up as well. While most of the nation laughed, a Brooklyn
shopkeeper named Morris Michtom decided to capitalize on the
story. Pulling two toy bears from the back of his stationery store, he
displayed them in his shop window. These homemade stuffed animals, sewed by his wife, quickly sold. Michtom ordered his wife to
make more of the tiny, buttoned-eyed bears, then picked up a pen
and wrote to the White House. A few days later he received a letter from the president giving the entrepreneur permission to call the
creatures "Teddy's Bear." Michtom, using the company name Ideal,
began to market the "Teddy's." Over the next few years the posses-
sive case would be dropped, and the teddy bear would become one
of the most popular toys in not only America, but around the world.

By the 1950s the teddy bear had been replaced in many children's hearts by electric trains that lit up, bicycles with horns, dolls
that cried, and cap guns that fired scores of shots in a minute.
There was still a good market for the stuffed creatures, and they
continue to serve as the big prize for winners at carnival games, but
the toy was no longer the bestselling children's item on five-and-
dime-store shelves. The teddy bear was not even the top money-

maker for the Ideal Toy Company. It would take a Pennsylvania man's visit to the apartment Elvis used in New York City to put the American spotlight back on "Teddy's Bear."

Kal Mann was a great songwriter, and in the 1950s he was also one of the most important figures in the Philadelphia music industry. A composer, promoter, record producer, and the cofounder of Cameo Records, Mann didn't just give birth to some great songs; he shepherded them at every stage, from recording to landing on the charts. Working with the likes of Dick Clark, whose *American Bandstand* was beamed daily from Philly to all of America, Mann got teens off their seats and on their feet, dancing to some of the best tunes of the early rock era.

During his long career, Mann teamed up with a number of talented songwriters. One, a Julliard-trained pianist named Bernie Lowe, was not only a writing partner, but the other half of Cameo Records, as well. As songwriters, the duo was also under contract with Hill and Range Music Company, the same firm that teamed with Colonel Tom Parker and published all of Elvis Presley's hits.

Mann and Lowe predated Elvis at the Nashville publishing house. Hill and Range had pushed the duo to help turn the company's Bill Haley and His Comets into teenager sensations. In short order the writers and publisher discovered that Haley was simply too old for the kids to relate to. They liked a few of his songs, but they couldn't connect with the balding singer on a personal basis. Haley was finally ruled out as an idol, and Hill and Range began to look for another "Great White Hope" who could sing R&B music. A year later, in early 1956, Mann and Lowe were brought back to Nashville to meet Elvis Presley, a young man who seemed to not only win hearts in the studio, but on the stage, as well. Like those at RCA Victor, the executives at Hill and Range thought that this performer might become the teen idol they needed. And they were right: within a few weeks of Mann and Lowe's meeting with Elvis, the singer had become a national sensation.

While Mann was impressed with the Memphis native as a performer, he was more struck by the character of the young man. Elvis was polite, considerate of others, and very humble. He listened more than he talked. He called the songwriter "Mr. Mann," and he always answered, "Yes sir" or "No sir" when responding to a question. Elvis was the type of kid with whom the songwriter enjoyed spending time.

In an effort to find out the type of music that Elvis wanted to record, Mann met with the singer a second time, in New York. On this occasion, Elvis asked Mann to accompany him to the apartment that the entertainer used in the city. As the two shared a soft drink and some conversation, Mann noticed the tremendous numbers of teddy bears that were sitting all around the small apartment. The animals came in all sizes and all colors. To Mann, it seemed that he had sat down in the shipping department of a stuffed-animal manufacturer.

"What's with the bears?" the songwriter asked Elvis.

"I like 'em, sir," Elvis replied. "They are my favorites."

At that moment, Kal Mann didn't know enough about Elvis to understand why a grown man would have such great affection for a child's toy. In time, the songwriter would discover that Elvis's childhood had been rather bleak. Raised in a tiny shotgun house in Mississippi, the surviving twin and only child of an unskilled couple from the wrong side of the tracks, the singer had grown up with little but dreams. His father had even served time in prison. When Elvis was thirteen, the family moved to the Memphis projects, but the poverty that had been a part of their life in Tupelo followed them to Tennessee. As a boy, an often lonely Elvis didn't have much in the way of toys. Now, as a young adult with money, he was making up for what he had missed in his youth. Little did he know that his toys would inspire one of his greatest hit songs ever made.

Mann returned to Philly and met with Bernie Lowe. Both men were determined to compose Elvis's next hit. Pulling inspiration from the stuffed animals he had observed in Elvis's apartment, Mann started a novelty number about a young man who wanted to be his girlfriend's teddy bear. With Bernie chiming in with musical riffs and lyrical imagery, the duo quickly created a very short and mild rock 'n' roll number. Once they had polished it, the men called in some local musicians and cut a demo. Through their contacts at Hill and Range, Mann and Lowe quickly got a copy of the demo to Elvis.

Elvis liked the song, as did producer Steve Sholes. Yet it would be Paramount movie producer Hal Wallis who decided that this song was destined for greater things than being just another RCA Victor release. Wallis had signed Elvis to star in a film the studio had christened *Lonesome Cowboy*. Besides his horse, a cowboy's best friend is supposed to be a song, and Hal sensed that "Teddy Bear" was the perfect song to be cast in that role.

Lonesome Cowboy would feature Elvis in his first starring role, and the script was tailored to both the young singer and his fans. In spite of the title, the film was set in modern times, and it embraced rock 'n' roll music. Wallis was determined to create a quality movie that could be aimed at the Elvis fan base. He accomplished his goal in spades.

In an attempt to look more like his screen idols Cary Grant and Tony Curtis, Elvis had his hair dyed black. It may have given him a more dramatic look, but it did not suddenly transform Elvis into a polished actor. Yet, much more so than in *Love Me Tender*, the singer showed some thespian potential under the veteran Wallis's direction. As his next few films would prove, if the Colonel had stayed out of the way, Elvis might have evolved into a very good actor. Yet with Parker pulling the strings, it never happened.

Lonesome Cowboy was an almost semi-autobiographical flick about a good-looking country kid who could sing. Character actor Wendell Corey played a washed-up country singer whose career was going down as Elvis's Deke Rivers's star was rising. Dolores Hart was the innocent and pretty love interest. Lizabeth Scott, who had worked with some of the greatest leads in Hollywood, was given the role of a manipulative female version of Colonel Tom Parker. This quartet of actors and some solid background players proved to be a great combination.

While *Lonesome Cowboy* was a musical, it was not like the B movies in which Elvis would star in the 1960s. This film was a drama, with music inserted in places that made sense in the context of the film. In that sense, the film can be compared to the Judy Garland–Mickey Rooney features of the 1930s, or even to a Doris Day movie of the early 1950s. Wallis needed original songs for the film's concert scenes, and he was on the lookout for real rock 'n' roll hits. When the producer heard the "Teddy Bear" demo, he knew he'd found just what he wanted for one of the film's most energetic performance scenes.

Elvis recorded the Mann-Lowe number somewhere between January 15 and 18. Record-keeping duties of these sessions was placed in the hands of Paramount, and the dates and times that each of the movie's songs were recorded has been lost. As had been the case with "Love Me Tender," the movie's songs were not recorded in a small studio; instead, the sessions were on the huge Paramount Scoring Stage. To a singer who was used to the intimate

Nashville style of recording, this was less than ideal. Fortunately, this time Elvis was surrounded by his own band, as well as by the Jordanaires. Two extra musicians were added to this mix—Tiny Timbrell, on rhythm guitar (something Elvis had played on many earlier records), and Dudley Brooks, at the keyboard. As the Jordanaires' Gordon Stoker and Hoyt Hawkins also sat down at the piano from time to time, just who was at the ivories for the final cut of "Teddy Bear" is still a matter of conjecture. Though nobody in the group liked working on the cavernous stage, the movie's songs were successfully recorded in time, and the production work of *Lonesome Cowboy* began on schedule.

"Teddy Bear" had been one of the session's easiest songs to record. Elvis copied the demo, right down to the ending tag, "just wanna be your teddy bear," and the group was able to quickly learn the number. Elvis had fun with the song, so there was little pressure on the stage as the musicians played with the funny little ditty. The song's tone reflects the same mood that Elvis produced on "All Shook Up." Take thirteen of the song was used as the final cut. The recording of "Teddy Bear" proved to be a walk in the park compared to that of "Loving You," another song that was slotted for the film. Forty different takes were made of the Jerry Leiber–Mike Stoller composition before Elvis decided he had done the number justice. Ultimately, Paramount liked "Loving You" so much that, just as Fox had done with "Love Me Tender," they changed the title of the movie to the name of the song.

Executives at RCA Victor believed that two strongest numbers in the *Loving You* score were the title cut and "Teddy Bear." On June 11, it released a single that consisted of these two songs. The record did not designate either side as A or B, and DJs played both sides when they first received the new product. Thanks to requests from callers, radio stations soon decided that "Teddy Bear," listed on the record as "(Let Me Be Your) Teddy Bear," was the one that most fans really wanted to hear. And why not? Millions of American girls were already wishing that Elvis would come home with them and be their teddy bear. This was their song.

The Mann-Lowe novelty rocker hit the top of the *Billboard* pop charts on July 8, 1957, one day before the premiere of the movie *Loving You*. Thanks at least in part to the popularity of the motion picture, the Elvis single held the #1 spot for most of the summer. It would take another movie song, Debbie Reynolds's "Tammy," to knock "Teddy Bear" out of the top spot. Still, this third #1 Elvis hit of the year held the #2 spot for several more weeks. In total, it stayed on the charts twenty-five weeks, eighteen of which were spent in the Top 40. Meanwhile, "Loving You" managed to peak at #20. In a sign that older country audiences might have been ready to hand Elvis over to the younger pop crowd, "Teddy Bear" topped the country charts for a single week.

Thanks to the success of the single and the blockbuster movie that contained the song, sales of teddy bears skyrocketed across the country. This time, the stuffed creatures weren't just for children—teenage girls and young women were sleeping with them, too. And millions of the creatures were given the name Elvis. Factories, not only in the United States, but around the world, put on second shifts to try to keep up with demand.

Beginning in late June, the United States Postal Service was flooded with thousands of boxes containing teddy bears addressed to Elvis Presley in Memphis. By late fall, the singer, who had recently purchased his Graceland mansion, was literally swimming in fluffy bears of all colors, shapes, and sizes, all sent by adoring fans. By Christmas, the invasion of the bears was threatening to completely consume the singer's home. On December 26, 1957,

Elvis quietly donated thousands of the teddy bears to the National Foundation for Infantile Paralysis.

Kal Mann would never pen another #1 hit for Elvis, but he would write and produce legendary songs for Bobby Rydell, Chubby Checker, the Dovells, Dee Dee Sharp, and the Orlons. Mann, who today is remembered as the man who kept America dancing, is responsible for such beloved numbers such as "South Street," "Let's Twist Again," "Bristol Stomp," and "Wah-Watusi." Not bad for a guy who didn't play an instrument and had to sing his compositions to his secretary in order to have them transcribed onto a musical page.

In the summer of 1977, twenty years after his "Teddy Bear" had topped the charts, Kal Mann took a trip to Music City to visit with old friends at the offices of Hill and Range Music. While he was there, one of the area's better-known singers walked in.

"Mr. Mann," a familiar voice announced. Mann turned to see Elvis Presley grinning, his hand extended. The singer was heavier, the voice a bit deeper, but the smile was the same as it had been the first day they had met.

"I think you might have it wrong," Mann answered. "By this time, considering all that has happened, I think I should be calling you Mr. Presley, and you should be calling me Kal."

Elvis shook his head. "No, Mr. Mann. That is not how it should be."

Before the two parted, the singer thanked the songwriter for what he had meant to his career. As the singer and the songwriter went their separate ways, Mann was again amazed by the entertainer's humble politeness. *I really like that guy,* he thought. Three weeks later, Mann was shocked to hear his "Teddy Bear" back in heavy rotation—and even more shocked that Elvis was dead.

JAILHOUSE ROCK

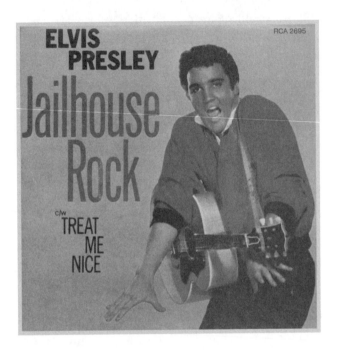

E ven before the second Elvis motion picture, *Loving You*, had been completed, a script was approved and plans were made for the next Elvis movie. Impressed with their work on *Loving You* for rival studio Paramount (though the film had not yet been released to the general public, it was available for review), MGM signed Jerry Leiber and Mike Stoller to compose the score of Elvis's next feature. Because executives at the studio were aware of the prolific nature of the R&B songwriting duo, they were initially less concerned about getting the songs than they were about making sure that the props for the prison drama were in place before shooting was to begin on May 13. But days turned into weeks, and weeks into months, and still no demo records had been sent to the producer's office. The studio began to get nervous.

In mid-April, MGM executives finally asked Leiber and Stoller to make a trip to New York City to update them on their progress. The two should have dreaded the trip—they'd written nothing. Instead, they figured that taking a little heat was a fair trade-off for a trip to the Big Apple. The duo could not wait to hit Broadway and search out all the spots on the Great White Way to party. What did wait was their work on the songwriting assignment.

As Leiber remembers, "We had been in New York for about a week, but had not settled down to write anything for the new film. New York was just too exciting. We were about to leave the hotel room for another assault on Manhattan when Jean Aberbach, of Elvis [Elvis Presley Music, a division of Hill and Range Music Company], barged in."

Aberbach wanted to hear the new songs. There were none, but Leiber assured the music-publishing representative that they would be written soon. Aberbach clamped his jaw, locked his teeth, and stared at the two writers in a threatening manner. Then he moved to the far side of the room, next to the suite's only exit.

"He pushed a large sofa in front of the door," Jerry recalls, "blocking the entrance, and with that, informed us that we were not leaving the room until we had finished the score and placed it in his hands."

Aberbach was a large man, much bigger and stronger than either Leiber or Stoller. The duo reasoned that even in a fair fight, Aberbach would be able to handle both of them. Rather than argue with this imposing enforcer, Stoller walked over to the rented upright piano and began to play on the keys. Jerry soon joined him with a pencil and some paper. For the next hour or so the two scanned the script, finding the marked spots where Elvis was supposed to sing a song. The songwriters noted four musical holes in the script, got a feel for the emotional needs of those scenes, and set to work.

One of the designated song spots in the script called for a huge production number set in a prison cell block. It seemed as though the scene was supposed to combine the feel of a tough Bogie or Cagney movie with the excitement of a Broadway show—a strange marriage, at best. As Leiber would later tell an interviewer, "I certainly would never have thought of a song like 'Jailhouse Rock' if somebody hadn't said, 'Look, there is going to a big production number in a jail.'" As the songwriters were themselves under house arrest, the inspiration for this session seemed obvious.

The title of the new song was the same as the working title of the movie, though the composers probably had a different reason for locking in on their "Jailhouse Rock" for the movie's spotlight number. The "Rock" in the title did, in one sense of the word, refer to rock 'n' roll (a term, invented by DJ Alan Freed, given to the popular music of the time), but it was also a reference to the nickname of America's most notorious prison, Alcatraz. Everyone who had watched jail films since the 1930s knew this handle very well. It was common to hear a character in an old Warner Brothers movie say, "Just got back from the Rock." Even the youngest film fan needed no translation—everyone knew that the guy was an ex-con who had just left toughest prison in the country. Although the prison in "Jailhouse Rock" was not Alcatraz, the term "the Rock" was so familiar to audiences that it immediately evoked thoughts of prisons in general. The other half of the title, "Jailhouse," was even easier, as it simply fit the movie's setting. It also sounded better than "Prison Rock," "Penal Rock," or "Big House

Rock." Once Leiber and Stoller came up with the song's title and had a clear image of the proposed set in their minds, the movie's hottest song almost wrote itself: all the songwriters had to do was remember the nicknames of the gangsters from the old Hollywood films of the 1930s and picture them at a prison party.

As the duo mainly wrote R&B music, they felt comfortable with this kind of driving material they felt was needed for this upbeat number. Yet they had to wonder if the studio was going to want something so hard-driving for a major film. This number rocked like nothing Elvis had put on vinyl—it was hardly fodder for a mom-and-pop crowd. But, outside the confines of their own hotel cell, the big city was calling, so rather than rework it or tone it down, the duo pronounced it finished and moved on to the next song.

As it turned out, it would be the movie's love songs that took the most time to pen that day. Yet, as Aberbach was holding down the couch that was blocking the door, it was work that had to be finished, or there would be no partying in New York.

"While Jean pretended to doze on the couch," Mike explains, "we hammered out 'Jailhouse Rock,' 'Treat Me Nice,' 'I Want to Be Free,' and '(You're So Square) Baby, I Don't Care.' We started writing at about 2:00 in the afternoon, and by 6:00 P.M. we were out on the streets again." As pleased as the team was to be strolling down Park Avenue, Jean Aberbach was even happier to have a quartet of solid songs to take back to Hill and Range, Elvis, and MGM.

Leiber and Stoller returned to their homes on the West Coast. On April 30, 1957, they were invited to meet Elvis Presley for the first time at his recording session for the new MGM film at Radio Recorders studio in Hollywood. Sensing that the invitation was less a request than an order, the songwriters arrived at the studio not long after Elvis had arrived.

Until that moment, the stellar writing team had believed that Elvis was little more than a backwoods hick who had gotten lucky and become a star. In their own words, they had "predetermined that Elvis was musically ignorant." When they met the singer for the first time and began to discuss music with him, they were shocked. Within minutes the songwriters discovered that Elvis was not only talented, but that he was humble and bright, too. He was familiar with almost all of their compositions—even those that had only been produced as obscure R&B recordings. More than that, Elvis was interested in finding out why the team had chosen certain arrangements, how they worked together when they wrote, and whether they had any specific disciplines that helped them remain creative. The songwriting team fell in love with Elvis. Instead of ducking out after the meeting, they stayed and helped with the session. Stoller even sat down at the piano and played "Treat Me Nice" for Elvis, teaching the young star the method he thought should be used when cutting the song. Elvis was so impressed with the writer's performance that he convinced MGM to cast Stoller in the role of the pianist in the film.

In addition to Leiber and Stoller, Elvis was surrounded in this session by regulars Scotty Moore, Bill Black, D. J. Fontana, and the Jordanaires. Dudley Brooks again worked the ivories when needed. But, even as well as the meeting with the songwriters had gone, the session was anything but smooth. It was Elvis who initially put the whole thing on hold.

Elvis had a habit of warming up by singing gospel quartet songs with the Jordanaires. RCA Victor had always cut Elvis some slack on this matter. They knew how much he loved religious music and how singing it sent his spirits soaring. RCA Victor figured that thirty minutes of gospel warm-ups were worth the cost of the studio time because they got Elvis focused and energized. MGM was not so kind. When the gospel singing began, the engineers and studio heads came down fast and hard. They informed the musicians that they were wasting valuable time and money, and that they all needed to get to work on the movie songs— now, not later! Elvis, who at the time had the reputation of being one of the least-spoiled men in show business, walked out of the session. If they were going to keep him from singing gospel, then he wasn't going to sing at all. The Presley strike went on for several days.

MGM finally relented, and Elvis came back into the studio on May 2. Singing his favorite gospel standards, he took even longer than usual to warm up. Then, just when it appeared that everything was on track again, a second emotional explosion occurred. Partway through the soundtrack session, MGM's engineer ordered Bill Black to switch from playing his much-beloved stand-up acoustic bass to playing a brand new electric Fender. That request was like asking a man to divorce his wife of thirty years and take up with an ugly woman he hated. Instead of plugging in, Black walked out. Again work came to a sudden and complete halt. Realizing that time was at a premium, Elvis knew that—with or without Black—it was time to rock, jailhouse style. He picked up the electric bass and played the bass lines until Black returned.

"Jailhouse Rock" was a joyful challenge to Elvis and his group. It was the hardest-driving song they had ever attempted. While other Elvis cuts had been rockers, none had the raw power of this Leiber-Stoller number. The song has an almost heavy-metal feel. Filled with an angry tone, the song forced the singer to dig down deep into his essence. Take after take, he tried to get it right, and, after hearing each playback, he shook his head. As they watched

Elvis attack and reattack their song, Leiber and Stoller realized two things about the man. One was that he had apparently boundless reserves of energy. Instead of fading, he became stronger with each take. The other observation was something that Steve Sholes had noted on the "Hound Dog" session: Elvis was a perfectionist. He would not give up until he thought that a song had been perfectly performed. Elvis's perfectionism drove everyone around him to reach beyond the limits of what they thought they could perform. Ironically, in many cases, this meant that after thirty or more takes had been recorded, one of the first takes was recognized as being the best. As was his nature, Elvis had to get through all of those less-than-perfect takes to accept the earlier effort. In the case of "Jailhouse Rock," take six was far from being the final cut, but it was the one that was released as a single.

In the film *Jailhouse Rock*, Elvis plays Vince Everett. Unable to control his temper, Everett gets into a fight, kills a man, and is convicted of manslaughter. His cell mate in the Big House teaches him how to play the guitar and arranges for him to appear on a network TV program that is being aired from the prison. His performance is a hit. Everett is soon released on parole, whereupon the budding rocker is scammed by one record label after another. Rather than be burned by another company, Everett and his pretty manager, played by Judy Tyler, start their own label. Naturally Elvis becomes a star. Then the old cell mate (played by Mickey Shaughnessy) shows up and produces a contract that had been drawn up in prison. The contract gives the former cell mate 50 percent of all of Everett's earnings. (Ironically, this was the same cut that the Colonel was taking from Elvis in real life, but in the movie, the percentage is deemed unfair.) A fight ensues and Elvis's character is struck in the throat, causing him to lose his voice. Naturally, to ensure a feel-good ending, he finally becomes able to sing again, and he finds true love in Tyler's arms.

Critics praised the movie, and Elvis's fans loved the music that made up the score. *Jailhouse Rock* had the feel of many other golden-age Hollywood prison efforts, and it would have been a good film even without the wonderful Leiber-Stoller score and an additional song, "Young and Beautiful," which was penned by the songwriting team of Aaron Schroeder and Abner Silver. Because this was an Elvis movie, however, everyone involved knew that the music had to be in the film. As solid as the film's production, direction, acting, and entire musical score is, there is no doubt that the cell-block dance number is not just the highlight of the film— it's also the most-remembered rock dance number ever produced by a major motion picture studio. Over time, this "Jailhouse Rock" bit has grown into almost mythic proportions in Hollywood history.

Elvis felt that "Treat Me Nice" was the best of the film's songs and perhaps the greatest number he had ever recorded. He predicted it would be his next #1 hit. As the singer would soon discover, the public would think otherwise.

On the day that Elvis's next single was shipped—September 24—the top song on the *Billboard* charts was "That'll Be the Day," the only #1 hit that Buddy Holly and the Crickets ever scored. In its initial week of release, "Jailhouse Rock" hopped onto playlists and began a twenty-seven week ride on the pop charts. Much to the singer's surprise, "Treat Me Nice" was deemed by the public as the lesser of the two songs, and the tune reached only #18 on the pop charts and #11 on the Country Disc Jockey chart. The movie's theme song did much better.

"Jailhouse Rock" would become the second Elvis #1 record penned by Jerry Leiber and Mike Stoller. On October 21, the song knocked the rockabilly duo the Everly Brothers and their "Wake Up, Little Susie" down to the #2 spot. "Jailhouse Rock" continued to reign for seven weeks, until Sam Cooke and "You Send Me" dropped the single to second place on December 2. "Jailhouse Rock" remained in the Top 5 for the rest of the year. On the R&B chart, the record held the #1 spot for five weeks. "Jailhouse Rock" topped the Country Best-Sellers chart for only one week, but remained on country playlists for twenty-four.

But the most incredible and surprising chart numbers for this Elvis single came from the other side of the Atlantic. In the United Kingdom, Elvis wasted no time climbing the playlist—"Jailhouse Rock" became the first single in British history to enter the charts at #1. The momentum for this unheralded leap to the top had come from just a couple of plays of the song on the BBC.

Fans would have to wait until November 8, 1957, to catch the nationwide release of the third Elvis feature film. By that time, everyone in the country seemed able to sing at least a few lines of the title tune. Long lines of fans hit theaters across the country, and it came as no surprise that, by the end of the first week, MGM had recouped all its outlay for production and advertising.

Elvis spent twenty-five weeks holding the #1 position on the *Billboard* pop charts in 1957. This kind of success is unparalleled in the history of entertainment. At the time, however, Elvis had other thoughts on his mind besides his enormous success. He had just received a draft notice from Uncle Sam. Elvis Presley's days as a civilian were numbered.

BLUE CHRISTMAS

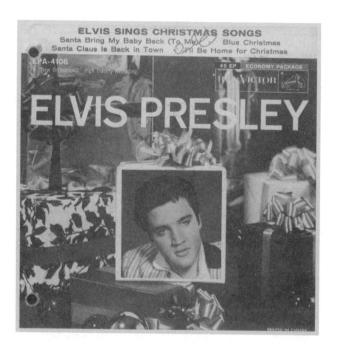

T he story of Elvis finding a Christmas standard dates back to a time long before the singer walked into Sun Studio or was discovered by Colonel Tom Parker. Though it was considered a "hillbilly" song until Elvis made it his own in 1957, in reality, "Blue Christmas" was written in New England, and was composed as something of a joke. This song's roots go back to a miserable commute from Connecticut to New York City and a man who just couldn't seem to catch a break.

As usual, Jay Johnson was running late. He had been slow getting started that morning, and the cold rainy weather wasn't helping at all. On top of that, his green 1939 Mercury convertible had developed a huge rip just above the driver's seat, and water was pouring through the growing hole onto his head. Pulling the car off to the side of the road, the forty-five-year-old Johnson rummaged among the papers he kept in his backseat until he found an umbrella. He pushed it through the hole in the canvas top, then hit the button that allowed the umbrella to open. Shifting into first gear, he eased the car back onto the road. With the umbrella shielding him from most of the water, Jay continued on to the Stamford, Connecticut, train station.

A script and commercial jingle writer for radio, Johnson was on his way to New York, in a daily commute that included a one-hour train junket. Johnson spent his time on the train catching up on the postwar news in the paper, working word puzzles, and scribbling down inspiration for story lines and songs. His daughter remembers her father as a man who was driven by creative challenges.

"He often wrote or worked as he rode on the trains," recalls Judy Olmsted. "I am sure that if he were alive today he would have had a laptop computer. He loved to play with words. He made up all kinds of limericks and poems. He wrote for some of the top shows on radio and, later on, television, too. He was a vaudeville veteran, played around with Broadway shows, and even published dozens of songs. Some of their titles were almost as funny as the lyrics. They included 'Peaceful,' 'Little Wedding Bells,' 'Telephone Fever,' 'Sunday Afternoon,' and one of my favorites, 'Peter Pan the Meter Man.' That title alone tells you how his mind worked." To Elvis fans it should be quickly apparent that Johnson and the rock singer did not appear to be cut from the same cloth, and that they had very little in common. But that was about to change.

On this bleak day, as the train rumbled toward the Big Apple, Johnson yanked a piece of hotel stationery from his briefcase. The holiday season was just around the corner, and tunes such as Irv-ing Berlin's "White Christmas" were being used in many of the radio shows for which he wrote. *Surely*, the writer thought, *I can come up with something more original than that.* As Johnson consid-ered the long list of Christmas classics he could use for one of his scripts, an idea began to take root. At first glance, it seemed almost too obvious. Given the success of "White Christmas" and the tremendous impact of blues music during the 1940s, surely, John-son thought, someone had already combined the two concepts into a song. A number about a blue Christmas seemed so natural. Yet, as he considered the idea, he thought, *what if no one has?* Picking up a pen, he scribbled down his initial thoughts.

> I expect to have a colorful Christmas
> tinged with every kind of holiday hue,
> and though I know I'll find every shade in the rainbow,
> this design of mine will be mostly blue.

These lines were destined to become the rough first verse of a lyric sheet that Johnson would call "Blue Christmas." Over the course of the next few days several more verses followed.

Once Johnson was satisfied with his lyrics and had assured him-self that he had written something unique, he met with friend and composer Billy Hayes. Though no one recalls what happened in that meeting, it is thought that Hayes offered a few suggestions about the lyrics. Perhaps that is why Johnson's first two verses were dropped. Using the writer's later lines, Hayes neatly wrapped the package with an appropriate musical score. The answer to "White Christmas" was then pitched to Choice Music. The music pub-lisher bought the rights to the number in 1948.

Choice Music immediately began to shop its new holiday number to recording artists. Bing Crosby, Bob Hope, and a host of other singers known for holiday tunes were not interested. Choice, a company that was known for its novelty songs, then attempted to interest Nashville artists in "Blue Christmas." Yet no one in Music City cared for the song. Finally, Hugo Winterhalter and His Orchestra, a pop band, cut the song.

Winterhalter had worked as an arranger for the likes of Count Basie, Tommy and Jimmy Dorsey, and Claude Thornhill before putting together his own group. In 1949 the bandleader had scored a minor hit with "Jealous Heart." When he recorded the Johnson-Hayes holiday offering that winter, Winterhalter's label, Columbia Records, hoped that it would be a hit. Instead, "Blue Christmas" barely touched the Top 10, peaking at #9. These modest numbers didn't forecast a long run for the new song. Most felt it would soon be forgotten.

Ernest Tubb must have heard the song because the Texas Troubadour worked it into his act at about that same time. In 1950, the country star recorded "Blue Christmas" for Decca Records. For the next five years Tubb's holiday song was a standard Christmas treat for radio listeners.

With its play on words and tone of heartbreak, "Blue Christmas" was as hillbilly as any song that appeared on the country charts. So many people identified it with Tubb that he was often referred to as the song's writer. In fact, Elvis probably believed that Tubb was the composer when he went into the studio to cut it. Tubb had done nothing to change the song's lyrics or score, but he had shaped it into a country music standard and put the song on the map.

By the mid-1950s almost every country act was using "Blue Christmas" in their November and December live shows. It was one song that put some twang in the mistletoe. "Blue Christmas" probably would have remained strictly a part of the Music City genre if not for the fact that RCA Victor wanted to find a way to recapture the success of Elvis's gospel EP *Peace in the Valley*. In a stroke of genius, the label decided to use Elvis to make some waves in the Christmas market.

Elvis had listened to a lot of country music in his youth. When he was at Sun Records he'd toured with a number of "hillbilly" acts. While performing on Grand Ole Opry, he took the time to have his picture made with one of his idols, Ernest Tubb. Tubb's impact on young Elvis probably pushed the singing sensation, years later, to record "Blue Christmas." Far from simply covering the country classic, however, Elvis rocked Christmas and turned it decidedly blue. In Elvis's hands, "Blue Christmas" was no longer a ballad, it was Memphis street-corner blues. In a recording that lasted only three minutes, Elvis made the Christmas song a rock standard, and he gave RCA Victor another huge-selling extended-play 45.

Elvis cut "Blue Christmas" on September 5, 1957. It was during this session that he also laid down the final version of "Treat Me Nice." This session, held at Radio Recorders in Los Angeles, was not as productive as RCA Victor had hoped. It was difficult for Elvis and his regular group of musicians to get into the Christmas spirit with a summer wind blowing through their hair every time they stepped outside. The results of the session were mixed at best, but the recording that came about that day would be issued in three different formats: a single, an extended-play 45 called *Elvis Sings Christmas Songs*, and an LP titled *Elvis's Christmas Album*. When released in November, RCA would find that there was gold in every format during the holiday season.

Elvis's recording of Johnson's and Hayes's song would generate more royalties for Johnson than all of his other songs combined. First released in 1957, Elvis's "Blue Christmas" would never hit the official Top 10, but for a decade it would consistently rule the Christmas Singles chart. In that sense it was a true #1 hit. "Blue Christmas" also opened the door for scores of other singers to embrace Jay Johnson's answer to "White Christmas." Thanks to Elvis, the Jay Johnson–Billy Hayes song has become the gift that keeps on giving.

"I will tell you this," Judy Olmsted says with a laugh. "It wouldn't be Christmas at our house without 'Blue Christmas.'" And a host of Elvis music fans would probably agree that, while there have been many great secular holiday classics, a real Christmas isn't complete until it's sung blue by the King of Rock 'n' Roll.

DON'T

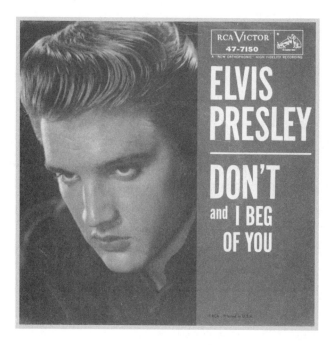

When Elvis Presley asked songwriter Mike Stoller to appear in the film *Jailhouse Rock*, Stoller had no idea that his cameo would lead to another huge hit for him and his partner Jerry Leiber. But work on the prison-theme musical put Elvis and Stoller together on a constant basis, and during their time together a solid friendship was forged, paving the way for a brand-new song that would help to redefine the direction of Elvis's career. During their breaks from shooting the film, Elvis and Stoller talked about everything from personal tastes in food to favorite songs and singers. Ultimately, on a Friday during some time away from filming, the young man who had just cut the duo's driving rocker "Jailhouse Rock" and who had made Leiber and Stoller's "Hound Dog" famous almost shyly asked Stoller if he and Leiber would create something new for him.

"On the set one day," Stoller recalls, "Elvis asked me if Jerry and I would write a love song for him." To many, the fact that Elvis wanted to record a ballad would have seemed strange. This was the King of Rock 'n' Roll, and Elvis was beloved as the man whose music reflected that title. Millions saw him as the symbol of the rebellious attitude of a new generation. But, during conversations with Elvis, Stoller discovered that the entertainer deeply loved the music of the previous generation's crooners. Elvis listened not only to R&B, rock, and gospel, but to the songs of Dean Martin, Tony Bennett, Frank Sinatra, and even Bing Crosby. And, because this type of music was so important to him, Elvis wanted an opportunity to try his hand at a song that coupled dynamic emotions to lush orchestration. In a very real sense, tackling a song like this had nothing to do with pleasing the fans; he wanted to do it for himself.

Feeling that they knew exactly the type of love song Elvis wanted to record, the R&B songwriters put their own musical tastes on the back burner and went to work in what was a new area for them. After discussing a number of different ideas and themes, Stoller and Leiber ultimately decided on exploring the pain of love. The inventive ballad that resulted from this concept examined a different take on the same idea that Otis Blackwell explored in "Don't Be Cruel." With that fact in mind, it is hardly surprising that the new song's title was "Don't." In early June, Stoller brought the number to the *Jailhouse Rock* movie set.

"We wrote 'Don't' on the weekend," Stoller explains, "and on Monday when I played it for him, Elvis smiled and said, 'That's real pretty. That's just what I wanted.'"

Because of the many demands now placed on his life, Elvis would not cut the ballad until September 6, 1957, in the middle of a three-day session that had originally been set aside for work on an extended-play Christmas 45. Elvis was much more enthused about the ballad than he was about singing Christmas standards in the middle of a heat wave.

Once again the studio of choice was Radio Recorders in Hollywood. The Jordanaires were on hand, as were all the other regulars: Scotty Moore, Bill Black, and D. J. Fontana. Dudley Brooks was again brought in for keyboard work. Until this point, Elvis's recordings had always maintained a fraternity-type environment. As the group readied to attempt "Don't," the boys' club was invaded by Millie Kirkham. Kirkham had a dynamic soprano voice that added a new dimension to the tight studio sound.

Had Elvis recorded "Don't" in the early 1970s, a huge orchestra would have been employed in addition to his standard band and backup vocals. As Elvis thought so much of the Sinatra and Martin hits, this might have been in the singer's original plans for "Don't." But this was 1957, not 1975, and at this time the Presley sessions were fairly elementary in nature and production. In retrospect, this would prove to be fortuitous. If a 1970s Elvis production technique had been employed in the "Don't" session, the essence of what made this newest Leiber-Stoller song a classic would surely have been lost.

Using a very light musical framework that was driven much more by the background vocals than by the song's instrumentation, the arrangement for "Don't" had the kind of feel that Mel Torme and Tony Bennett invoked in many of their jazz ballads at the time. The resulting intimacy fully captured the pleading tone of the song's lyrics. In fact, Elvis's startlingly clear vocals are so richly spotlighted that "Don't" is almost a musical love prayer. Because of the honesty heard in the singer's voice, it really seems that he had been brought to his knees by hearing, over and over again, the simple word "don't." Because of that word, his life was not worth living; because he could not get his lover to take the leap of faith that was necessary for their love to grow, he knew that love was doomed. Ultimately, thanks to the way that Elvis sold it, "Don't" is one of the most beautiful and haunting songs Presley ever recorded.

Maybe because he had four months to consider exactly what he wanted to do with "Don't," the session went very smoothly. It would take only seven recording efforts to please Elvis and producer Steve Sholes, thus becoming one of the easiest early hits the singer every recorded. Best of all, almost everyone in the studio agreed that "Don't" was a masterpiece. Much more than "Hound Dog" or even "Jailhouse Rock," this was the kind of song that Elvis wanted to be remembered for.

As the new recording made the rounds at RCA Victor, no one questioned its quality. It was an almost unanimous opinion that their top singer had never sounded better. But some of the label's executives were concerned about what they viewed as "the rather suggestive nature" of the lyrics. As far as Elvis was concerned, this was a love song, but many at RCA Victor feared that mothers and fathers of fans would hear the lyrics and think that the young protagonist is begging a girl to give up her virginity. They argued that, while the number would be fine on an LP, it could not be released as a single that received daily exposure on the airwaves. A few people at RCA Victor even expressed concern that some radio stations would ban the song.

As the debates over the potential marketing problems posed by "Don't" continued, Elvis scored a monster hit with the "Jailhouse

Rock" single, as well as with the movie *Jailhouse Rock*. Now a certified international star, Elvis was becoming as well known in every
corner of the world as the president of the United States. He lived
in luxury, drove the finest cars, and was a moneymaking machine for
his manager Colonel Tom Parker, the Hollywood film studios, and
RCA Victor. He was also quickly growing into one of the nation's
most generous taxpayers. But that did not keep the United States
Army from sending Elvis a draft notice on December 19, 1957. And
just as "Jailhouse Rock" began to slide down the charts, the singer was
scheduled to report to the service for active duty.

It was Paramount Pictures who saved Elvis from the military for
a few months. By the time the draft noticed reached Graceland,
the studio had already signed Elvis to star in the movie *King Creole*. Set to be filmed on location in New Orleans, using a book by
the legendary Harold Robbins as the basis for the script, with a
long list of Hollywood's brightest new stars already signed to costar
with the singer, Paramount had far too much invested in the film
to cancel production. So the company asked for and received a
deferment for Elvis until his work on the movie could be completed. Elvis was in the midst of making the film when RCA Victor matched "Don't" with "I Beg of You" and shipped the single to
radio stations and record outlets. Though some at the record label
still felt that releasing "Don't" as a single was risky, Elvis had been
so busy making movies instead of records that RCA Victor didn't
really have much choice in the matter. There just wasn't much
Elvis material left in the vault that had not already been released.

As some RCA Victor executives held their breath, "Don't" was
released the first week of January 1958. Everyone at the label
expected to catch some flack from church groups and perhaps
PTAs because of the perceived nature of the song's lyrics. But the

protests never came. Why? The reason might be due, in part, to the success of the Elvis gospel recordings. In addition, when Elvis performed "Peace in the Valley" on *The Ed Sullivan Show*, Sullivan had put his arm around the singer and called him "a really fine and decent young man." Once Elvis was deemed respectable by Ed Sullivan, and once fans learned of his deep Christian faith via his gospel music, the once-demonic image of the singer was somewhat tamed. Many who had previously railed against the singer now seemed to view him as something close to an altar boy. For this reason, no one wanted to hear anything bad in an Elvis song. As far as the now-adoring public was concerned, it simply was not possible that Elvis, in the song, was begging for sex. No—the song was definitely about a fine, upstanding boy asking the love of his life to trust him, and to give him a chance to prove his devotion.

As with almost all of Elvis's major releases to date, "Don't" quickly climbed up to the #1 spot on the pop charts. The single reached the top of the playlist on February 10. It would hold its place there until the Champs and their "Tequila" knocked it out five weeks later on March 17. The single remained in major rotation for sixteen weeks on *Billboard's* pop playlist. "Don't" stalled at #2 on the country side, again signaling that Nashville was almost finished with rock's king. "Don't," a decidedly un-R&B single, peaked at #4 on the R&B chart.

Even though it didn't quite match the numbers of "Jailhouse Rock," "Don't" was still a huge success, and it proved that an Elvis ballad could be fully accepted by those buying rock 'n' roll music. Due at least in part to the public's reaction to "Don't," this type of song would become a staple of Elvis music for years to come. Yet, while it sold in the millions, established a new tone for the singer, and widened the public's perception of Elvis's unique talents, there was a sad side to this single as well. It involved Elvis and the song's writers.

It's indisputable that Jerry Leiber and Mike Stoller were the best songwriting team of the rock 'n' roll era. During their careers they produced scores of classic hits, and the duo created songs that remain some the best-known numbers in the world today. With hits that include "Along Came Jones," "Charlie Brown," "Fools Fall in Love," "Is That All There Is," "Kansas City," "Love Potion Number 9," "Only in America," "Poison Ivy," "Ruby Baby," "Yakety Yak," "Searchin'," "Spanish Harlem," "Stand By Me," and "Riot in Cell Block #9," these two men proved time and time again that they had their fingers on the pulse of American pop music. There is little doubt that their genius could have created many more Elvis hits. Except for one lone cut that was cowritten with Jerome "Doc" Pomus in 1962, Elvis would never again top the charts with a Leiber-Stoller number. Why did this successful pairing of writers and singer end? In short, it was the Colonel.

Leiber and Stoller loved working with Elvis. They respected the singer's work ethic, his knowledge of music, and his quest for perfection when he performed and recorded. What they could no longer stomach was Tom Parker. Unlike many up-and-coming song-writers who needed a break and would give up a portion of the publishing rights of their song to the Colonel just to gain an Elvis cut, Leiber and Stoller were so successful that they did not need another Elvis cut. Rather than bow to the manager's demands for a piece of the action, the songwriting duo took a stand. They wanted total control of the publishing end of their own creations. That stand cost them the opportunity to write anything else for Elvis. Other well-known song scribes would follow suit and take their own stands in the future, and each of them would subsequently be ousted from Elvis's realm. Many of the industry's most respected composers flatly refused to share their best work with Elvis because they could not, or did not want to, deal with the Colonel's demands.

The Elvis song well was hardly dry when Leiber and Stoller walked away: a host of great writers were waiting in the wings with new material for Elvis. But over time, as Parker shut off more and more creative avenues with unreasonable publishing demands, the well would begin to dry up, and the quality of Elvis's recordings would suffer. Though Elvis could not say no to the demands of the United States Army, the singer could have told his manager, "No, I want to continue to use the best writers even if we don't get publishing rights." Elvis didn't assert himself on this matter, and in time his work would suffer because of it. If only he had said "don't" to the Colonel, he might have scored more #1 records, and who knows what Leiber and Stoller could have created as a follow-up to their first three monster hits for Elvis Presley.

WEAR MY RING AROUND YOUR NECK

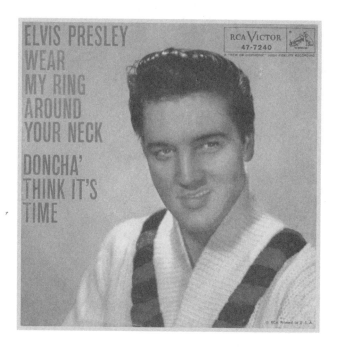

When Bert Carroll and Russell Moody composed "Wear My Ring Around Your Neck," the song seemed more a novelty number than an R&B or country classic. R&B hits were usually more adult in theme, and they often embraced smoldering emotions and life-changing issues. This song, which deals with high school romance, seemed destined for the pop market. And, judging by the song's merits, even that did not offer great potential.

The inspiration for "Wear My Ring Around Your Neck" was a 1950s phenomena in which puppy love combined with surplus cash to produce a symbol that could be found on every high school campus and in thousands of malt shops and juke joints all over the United States. Thanks to the economic boom that occurred after the end of World War II, middle-class families had extra income to spend on items that had once been reserved for the wealthy, such as second cars, weeklong vacations—and high school class rings. Along with a car—in this case often a jalopy or hot rod— the class ring was a symbol of status for most high school boys. Large, shiny, and etched with information that made the jewelry unique to each school, these rings were personal affirmations of academic accomplishment and social significance. Millions were purchased each year as a rite of passage. Who knows how many potential dropouts hung around just to get a class ring?

Carroll and Moody noted the importance of the class ring, as well as how its importance was magnified when a boy felt so deeply about his girlfriend that he gave his ultimate status symbol to her. As she usually had her own class ring already on her finger, the issue of how best to sport this new hunk of jewelry became a major dilemma. Some girls, in a kind of symbolic wedding ritual, looped yarn around the ring and wore it on the third finger of their left hands. But the rings were heavy and bulky, and they were impractical and uncomfortable for most girls to wear on their hands. Instead, a girl often looped the ring through a necklace and wore it around her neck. By the mid-1950s, this method of displaying that a girl was "going steady" became so popular that jewelry stores sold special necklaces that had a ring clasp already installed on them. Not only did the guy have to give up his ring to his girlfriend, he was now expected to purchase *another* piece of jewelry to properly display it.

In composing an ode to this tradition, Carroll and Moody put together a set of lyrics that were elementary at best, and chauvinistic at worst. With lines like "show the world you're mine, by heck" and "they say that going steady is not a proper thing," the rhymes and meanings often seemed forced and poorly thought-out. Then again, there aren't many great words that rhyme with "neck," and high school kids tended to "go steady" with each other at what seemed like the drop of a hat; they didn't spend a lot of time thinking of the moral implications of the act. On the other hand, the idea that, by having a girl wear his ring, a boy could prove to the world that she was his displayed an almost caveman mentality. Of course, in defense of this kind of thinking, the women's movement has not fully taken root, men still controlled the business world, and, more often than not, a high school girl's future dreams centered around being a housewife, not a tycoon. So the lines probably did fit the times. What they did not seem to fit was a singer like Elvis Presley.

By this time, Elvis was twenty-three years old. While he was the nation's top teen idol, he was no teen himself, and he was long past wearing high school rings and letter jackets. A casual observer might conclude that the song would have been much better suited to Paul Anka or Ricky Nelson, both of whom who were still of the age to go steady. So why was RCA Victor producer Steve Sholes drawn to the number?

The reason that Elvis recorded "Wear My Ring Around Your Neck" probably had little to do with the song's rather sophomoric theme. It had to be the tune's driving rock beat. The suits at his record label didn't mind if Elvis chose to croon from time to time, but they wanted to keep his hard edge as well. Elvis's last single had been a ballad. The powers at RCA Victor thought it was time for another up-tempo release. And "Wear My Ring Around Your Neck" had much more potential to be a rocking tune than did most of the demos that had recently been delivered to either RCA Victor or Hill and Range Music Company.

Another element that must have played into the final decision to record this particular song was that the clock was quickly ticking down to zero for Elvis the civilian. The singer was due to report for military service in less than two months. Given his movie work, there were few open dates left for recording, and RCA Victor had to have some product to issue while the singer was in the army and away from their recording studios. The company feared that, without new records, Elvis would be forgotten. Sholes had to choose the best of what was on hand and use it, even if the song's lyrics or theme were not up the standards that had been established by previous releases. Or in this case, even if the subject matter seemed rather juvenile for a man of Elvis's age. Ignoring all of the reasons why they should pass on "Wear My Ring Around Your Neck," the decision was made to record it.

"Wear My Ring Around Your Neck" was recorded on February 1, 1958. As Elvis was busy filming his fourth film, *King Creole* (which, at the time, was still titled *A Stone for Danny Fisher*) session time was again booked at nearby Radio Recorders in Hollywood. Joining Elvis for this session were all of his regulars, including Scotty Moore on guitar, Bill Black on bass, D. J. Fontana on drums, Dudley Brooks at the piano, and The Jordanaires as the back-up vocalists. Another guitar was added, and this time it was played by West Coast session musician H. J. "Tiny" Timbrell. It took the group some time to get a satisfactory take of the up-tempo rocker, and Elvis was still not satisfied when they finally called it quits on the number and moved on to other songs. Elvis felt that this "Ring" did not shine. He vowed to Sholes that he would come back and fix it when he got another break from the production of the new film.

It would be twenty-five days before Elvis returned to Radio Recorders. He'd had more than three weeks to consider what he viewed as the problems with "Wear My Ring Around Your Neck." He and Sholes discussed the problems and ways in which they might fix them. Both realized that their only chance to make the song right was at that moment. Elvis was just too busy to come back to the studio yet again. First, they beefed up the piano part. Then, much as he had done on the 1956 monster hit "All Shook Up," Elvis used his hands to slap out a percussion beat on the back of his guitar. In truth, a drum would have produced a much higher-quality sound. And in retrospect, considering all the time and effort that went into this recording, it seems strange that Sholes did not simply record Elvis playing a bongo set. There had to be one around the studio. Certainly the sound would have been far superior. But perhaps Elvis simply felt more comfortable creating this added element to the recording in same manner that he often used while listening to music at home. In the end, the singer was not credited as the "guitar slapper" in the final recording's notes, but the song now had a driving rock beat and an R&B feel. Speeding like a race car, the final version's melody seemed to demand an answer to the song title's offer.

"Wear My Ring Around Your Neck" was paired with "Doncha' Think It's Time," another song from the February session, and the single was shipped the first week of April, just a few days after now–Private Presley had begun basic training in Texas. As all of the A sides of Elvis's RCA Victor singles released since 1956 had reached #1 on the pop charts (the records that did not hit the top spot were either extended-play 45s or B sides), the record label expected no less than the top of the charts with this ringer. But, thanks to the magic of a medical practitioner, Elvis's latest cut stalled at #2.

David Seville's novelty hit "Witch Doctor" topped the charts on April 28, thus making "Wear My Ring Around Your Neck" a bridesmaid rather than a bride. The good doctor held the charts for two weeks, then the Everly Brothers' "All I Have to Do Is Dream" grabbed the #1 spot and held onto it for the next month. For the first time since he had signed on with RCA Victor, Elvis was shut out of the top spot. Some felt that at least a part of Elvis's market power had been lost when he entered the service, which caused him to lose the national spotlight that had brightly shined on him for two years. In fact, Elvis's #2 position on the pop charts was really due to bad luck and bad timing. Everyone loved "Witch Doctor." It was so cleverly and creatively produced that it appealed to ages ranging from six to sixty. Even Elvis could not claim that broad a demographic base. If the Elvis single had been released two weeks earlier or two weeks later, the good doctor would not have been on call and "Wear My Ring Around Your Neck" would have probably claimed the top spot. However, "Ring" would still score a #1 position on the charts.

For some mystical reason, the R&B crowd loved "Wear My Ring Around Your Neck." As this single did not contain the emotional depth that was often favored in this genre, what must have appealed to fans was the way in which Elvis attacked the song. During the recording session, Elvis had drawn from his Memphis experiences with African American music. The raw edge that his vocals exhibit in the song would not be evident in the post-service Elvis. But, as of the recording of "Wear My Ring Around Your

Neck," Elvis had not yet been totally tamed, and the singer hit the notes in a way that would have made Little Richard proud. Coupled with solid, driving instrumentals, especially Fontana's machine-gun drum licks (which, for the most part, had been unheard since "Hound Dog") and Elvis's own guitar slaps, this "Ring" did rock. Thus, the uninhibited nature of the session probably made the song an R&B favorite.

In hindsight, it is doubtful that any teen idol of the time, even one as popular as Ricky Nelson, could have driven "Wear My Ring Around Your Neck" into the Top 10. In order for the number to work, it took the kind of energy and punch that few white artists besides Elvis possessed. This fact was painfully displayed when Pat Boone covered Little Richard's "Tutti Frutti" and Fats Domino's "Ain't That a Shame." Both of Boone's cuts hit #1, but neither contained even of a fraction of the power of the original recordings. In truth, they were bland efforts. If Pat had cut "Ring," the result would surely have been the same kind of lifeless single. And, because of the changes that took place between 1956 and 1958, it is highly unlikely that the record would have created much chart action, either.

In the two years since Elvis earned his first #1 hit, America had grown. African American artists now found the pop charts opening up to their efforts. They were also being featured on TV shows like *American Bandstand* and *The Ed Sullivan Show*. With this new "soul" added to the rock 'n' roll mix, white artists found it difficult to compete with real R&B music. White artists' covers of black artists' hits were also being phased out. Elvis was one of the reasons that the door had opened, and he was also one of the few white singers who could do justice to the genre created by African Americans. Perhaps that is why, even when singing a number whose lyrics were not carefully conceived and were certainly aimed at an age group beneath his own, Elvis could still generate fire, passion, and a #1 record. The same could not be said of the song's writers.

Bert Carroll and Russell Moody never composed another song that topped the major charts. They would not be employed to write another song for Elvis, either. Still, the inspiration they found in high school romance did give Elvis one of his last chances to really rock. That makes the writers' R&B chart topper a real gem.

HARD HEADED WOMAN

onsidering the profits that MGM had generated from its rather serious musical drama *Jailhouse Rock* and the success of its own, more lightedhearted, *Loving You*, Paramount Studios sensed it had a real movie star on their hands in Elvis Presley. Instead of sticking the Memphis singer in a low-budget Hollywood formula film, they opted to purchase the rights to bestselling author Harold Robbins's book *A Stone for Danny Fisher*. Then, as if to prove that they were serious about making Elvis an actor, Paramount brought in a director who was responsible for some of the most renowned movies of all time.

Over the previous three decades, Michael Curtiz had proved time and time again that he could pull fantastic performances from both great and average actors. The native of Hungary had done just that in films such as *The Third Degree*, *Angels with Dirty Faces*, *Four Daughters*, *Virginia City*, *The Adventures of Robin Hood*, *The Sea Hawk*, *Mildred Pierce*, *Night and Day*, and *Casablanca*. Although he was more than seventy years old when he was hired to direct Elvis's next film, Curtiz still had the style, drive, and energy that was needed to produce another classic. Needless to say, Elvis was genuinely excited to be working with a man who had guided the likes of Errol Flynn, Humphrey Bogart, and Joan Crawford.

By this point in his career, Curtiz did not have to work. He now took jobs only when they interested him, and the project had to have the solid support of the studio that was making it. Before he agreed to direct *A Stone for Danny Fisher*, he made sure that Paramount would give him a large budget, a great script, a dynamic supporting cast, and the freedom to create the moody environment that was necessary to successfully bring Robbins's novel to the screen.

The story, with its gritty underworld theme, seemed better suited to an actor such as Humphrey Bogart than it did to Elvis. Even before production had begun, many critics predicted that the singer would fall flat in this role. But Paramount seemed sure that Elvis could carry the load. So did the veteran director. If they had any concerns, they did not show them.

Unlike most movies that excited middle America, this was a ghetto tale—a movie in which moral choices are anything but clear. Each day in Danny Fisher's world seemed hopeless, and the director was determined to capture that emotion and burn it into the film's soul. One of the movie's most famous songs begins, "If you're looking for trouble, you came to the right place." This movie echoes that despairing reality time and time again. The story was a combination of *Casablanca, Rebel Without a Cause,* and *Blackboard Jungle.* Therefore, while it would have been easy to use color film, Curtiz determined that the seedy nature and setting of the story required that the film be shot in stark black and white. Critics viewed this as another strike against the film. Some at Paramount worried that fans would assume that the use of black and white meant that this motion picture had been cheaply put together. Once again, Curtiz showed no signs of worry.

The Robbins novel centered on the saga of a tough Bourbon Street kid who climbs up from working small jobs for the mob to becoming a championship-quality boxer. Curtiz and others didn't think that Elvis's fans would embrace the fight angle, and the movie's script has Danny Fisher quitting school to work as a busboy. Falling in with a bad crowd, Fisher commits a robbery. Then love, in the shape of Dolores Hart, sets him straight. The reformed Danny works his way up from the bottom of the socioeconomic ladder by singing in a club that is frequented by a hood (played by Walter Matthau). In the club, Danny is tempted by the hood's gal pal, a beautiful vamp (played by Carolyn Jones). Dean Jagger plays the deeply moral father who knows that tough love is the only way to straighten out Danny's life. After numerous false starts and tragedies, Danny makes himself into a success and, in true Hollywood style, the film ends happily.

Curtiz didn't mind Elvis singing in his movie. The director felt that it was smart to take advantage of Elvis's unique talent and popularity. But when the move from boxer to singer was made, the director wanted a guarantee that the songs provided for the score would be as good as his picture. His thirty-one years in Hollywood had taught Curtiz that a mediocre musical score can drag down even the best of films. He was not going to approve songs that were less than great. The songs had to be tough and "real," and they had to reflect the tone of the movie as it was directed by Curtiz. In contrast to the colorful show standards found in movies such as *Singing in the Rain*, the musical numbers found in this film had to possess the black-and-white atmosphere and raw emotions the director was employing in each scene of *A Stone for Danny Fisher*.

Feeling the pressure to bring a new level of music to the production, Paramount did not follow the formula it had used in the first three Elvis films. This time, instead of simply giving the musical responsibilities to a single songwriter or songwriting team, the studio allowed many different composers, with all kinds of musical backgrounds, to read this new script. Landing a tune in this movie became a competition, and the level of writing found in the ten songs that made their way into the film would reflect the production team's push to uncover the very best music available.

Because Elvis was playing a New Orleans nightclub singer, the songs had to have a rock 'n' roll feel coupled with an authentic Dixieland foundation. Crafting this marriage of musical genres was not easy, and most of the songwriters whose demos received favorable reviews either had deep musical roots in the blues or had spent some time in Louisiana.

Leiber and Stoller's submission, "King Creole," earned a place in the film, and the song would also be used as the revised title of the film. Fred Wise, Ben Weisman, Sid Wayne, Roy C. Bennett, and Rachel Frank landed songs in the movie, as well. But it was the work of two other writers that stood out in the coarse *King Creole*. Ironically, RCA Victor and Elvis had discovered these men's talents when they contributed one of the original songs for Elvis's 1957 Christmas music sessions.

Little did Aaron Schroeder or Claude DeMetrius realize when they submitted "Santa Bring My Baby Back to Me" for Elvis's consideration that the number would open up the door for a chance to write for the movies. Yet, due in part to that song, these men were two of the many who received invitations to submit songs for *A Stone for Danny Fisher*. Understanding the script and the film's needs, Schroeder landed a two tunes in the score: "Dixieland Rock" and "Young Dreams." Both songs perfectly captured the mood needed for two specific points in the motion picture. Each number also seemed to have solid marketing possibilities. But ultimately, neither would become a single. Instead, it was a hard-driving DeMetrius composition that most fully defined the film's mood and that offered RCA Victor its best up-tempo Elvis number since "Jailhouse Rock."

Though the writer did not share his own inspiration for the composition with the press or with Elvis, the few interviews he gave over the course of his life seem to indicate that the tone of "Hard Headed Woman" had been influenced by a failed first marriage. Having also written such songs as "Mean Woman Blues" and "Ain't That Just Like a Woman," DeMetrius seemed to have little trust for the opposite sex. His music often voiced the opinion that women offered little but trouble. In "Hard Headed Woman," there was an angry tone that seemed to embrace the continuing emotions that flowed through the film itself. This lack of trust, combined with image of the druglike trance that women induce when plying their magic on men, fit perfectly into the rebellious nature of the movie. The liberal use of references to Adam and Eve, Jezebel, and Samson and Delilah also showcased DeMetrius's knowledge of the Bible. Here, in a musical nutshell, was the movie's theme of good versus evil. "Hard Headed Woman" was a morality play, completely tied up in just two minutes of frantically paced words and music.

Elvis brought the energy necessary to perform "Hard Headed Woman" into the January 15, 1958, West Coast session that produced all of the *King Creole* tracks. In addition to the regular Elvis sidemen who had worked on all of the Elvis hits (with the exception of "Love Me Tender"), a small orchestra was brought in to give the movie tunes the necessary Dixieland feel. Joining Elvis for the first time were Ray Siegel on bass and tuba, Mahlon Clark on clarinet, John Ed Buckner on trumpet, Justin Gordon on saxophone, and Elmer Schneider on slide trombone.

The session was dynamic. Each song recorded for *King Creole* has an energy that simply is not found in previous or later Elvis soundtracks. Part of this has to be attributed to the thrill that Elvis felt working with legendary director Michael Curtiz. Yet perhaps the quality and excitement found in these ten songs also had their roots in fear. The singer wondered if his upcoming two-year hitch in the army would ruin his career. He was honestly scared that no one would remember him when he mustered out. This album represented a chance for him to make a lasting impression on his fans by saying, "I may be gone, but after you hear these songs, you will know that I am still the King."

"Hard Headed Woman" was the crowning achievement of the session. A feverishly paced song, it oozed a kind of raw sex appeal that had not been present in the singer's most recent recordings. Making the number even better was the way in which Elvis embraced an African American style of singing. Elvis had been around black music all his life. He had spent time in African American churches, singing along with gospel choirs, and he had jammed with blues artists in Memphis. He knew the mannerisms of African American music, and he felt the soul that was a part of this genre. This was evident in his previous recordings of "Tutti Frutti" and "Ready Teddy." Elvis didn't refine or clean up these songs, as Pat Boone did when he recorded them; he didn't make them another piece of musical white bread. Elvis plunged into these numbers with an emotion and drive that was simply not found in pop standards of the day. He rediscovered this energy and enthusiasm when he ripped through "Hard Headed Woman" in a dynamic fashion that other white artists could not touch. Elvis didn't as much sing it as vocally *feel* it. Perhaps that is why this song came together so easily and quickly in the studio. It was ultimately decided that take number ten would be the cut destined for release as a single. It was also determined that the song would not be released until Paramount began the new film's publicity push.

Elvis finished his work on *King Creole* on March 10. Two weeks later he began basic training at Fort Hood, Texas. This large step, from being the most famous man on the planet to becoming an army private, would be the first in a series of traumatic blows to strike Elvis over the next few months.

At about the same time that RCA Victor shipped "Hard Headed Woman" to radio stations and record outlets on June 10, the singer's mother, Gladys Presley, became ill. She was taken to a Memphis hospital, where she would still be hospitalized when "Hard Headed Woman" knocked "The Purple People Eater" off the top of the *Billboard* charts on July 21. The single would also hit #2 on the Country Best-Sellers chart. But country stations were tiring of the rock star. "Hard Headed Woman" would be the highest-ranked Elvis song in country music until 1977.

On July 1, 1958, with "Hard Headed Woman" still at #1 on the pop chart, *King Creole* hit theaters. It quickly became the most successful motion picture with "king" in its title since *King Kong*. Yet, although he ruled the music charts, and critics gave Elvis terrific reviews for his acting, Private Presley did not care. On August 4, when Ricky Nelson's "Poor Little Fool" replaced "Hard Headed Woman" at #1, the singer didn't even notice. A day later, a distraught Elvis boarded a train for Memphis to be with his ailing mother. On August 14, Gladys Presley died at the age of forty-two.

For Elvis, life would never be the same. On September 22, the man who had hardly traveled at all before becoming a national star, found himself on the USS *General Randall* with hundreds of other soldiers, headed to Germany. With no more movies to be released, only a few records in the RCA Victor vault, and a host of new rock 'n' roll stars ready to take his spot, Elvis truly believed that his last #1 song would be the Claude DeMetrius number. A host of critics predicted the same thing. While this would not be the case—he would actually return from his stint in the military more popular than ever—much of the energy that had infected Elvis's music would be lost. The King would never again rock with the enthusiasm and force that had been captured on "Hard Headed Woman."

ONE NIGHT

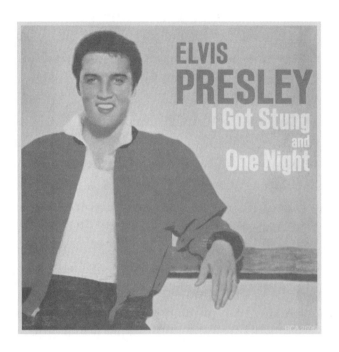

Elvis first opted to cut Dave Bartholomew and Pearl King's "One Night" during a January 1957 recording session. Elvis had heard blues singer Smiley Lewis's version of the song and had fallen in love with it. Yet, for much the same reason that the original Imperial-label recording had failed to find any mainstream airtime, Elvis's version was all but buried by RCA Victor as soon as it was cut. It would take a widely scattered and seemingly unrelated chain of events, some whose origins went back to about the time that Elvis was born, before the song found its way out of the RCA Victor vaults. Even then, Elvis would have to play with the original lyrics before the song could be released. Therefore, when it did hit the airwaves, "One Night" was not in the form that Elvis had wanted. This version, he felt, had little of the real passion of the original Lewis cut. The story behind "One Night" begins with a blues singer who probably should have become a legend, but who is now little more than a footnote in music history.

Smiley Lewis was already more than forty years old by the time Elvis became familiar with his version of "One Night" (which was titled "One Night of Sin"), and he had been singing the blues for three decades. Just after World War II, the Louisiana native became a fixture on the New Orleans R&B club scene. A solid vocalist and a dynamic song stylist, Lewis first signed with DeLuxe Records in 1947, then Imperial in 1950. Two years later he scored a minor R&B hit with "The Bells Are Ringing." In 1955 Smiley's "I Hear You Knocking" climbed a bit higher on the charts, and things started looking bright for the entertainment veteran. But, even though he wrapped his roaring voice around great numbers such as "Blue Monday" and "Lost Weekend," he could not move onto the national pop charts. Ultimately it would be another French Quarter sensation, Fats Domino, who would pick up many of Lewis's cuts and make them into national hits. Even Domino didn't feel secure enough to tackle "One Night," however, and the door to recording the song was thus left open for Elvis.

Dave Bartholomew was the real force behind both "One Night" and Domino's career. Another product of Louisiana, Dave was a child prodigy. In 1934, when he was just fourteen years old, Bartholomew was playing with the likes of Professor Claiborne Williams's big band. Five years later Dave became a featured act on the SS *Capitol*, a Mississippi riverboat. After an army stint during World War II, Bartholomew returned to New Orleans, formed his own orchestra, and invented "big beat" music, a forerunner of rock 'n' roll.

During a Houston gig the conductor, songwriter, and arranger met Lew Chudd of Imperial Records. Chudd immediately signed Bartholomew to a recording contract. At Imperial Dave became friends with Antoine "Fats" Domino and, as pop music morphed into what is now known as rock, this duo helped changed the course of African American music's influence on the country and the world.

Over the course of the next decade Bartholomew and Domino cowrote scores of hits, including "Ain't That a Shame," "Blue Monday," and "I'm Walkin'." Not only did Bartholomew help pen and arrange these hits, he produced them, as well. As a result, Bartholomew became the guiding force behind other performers, including Lloyd Price and Smiley Lewis. Elvis Presley grew to know and appreciate Dave's work in both songwriting and producing.

Since his days at Sun Records, Elvis had been a fan of Fats Domino. He felt connected to the African American performer who, like Elvis, easily drew inspiration from blues, country, and pop genres. Though he would eventually record "Blueberry Hill," Elvis believed that Domino's recordings were so well done that it would be senseless to cover them: any new version would pale in comparison to the original. Elvis's wisdom in this regard would be proved time and time again, as no one who attempted to cover a Fats Domino song ever produced a version that could rival that of the piano-pounding blues singer from New Orleans. But when Fats and Imperial passed on to the opportunity to bring another Bartholomew standard to the world, Elvis jumped at the chance to make it his own.

While Elvis had too much respect for Domino to cover one of his songs, he had no qualms about covering a Smiley Lewis cut. Elvis loved Lewis's music, but he also knew that few outside of New

Orleans had heard it. The artist and his songs were almost unknown, and they were completely unappreciated in mainstream music circles. On top of that, Elvis felt that Lewis's work had real grit, something the teen idol admired. To reach their full potential, Lewis's songs demanded a lot of heart and soul. Most popular singers simply did not have the capacity to do these numbers justice. This was particularly true of "One Night." Yet Elvis felt that he could tackle this song and make it a hit.

Elvis cut "One Night" for the first time during a January session that was devoted mainly to the *Loving You* soundtrack. The singer cut it almost exactly as had Lewis, including the line "One night of sin is what I'm now paying for." Presley hoped that the number would make it into the film. But the song was far too earthy for even RCA Victor, much less Paramount, to even consider. Horrified as to what religious leaders and parents would think, the Hollywood studio dismissed it, while RCA Victor stuck "One Night" in the vault and locked it up tight. The song was deemed much too hot and controversial for public consumption.

Elvis did not give up on the song. He continued to play with it during his spare time on the set of *Loving You*, finally rewriting the lyrics that he felt were holding the song captive. It was Elvis himself who reworked "One night of sin is what I'm now paying for," into "One night with you is what I'm now praying for." On February 23, 1957, at Radio Recorders in Los Angeles, the singer showed up with his new lyrics, feeling sure they would meet with his label's approval. Reflecting the number's roots in the blues, Elvis sang it as a New Orleans shouter, an emotional ballad that screamed pain and heartache. He continued to hope that the song would make it into the soundtrack of *Loving You*, and he believed that his changes would do the trick.

Other than Dudley Brooks on piano (in one of his initial team-ings with Elvis), the rest of the crew for the session consisted of the normal bunch of Elvis players, including Scotty Moore, Bill Black, D. J. Fontana, and the Jordanaires. The tenth take of the new "One Night" was chosen as the best. After hearing the playback several times, Elvis left the studio, somewhat convinced that the song would be his next single. But RCA Victor was still scared to death of the song, and it buried this second version just as it had done the first. Ultimately, it would take the success of another movie's soundtrack and a certain invitation from Uncle Sam to get the label to reconsider the value of "One Night."

Because legendary Hollywood director Michael Curtiz wanted *King Creole* to reflect the coarse image of the New Orleans slums, as well as the essence of the French Quarter's blues heritage, some of the songs used in the 1958 film pushed the envelope a great deal more than did standard Elvis recordings. One in particular, "Trou-ble," by Jerry Leiber and Mike Stoller, screamed out "I'm evil," and "If you are looking for trouble, you came to the right place." Though it was not released as a single, "Trouble" received a lot of radio play. Much to the surprise of RCA Victor, no groups rallied to have either the song or the *King Creole* album banned. Yet, even though "Trouble" had managed to escape controversy, "One Night" was still deemed too hot to even consider for mass release.

It took the United States Army to pave the way for the cover of the Smiley Lewis record to reach the public. RCA Victor tried to get Elvis into the studio several times before he left for military service, but these efforts were met with very little success. While one summer session produced four songs, others that had been set up to take place before Elvis shipped out to Europe fell through. It seemed that Colonel Tom Parker always had Elvis busy doing

something else. What RCA Victor didn't realize was that Parker
didn't want a new Elvis single coming out every two months. The
Colonel felt it was best to make the singer almost disappear while
he was in uniform. Then, when he returned to the stage in two
years, the public would be lusting after all things Elvis. It was
Parker's view that, when the army finished with his singer, Elvis
could literally be relaunched with even more success than he had
experienced in 1956. Had the label's executives been made privy
to this plan, they probably would have kidnapped Elvis and forced
him to record more new material before he left the country. RCA
Victor had far too much invested in the singer not to continue to
push the Elvis product; it would not have even considered the gamble that Parker was willing to take. Yet, thanks to Parker keeping
Elvis away from the studio, a song the singer had pushed for almost
two years would finally get its chance to shine.

   With little else in the Elvis vault to choose from, in October
1958 RCA Victor finally opted to release the second, cleaned-up
version of "One Night." Teamed with "I Got Stung" on the flip
side, the hard-hitting blues number was shipped on October 21.
Two days later, just as radio stations were beginning to play the
single in the United States, and a few days before stations in
Britain and Europe would spin the record, Private Presley received
a pass. He used his time away from the base to watch Bill Haley and
His Comets perform in Frankfurt, Germany. After the show, Elvis
met Haley backstage. It would be the only time the two men who
represented the foundation of rock 'n' roll would ever meet, and a
photo of that meeting was seen in papers worldwide the next day.
Most of the captions to the photo mentioned Elvis's new single.
This proved to be a public relations blessing, because folks now
knew about and wanted to hear the latest Elvis song.

"One Night" did not create the controversy that RCA Victor had feared. Yes, listeners understood that the song's protagonist was asking for a great deal more than a simple kiss. Nevertheless, compared to the likes of Jerry Lee Lewis, Elvis no longer struck much fear into the hearts of religious leaders or conservative parents. Many of them reasoned that if he was serving our nation as a soldier, and if he loved gospel music, then he must really be a solid, decent young man.

"One Night" spent seventeen weeks in the Top 40. On the pop chart, it peaked at #4. On the R&B charts it topped out at #10. Country stations had pretty much backed away from Elvis at this point, and "One Night" lasted about one night on the country chart, peaking at #24. But far away, in a more liberal place that was more open to racy lyrics, Elvismania was peaking, thanks to having the singer stationed next door in Europe. In England, the single reached the top of the charts.

Just as Elvis had, England loved "One Night." BBC listeners could not get enough of this New Orleans blues ballad. A week after its release, it became the most-requested song on the British airwaves. Record stores could not keep up with demand. For three weeks in November, America's king ruled Britain.

Today, "One Night" is one of the least-remembered Elvis hits. It is rarely played on oldies stations, and even most Elvis fans cannot remember all of its words. But many music critics and scores of artists still cling to the song as if it were made out of pure gold. To them, "One Night" represents the untamed Elvis, a young man who could wail like no other singer of his era. In their eyes, this release fully captured Rock 'n' Roll's rebel with a musical cause. Perhaps that is why, although a host of the best-known Elvis hits are rarely covered by popular artists, "One Night" has been rerecorded scores of times by the likes of Bad Company, Rick Nelson, Etta James, Tom Jones, Sean Lennon, and Albert King. Yet none of these recordings have come close to making listeners believe the emotion behind the lyrics as much as Elvis's version does.

In 1983, RCA Victor unearthed the original January 1957 cut of "One Night." In the twenty-six years since it had first been recorded, times had changed a great deal. No longer fearing a negative response from critics, PTA groups, or religious leaders, the label released this version of "One Night," sin and all. By this time the raw and powerful Elvis of the 1950s had been all but forgotten, replaced by the image of a bloated singer who performed lush ballads with huge orchestras and scores of backup vocalists. For those who had never heard Elvis's second version of the song, "One Night" shocked listeners, not because of its restored lyrics, but because of its potency, energy, and drive. The 1983 release of the song on the *Elvis: A Legendary Performer* series of albums allowed a new generation to understand that Elvis had been more than just another popular singer; he was a real rocker with soul.

A FOOL SUCH AS I

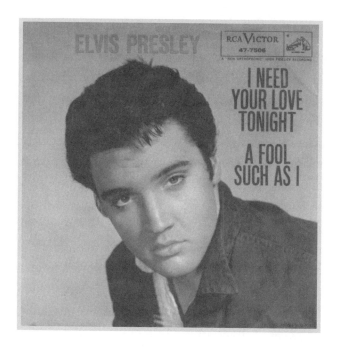

n June 1958, Private Elvis Presley had a brief leave before getting ready to ship out with his army unit to Germany. Using
two of these days, the singer returned to the studio to cut five
new songs. Four of these numbers reflected the rocking Elvis, and
the session marked one of the last times that Elvis fully threw himself into the genre he'd helped jump-start. The lone remaining effort
represented something completely different—a tip of the hat to a
country music veteran who had once helped a struggling Elvis establish himself as an entertainer. To this day "(Now and Then There's)
A Fool Such as I" stands apart from almost all other Elvis recordings. Not country, definitely not rock, and not really pop, the record

neither mirrors anything the singer had recorded previously, nor foreshadows any of his future work. Nevertheless, the recording remains distinctly Elvis. This single, which seems completely out of touch with the rest of Elvis's career, emphasizes just how difficult it is to pigeonhole either the man or his music.

By the time that Elvis cut his first record for Sun, Hank Snow had run up five monster country music hits. As a teen, even before World War II, this native of Canada had run away from home to escape his abusive father. After spending time on the high seas, he came back to dry land to try his hand as a singer in the mold of his idol, Jimmie Rodgers. Snow was not the same kind of vocalist as "the Singing Brakeman," but he did have a knack for uncovering great songs and putting his own unique spin on them. Still, it took him fifteen years of playing gigs throughout Canada and the United States before Snow finally landed in Dallas and earned a national hit in 1949. Already thirty-five years old, Snow soon joined the Grand Ole Opry, and he remained a solid force in country music for fifty more years. Even in the face of mega sales by the likes of Garth Brooks, the Dixie Chicks, and Shania Twain, Snow remains one of the top twenty-five country music recording artists of all time. With scores of hits, sixty-five charting records, and a huge legion of country acts who were influenced by his work, it is perhaps this Hall of Famer's connection with Elvis that is the man's most overlooked contribution to show business.

In 1954 and 1955, Elvis, Scotty Moore, and Bill Black participated in a series of country music package shows. Hank Snow was usually the headliner at these concerts. Being the top draw on the bill, Snow closed the show. Performing songs such as "I'm Movin' On," "The Golden Rocket," and "The Rhumba Boogie," the short man with the deep voice and gentlemanly manner usually brought down the house, leaving the crowds begging for more. Then Elvis came along.

The first night that Elvis opened directly in front of Snow was said to be one of the worst of the country singer's life. Elvis, with his swiveling hips and rockabilly numbers, literally drained the crowd dry. They had no energy left for Snow. As the country music giant stood in front of the microphone and rolled through his hits, folks sat there as if they were in a trance. No matter how hard he worked, the only time he elicited an enthusiastic response from the hundreds in the audience that night was when he mentioned Elvis's name. This did more than discourage the singer; it angered him. After finishing his set, he walked offstage and called the show's booker. Allegedly, his exact words were, "Never place me behind that SOB again."

Later in life, Snow remembered it differently. Yes, the audience he faced that night had been worn out and unresponsive; yes, he had called the booker; and yes, he had asked to never again follow Elvis. But Snow argued that he never called Elvis any names. Instead, he claimed that he simply reported back that the young man from Memphis was a huge audience pleaser who would soon be a big star. So, Snow argued, let's make *him* the closer.

Though his description of the events of that night is still debated to this day, what cannot be argued is that, from the start, Snow recognized Elvis's potential. The country star honestly thought that the young man had the chance to become the next Hank Williams. Snow also realized that the young crowd who clamored for Elvis would bring a new and vibrant audience to hillbilly music. By doing so, this audience would put more money into everyone's pockets.

Bob Neal was booking Elvis at this time, and he was putting together a lot of Snow's dates, as well. Sensing there was money to

be made, the Canadian singer attempted to hammer out an agree-
ment between Elvis, Neal, and himself for future representation.
But Snow made one mistake. Legend has it that it was either Snow
or his son Jimmy who told Colonel Tom Parker about the hot new
prospect. The minute the smooth-talking Parker came into the
mix, Snow's chances of controlling Elvis quickly went out the window. Within a year, Bob Neal had lost out as well. Still, the
Colonel could not keep Snow and Elvis from visiting backstage
between shows. Elvis asked Snow a lot of questions during these
gab sessions, and Snow freely shared his ideas and suggestions. Yet
these words of wisdom were just a part of the lessons the new singer
learned from the veteran.

Though their styles were much different, Elvis studied the way
that Snow worked a crowd and sang his songs. While the man himself seemed reserved behind the microphone, Snow's outfits were
flashy. He dressed for the crowd. With his tailored, embroidered
stage costumes, he looked every bit a star. Each moment he spent
onstage reinforced, through his dress, his actions, and his words,
that he was the man in charge. This command, this assurance,
combined with a humble nod to the fans' wishes, put Snow head
and shoulders above almost everyone else who worked those country bills. Elvis borrowed what he could from Snow, especially in
regard to his flashy manner of dress and his sincere communication
with crowds, and he used it to his advantage onstage.

Elvis was especially touched by the sincere manner in which
the country music star wrapped his voice around a ballad's lyrics.
Snow tended to slide from one note into another, often blending
two different words together. There was no one in country music
who sounded like Hank Snow. His voice and style were unmistak-
able, and this fact was not lost on Elvis. It was Snow who helped

teach Elvis that, on records, the voice had to be so distinctive that everyone would know from the first note who was singing.

During his days with Sun Studio, Elvis finally realized his life-long dream to work the stage of the Grand Ole Opry. Snow was there to encourage him. When Elvis fell flat that Saturday night, Snow told him not worry about it, and to move on. He assured Elvis that success would find him very soon. He was right.

By 1958 Elvis ruled rock 'n' roll music, and the popular teen idol had lost track of his former traveling partner. Though they both were recording for RCA Victor, Snow and Elvis were now on much different paths. Yet in that June 1958 recording session, Elvis would not just reconnect with the country music star, but he would also pay tribute to Snow's influence on his career.

On June 10, in RCA Victor's Nashville studios, Elvis gathered his musicians together once again to try to recapture music magic. But this time, two of Elvis's bandmates were missing. Scotty Moore had left the band to work for a Memphis label, and Bill Black had formed his own combo and was recording songs for Hi Records. Black would chart seventeen times with his group before dying of a brain tumor in 1965. He would never work with Elvis again. Moore would be back, but it wouldn't be for several years. Besides these two pickers, another old friend was absent as well.

Hugh Jarrett, who had been a regular at Elvis's sessions since "I Want You, I Need You, I Love You," had left The Jordanaires. His bass part was now being sung by Ray Walker. In his debut session with Elvis, Walker would find himself so dramatically spotlighted that his voice would become the strongest identifying feature of the next Elvis hit.

Elvis had long loved the old Snow standard "A Fool Such as I." He had watched the country singer perform the number countless times in concert, had spun the record scores of times on his turntable, and had even plunked nickels into jukeboxes to listen to it while on the road. Like thousands of others, Elvis was most caught up by the ballad's pacing. It was infectious. The easygoing phrasing that Snow employed when he sang "Fool" captured a sincerity that was rarely heard on an up-tempo love song. As the number was largely unfamiliar to pop audiences, and as it had only hit #3 on the country chart six years earlier, Elvis figured he could salute Hank without being lost in his shadow. Elvis needn't have even worried about that: although his vocals would strongly reflect the same style that Snow had employed on the original, Elvis dreamed up a gimmick that would move his recording to a different level.

Working out the backup vocals with the Jordanaires, Elvis asked Ray Walker to sing a strong, echoing bass line whenever Elvis sang, "Now and then there's a fool such as I." Not satisfied that having Walker just sing behind him would be enough to really emphasize this vocal kicker, Elvis also had the singer open each verse with a solo line of "Now and then, there's a fool such as I." This opening was dropped down a full octave lower than that of the line Elvis was singing. The effect was startling: it was as if the floor had fallen out from underneath the song.

The session had been set up just as it always had been, with Elvis on one mic, the quartet on the others. But Elvis felt that the setup did not emphasize Walker's vocals enough, so he asked the backup singer to move over and share his microphone. Elvis knew that this would make the bass vocal as strong as his own, thus creating an almost duet effect on the song's most important line. It was a stroke of genius, and it made this recording one of the most unique of Elvis's entire career. Twenty years later, using a different gospel singer, J. D. Sumner, Elvis would once again share the glory with a bass solo vocal on "Way Down."

Elvis fans felt that the casual but heartfelt emotion the singer infused into every word of "Fool" marked one of the most unique interpretations of his recording life. The song was both fun and hauntingly sad at the same time. To millions of minds, this was Elvis's genius at work. Yet, except for a vocal "dance" found in the second verse, where Elvis swung his voice in the same kind of way he often moved his hips on stage, creating a bit of a hiccup phrasing element, the rest of Elvis's work on "Fool" was a direct reflection of Snow's original. In some places, the recording is actually is a mirror image of the country cut.

As was usually the case, Steve Sholes and RCA Victor were satisfied with "A Fool Such as I" long before Elvis was. He kept recutting it, over and over again, until he was convinced that the old Snow tune had been done as well as he and his band could perform it. Then, after listening to several playbacks, he chose the ninth take as his personal favorite. One day and four songs later, Elvis walked away from RCA Victor, not to return for almost two years.

Fifty weeks after Elvis was inducted into the army, on March 10, 1959, his "A Fool Such as I" was shipped. "I Need Your Love Tonight," another of the June session cuts, was placed on the B side. Half a world away, Private First Class Elvis Presley was manning a tank and not keeping close tabs on what his songs were doing on the charts. As a result, he had no idea that a bad decision by his record label would keep him from celebrating another American chart topper.

On paper, it would be the Fleetwoods' classic "Come Softly to Me" that would keep "A Fool Such as I" from hitting #1 on the pop charts. But in truth, the single's chance at a #1 spot were killed by a decision made at RCA Victor. The flip side of the new Elvis record, "I Need Your Love Tonight," was such a strong song that it gained almost as much airtime as did "Fool." As a result, some stations ignored the ballad, focusing instead on the rocker. Others chose the country cover and forgot about the one that really moved. This double-sided war over radio play created an atmosphere in which "Fool" was stopped in its tracks by the success of its own B side. Ultimately "I Need Your Love Tonight" would hit #4 the week that "Fool" hit #5. Then "A Fool Such as I" would go on to jump over "Love" and land at the #2 spot. Had RCA Victor simply released each number separately, backing them with weaker B sides, both singles would probably have topped the charts on their own.

Although Elvis was shut out of the #1 spot on the pop charts, RCA Victor figured that the single would mark the singer's return to the upper level of the country playlists. After all, the Bill Trader–penned classic had strong country roots. But country stations did not even acknowledge the single. It was as if they were saying, "This is a Snow hit—no new version need apply." Nevertheless, Elvis would still earn a #1 spot with the country cover.

At the same time that "A Fool Such as I" ran out of gas in the United States, it was picking up steam in Great Britain. On April 4, Elvis registered his fourth #1 hit in the United Kingdom. "Fool" would become one of the most successful Elvis hits ever to cross the pond and land on the British Isles.

In retrospect, it seems strange that a song that first became a hit in country music would have to be exported to another country to top the charts. But perhaps this record was a testament to the ability of Elvis Presley to make his music something more than country, rock, or pop, or even American music as a whole. When Elvis sang now, he sang the music of almost the whole wide world.

A BIG HUNK O' LOVE

The world of popular music would have been a much different place without the influence and direction of Aaron Schroeder. A man who could write and produce #1 songs, spot and develop budding superstars, manage and direct artists, and, during his five-decade career, understand and oversee every facet of the music business, Schroeder was a unique talent who was driven to create. Without his drive, scores of great records and incredible artists would never have become a part of the American musical landscape. Aaron was there to birth such great acts as Barry White and Gene Pitney. As a publisher, he gave the world Jimmy Hendrix's "Purple Haze" and the Fred Neil classic "Everybody's

Talkin'." His compositions were recorded by hundreds of performers, from Sinatra to the Beatles. Schroeder was even responsible for all of the theme songs to the much-loved Hanna-Barbera cartoons. And in the case of Elvis Presley, had it not been for Schroeder's input and creativity, the King's career would have been shortened by sixteen records. This marriage of songwriter and artist began just as Elvis emerged onto the national scene.

When RCA Victor signed Elvis in 1956, the company used its grapevine to get the word out to songwriters that material was needed for a hot new rock 'n' roll artist. Aaron Schroeder was one of hundreds who got the message and responded. From his New York office in the famous Irving Berlin Building, the composer assembled many of his friends and cowriters to sift through existing songs and to create new music for the teen sensation. Ultimately, this quest would lead to Schroeder landing a spot on Elvis's first Christmas release, as well as to scoring a number on the *King Creole* soundtrack. While neither of these songs would become hits, they did lay a foundation for the future, and they opened the door for every demo that Schroeder chose to send to Elvis over the next six years. Though he would eventually write more #1 records for Elvis than any other composer, in 1958 Schroeder was still trying to dial the right combination of words and music to land an Elvis single.

"Aaron worked with a lot of writers," his wife, Abby, recalls. "He was always spotting new talent, giving writers their first breaks, making a place for those who were trying to break into the music business."

Schroeder's receptive attitude opened the door for a lot of new faces in the music business, and the relationships between the established writer and the "new blood" brought forth inspiration that produced a lot of hits. It would be in this type of collaboration, a first-time teaming, that would generate Aaron's initial Elvis chart topper.

When Schroeder wrote with new writers he usually took the lead, and he was almost always the catalyst that moved the number along. He was the one whose ever-expanding mind seemed to first lock onto an idea that had real market potential and discard others that, while solid, did not speak to that day's need. Part of the songwriter's success had to be traced to his ability to understand his target audience.

Unlike many writers who composed with little thought of their song's potential, when Schroeder wrote, he considered more than just the idea; he thought of the audience for that idea. This ability to project his concepts into the marketplace as he wrote them made Schroeder unique. He was more than an artist: he was a visionary. He even studied the artists who needed songs, as well as the market that bought each artist's records. Due to this study, Schroeder was able to sense the direction that music was going in before it had arrived there. As a result, he was able to give record labels the songs they needed when they needed them. It was this ability that brought so many artists back to the writer's office time and time again.

Schroeder's first cut came as a teen, with the Rosemary Clooney song "At a Sidewalk Penny Arcade." The song was not a hit, but it did plug the budding New York writer into the music business. Over the next few years Frank Sinatra, Nat King Cole, and Tony Bennett would cut tunes written by Schroeder, and by the mid-1950s he was recognized as one of the best of a new breed of popular songwriters. While most pop tunesmiths ignored the advent of rock 'n' roll and concentrated on churning out Sinatra-type ballads, Schroeder jumped into the developing genre with both feet. Even before Bill Haley and His Comets recorded "Rock Around the Clock," Schroeder was writing songs for this new sound. And, because he was still in his early twenties, he understood the youth market better than most of the other established writers of the era. When the word came down the pipeline that RCA Victor needed songs for Elvis, he was ready.

"Aaron had been listening to Elvis records," Abby explained. "He knew Presley's music and could sense what made the singer unique."

When a new writer, Sid Wyche, came to Schroeder to pitch some of his ideas, Schroeder opened his door. The two decided to try to write some things together. As RCA Victor was looking for new Elvis cuts, the duo sat down and compared notes. In Schroeder's case, this review took a while. He had a huge book in which he wrote down everything from ideas to song titles to abstract lyric lines. On this day, with Elvis in mind, the songwriters pulled an off-the-wall concept from one of the pages and set to work. At first this concept sounded more like a Valentine's Day recipe than a song, but with the master's touch and an enthusiastic contributor's input, the wild idea would blossom into Elvis's most successful record of 1959, and his last hot rocker until "Burning Love."

Schroeder and Wyche built their song around a beehive. "Honey" was a popular pet name for a lover, and the duo used this idea to create a hive filled with sweet nectar. The singer opened with "I ain't asking much of you," and a few lines later added, "all I want is all you've got." In three verses, in which everything from wishbones to a rabbit's foot were employed, the song begs not for a kiss or a hug, but for everything a woman could offer a man. If the lyrics did not incorporate so many childlike images, they would be shocking. The words begged for action. But the song's raging tune demanded it.

When Schroeder and Wyche completed "A Big Hunk o' Love," they sensed they had created something special. This was a wild rocker. It had a edge like "Hard Headed Woman" and "Trouble," but it also had a pulse that resembled Jerry Lee Lewis's hits "Breathless" and "Great Balls of Fire." In other words, this song was the kind of number that kids loved—and that parents hated.

Schroeder put together a demo of the song that pushed the limits of rock music at that time. With a pounding piano, loud guitars, and a screaming vocal, "A Big Hunk o' Love" was almost orgasmic in presentation. Considering the softer hits that topped the pop charts at the time—"Venus," "Smoke Gets in Your Eyes," and "Come Softly to Me," among others—this was a much different breed of song. Even as he shipped it off for Elvis's consideration, Schroeder had to wonder if this hot number was not a year or two too late. In truth, it might have been six years too early. The Rolling Stones would have loved this kind of song in 1966.

Producer Steve Sholes liked "A Big Hunk o' Love" as soon as he heard it. This new number would require Elvis to pull deeply from his rockabilly roots, a genre the producer wanted to again embrace. But the song was just the opposite of what Elvis's manager had in mind. Shocking the world with "the Pelvis" had been the right way to introduce the singer to the world, but now the Colonel was looking to move Elvis into a more mainstream pop mode. By doing so, the manager believed, Elvis was assured staying power. Parker now wanted a toned-down Elvis who crooned in the mode of Sinatra or Crosby. "A Big Hunk o' Love" was not a ballad, and it certainly did not have that safe, middle-class feel that the Colonel wanted to push.

As Parker was rarely in the recording studio, Sholes was unconcerned about getting the song past management. Besides, he knew that the songwriters would give the Colonel the publishing cut he always demanded in order to assure a single. The producer did wonder, however, whether Elvis would want to really get into the number and generate the power required to make it a strong record. In addition, Sholes knew that the lyrics would have to get by the censors. After all, much like in the ballad "Don't," the protagonist of "A Big Hunk o' Love" was asking for much more than dinner and a movie. Would radio stations play a song that featured a message so overtly sexual?

Sholes decided to take a chance on the theme, and he scheduled "A Big Hunk o' Love" to be recorded during Elvis's next session. Now the problem became finding the time to cut the number. Elvis was in the military, and soon he would be sent out to Europe. On top of this, Elvis's mother was very ill, and the singer was deeply concerned about her health—so much so that, except for his time spent on duty, he didn't like to leave her side. And then there was the Colonel.

Parker was using every trick in his book to keep RCA Victor and the company's hottest property on different sides of the street. The manager didn't want Elvis in the studio. He wanted America to be so starved for Elvis material that, once the singer returned from service, the public would purchase anything and everything Elvis. The release of new records during this time would throw a wet blanket on the Colonel's plans. Despite Parker's efforts to keep the two apart, on June 10, 1958, Elvis finally came to RCA Victor's offices in Nashville for a much-needed two-day recording session. "Big Hunk o' Love" was one of five songs cut during those two days.

The Schroeder-Wyche number sprang to life in the famed RCA Studio B. With Bill Black and Scotty Moore now pursuing their own careers, Nashville session players supplied the music for the session. Hank "Sugarfoot" Garland was assigned to the bass guitar. On piano was the legendary Floyd Cramer. D. J. Fontana was still with Elvis and on drums, but another drummer, Buddy Harman, was brought in as well. As always, the Jordanaires were also in place, and they helped Elvis prepare for the real session that lay ahead with a spirited gospel music song session. Rounding out the group with his guitar, as well as serving as session producer, was Mr. Music City himself, Chet Atkins. Having the world's greatest guitar player filling in for Scotty served to put Private Presley at ease.

To make "A Big Hunk o' Love" work, Elvis had to pull out a rebellious spirit that the army had somewhat tamed. He had to again be young, wild, and hungry. He had to get back to the crazy and unreserved enthusiasm he had exhibited in his early live shows. In other words, he had to get worked up. It was not easy to get the soldier into a lather, and when he did get there, some of the musicians were lagging behind. As a result, the song did not come together very quickly. As the men worked against the clock, knowing that this would be their last session for almost two years, frustration set in. Eventually the plug was pulled, and "A Big Hunk o' Love" was left unfinished. This is probably why the Schroeder-Wyche number was the last of the five session songs to be released.

Later, when the label needed a new single, Sholes and Atkins revisited the session, carefully studying the various takes of the Schroeder-Wyche number. Pulling pieces from several different takes, a single version was spliced together. It was ultimately decided that this blended cut was good enough to be released as a single. With nothing new to slap on the B side, RCA Victor pulled a rejected ballad from Elvis's earlier work from the vault. "My Wish Came True" was used as the flip side to the new Schroeder-Wyche rocker. This union of a strong song and a weak one did fix a problem that had plagued the last Elvis single. Unlike "A Fool Such as I"/"I Need Your Love Tonight," two strong songs that ended up competing against each other, resulting in neither reaching the #1 spot, there would be no doubt about the side that DJs would play this time. Only one of these songs sounded commercial.

"Big Hunk o' Love" was shipped out the first week in July and hit the charts on July 13, 1959. It quickly became the fastest-moving song in the nation, and it surfaced in the Top 100 the next week at #43. Two weeks later, on July 20, it was at #9. By August 10, the song had knocked Paul Anka's "Lonely Boy" off the top of charts. The Elvis song held the #1 spot for two weeks until it was replaced by the Browns' "Three Bells" on August 24. "Big Hunk o' Love" would join "Stagger Lee" as the only two real rockers to hit the top of the charts in 1959, a year that saw "The Happy Organ" hold the #1 spot for a week in May. Times were changing, and the rock was being squeezed out of rock 'n' roll.

Looking back, "A Big Hunk o' Love" is one of the most unusual of Elvis's hits. With its driving piano and edgy lyrics, the song sounds more like a Jerry Lee Lewis number, and it certainly was not a reflection of the musical tastes of the very late 1950s. Rabid in nature and rebellious in tone, it flies in the face of the respectable image that the young soldier was then presenting. In terms of #1 hits, it represents the closing of a chapter. On his next single, "Stuck on You," a newer, softer Elvis would emerge.

The "Elvis for Everyone" that was being molded by Colonel Parker might well have saved Elvis's career. At the time, clean-cut teen idols dominated the pop playlists. Raw was out, and polish was in. Therefore, it is hardly surprising that "A Big Hunk o' Love" represents the kind of song that Elvis would not revisit for almost a decade. Amazingly, the music that would herald the next, more mellow, chapter in Elvis's career would again be Aaron Schroeder's.

STUCK ON YOU

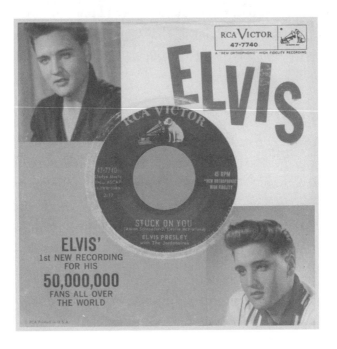

ELVIS' 1st NEW RECORDING FOR HIS 50,000,000 FANS ALL OVER THE WORLD

O n a snowy March 5, 1960, Sergeant Elvis Presley was discharged from the United States Army at Fort Dix, North Carolina. Newspapers around the world fought to get the final pictures of the singer in his military uniform. Elvis, looking much more mature and confident than he had two years before, was nevertheless a bit frightened and very unsure of the way the entertainment world and the public would welcome him back. The sound of rock 'n' roll had changed. Acts that had been on top of the charts when he had gone into the army now couldn't buy a hit. Pat Boone had not had a #1 hit since 1957. Chuck Berry seemed to be washed up. Bill Haley and His Comets were considered middle-aged men. What if Elvis's time had come and gone, too? What if the world wasn't interested in hearing more of his music?

Perhaps that is why he carefully answered one reporter's question about his future as a singer by saying that he was going to devote himself to his acting career, not his musical career. These were obviously not words that RCA Victor wanted to hear. The label had a long-term contract with the singer and it was out of Elvis material. He was needed in the studio ASAP.

Initially Elvis bypassed the recording studio, opting instead to first return home to catch up with his old life in Memphis. The singer visited with old friends, shopped for cars and clothes, and caught up on American television shows. He supposedly also spent some time learning the script for his first post-service movie, *G. I. Blues*. Still, even though Elvis had not been to the recording studio and there was nothing left to release, RCA Victor pressed forward and began selling "Elvis's new single." Using photographic images of a pre-service Elvis, the company printed a 45 picture sleeve that simply stated "Elvis' 1st New Recording For His 50,000,000 Fans All Over The World!" The identification number of the new single was 7740. In the middle of the sleeve was a hole for a record title to show through, but there was no title underneath the picture of Nipper, the RCA Victor dog. But that did not keep the company from accepting orders for the unknown new release. In fact, before Elvis finally made it into the studio on March 20, RCA Victor had registered 1,275,077 in sales units for mystery song 7740. It now seems a shame that some songwriter did not pen a tune with those numbers in the title and have it cut for this first Elvis single of the new decade.

Dozens, if not hundreds, of tunesmiths pitched their best material to RCA Victor for the session. The first Elvis song since his discharge would no doubt produce such a financial windfall for the songwriter that even signing off part of the publishing rights to the Colonel seemed insignificant. When the composers whose demos had been accepted for final consideration found out the presale numbers of this first single, they could not wait to see what song the label finally chose for the honor. In this case, cars, homes, and vacations were riding on RCA Victor's choice.

The tunes that made the final cut for the two-day session were "A Mess of Blues," "Soldier Boy," "It Feels So Right," "Make Me Know It," "Fame and Fortune," and "Stuck on You." "A Mess of Blues" was similar to the kind of songs Elvis had been cutting in 1957. It was more R&B than pop and, given the songs that were in the charts at the time, it did not seem well suited to a 1960 market. Though it was a natural tie-in to both Elvis's recent military experience and his next film, "Soldier Boy" was not a very strong music vehicle. In truth, it was little more than an album cut. "Make Me Know It" was a rather pale re-creation of the sound that was featured in songs such as "Don't Be Cruel" and "Paralyzed." That left "Fame and Fortune" and "Stuck on You." The former was a ballad, and the powers at RCA Victor wanted something that rocked out of the box first, so "Stuck on You" won the lottery.

Aaron Schroeder, who had helped pen Elvis's only #1 hit of 1959, was the cocreater of the singer's first single of the new decade. Working with him this time was J. Leslie McFarland.

"He was a magical guy," says Abby Schroeder, smiling as she recalls her husband's friend and cowriter. "Oh, like all writers, he was a bit of crazy—wonderfully so, though. McFarland was really a touch of genius, a touch of torment. He would sometimes drink too much, but he was such a great guy when he was sober. And his songs were usually so good."

During his career McFarland would pen some classic cuts, the most-remembered being the haunting "Little Children," a Top 10 single for Billy Kramer and the Dakotas in 1964. But neither he nor Schroeder tried to make any larger-than-life statements in the demo they submitted to Elvis. Instead, the team found a gimmick—an old, well-known American saying—dreamed up a melody that echoed the feel of Otis Blackwell's "All Shook Up," and toned down the beat a little. The tune was great, but the real genuis was found in the song's message and presentation.

The writers used extremely simple but very creative, cute lyrics, as well as some stop-and-go pacing, to make the number stand apart from others being demoed for the session. They also penned a lot of "Uh-uh-uhs" and "Yes-sir-rees" to give Elvis some lateral movement and chances to be creatively quirky with his vocal inflections, as he had on hits such as "All Shook Up." The lyrics rang out in a fashion that reflected the lingo of the youth idol of the time, Ed "Kookie" Byrnes, a character in the TV show *77 Sunset Strip*, giving Elvis the chance to project a kind of casual cool in each verse. To Schroeder's astute mind, the song rocked enough for the kids while reassuring the adults that this Elvis was now the new, safe all-American model of the old rock 'n' roll king. Its lyrics and style also made it the perfect music vehicle to be quickly absorbed into pop culture.

Even though he was no fan of Colonel Parker, Aaron Schroeder sensed where the manager was taking Elvis. The writer realized that Parker wanted to reconnect fans with the Elvis of the old days, but in a respectable manner. In modern terms, Parker wanted to present Elvis Lite. In contrast to his last hit, the hard-driving "A Big Hunk o' Love," the singer needed a number that could be sung while wearing a conservative sports coat, a white shirt, and a tie. The new Elvis would reflect what middle America viewed as a proper and upstanding citizen. As a result, Schroeder made sure that the lyrics to "Stuck on You" were not sexual, but fun and playful. In every sense, this carefully crafted song was perfect for the singer and for the times.

While "Stuck on You" and the other tunes captured during this recording session would reflect a more mature style from Elvis, the songs would also give the singer a chance to perform with new technology. RCA Victor was now using stereo and three-track recording in its sessions, and Elvis's first single would be an example of how far sound recording had come in the last two years.

Not sure what to expect out of the singer in this first time back in the studio, RCA Victor executives assembled some familiar faces to make the transition easier. Guitarist Scotty Moore was there to greet Elvis, as was Hank Garland, on bass. D. J. Fontana was behind the drum set. Floyd Cramer was on hand to finger the keyboard, and the Jordanaires were ready for the backup. In fact, it was probably Elvis's gospel jam with the quartet that broke the tension that filled the studio. As Elvis attacked his favorite gospel tunes, everyone in the studio realized that RCA Victor's top act was back. And, while his hips didn't swivel as much, his voice was stronger than ever.

Quickly reclaiming his old confidence, Elvis listened to the demos, got a sense of what he wanted from each of the cuts, and set to work. The fact that "Stuck on You" changed very little from demo to final cut showed how firmly Schroeder understood not only the singer's strengths, but also the new direction in which Elvis was headed. In the demo, the phrasing mirrored that of some of his past hits. The occasional stopping of the musical instruments, which allowed Elvis's voice to set the pace and tone for the number's key phrases, also perfectly suited the singer and his fans. "Stuck on You" was not just written with Elvis in mind; it was arranged in such a way that it was guaranteed to strike a chord with his fans. It took only took three takes for the singer to nail the song.

After his work in the studio was finished, a very satisfied and relieved Elvis grabbed a train headed for Miami to tape an appearance on *The Frank Sinatra Timex Show*. From Tennessee to Florida, fans lined the tracks to try to catch a glimpse of the rock idol. When Elvis did appear, to wave or blow a kiss, women screamed and fainted. Based on the huge preorder sales for Elvis's next, as-yet-unknown single and the chaotic scene along his train route, it was obvious that the King had returned, and that his country was ready to hail him master over all.

As Elvis rolled down the tracks, receiving the kind of attention normally reserved for a president or royalty along the way, RCA Victor boxed and shipped his new single. Less than forty hours after the third take had been completed and accepted, 1.5 million copies of "Stuck on You" were headed to stores and radio stations. The strongest ballad that had been recorded during that session, "Fame and Fortune," was pressed onto the B side.

In late March, when radio stations received their copies of the new Elvis single, "Theme from *A Summer Place*," performed by Percy Faith's Orchestra, was the #1 song in the land. During the first week of April 1960, as Faith ruled the top spot on the chart for his sixth straight week, "Stuck on You" made the largest leap in the history of pop charts, jumping from #84 to #17 in seven days. On April 16 the Elvis single hit #6. A week later "Stuck on You" was #1, and its B side had jumped into the Top 20. The carefully crafted Schroeder-McFarland song was a monster hit, and it proved once and for all that Elvis was back.

On May 12 the singer appeared on television for the last time until 1968. As a favor to Nancy Sinatra, Elvis agreed to be officially welcomed back home by the Rat Pack. With a #1 song and a movie in the works, the timing could not have been better for Elvis, or for Sinatra. The rocker thrilled his fans by singing his newest hit, and he even had fun with the older generation, crooning Sinatra's hit, "Witchcraft." Ratings went through the roof. Perhaps the person who most enjoyed the show, however, was Elvis himself. "Stuck on You" stayed on top of the charts for four weeks. In doing so, it gave the singer new faith in his future. The song paved the way for a softer, post-service Elvis. Aaron Schroeder's next composition would serve to complete Elvis's evolution from rocker to crooner, killing the rockabilly rebel and transforming Elvis into the most powerful and universally loved entertainer on Earth.

IT'S NOW OR NEVER

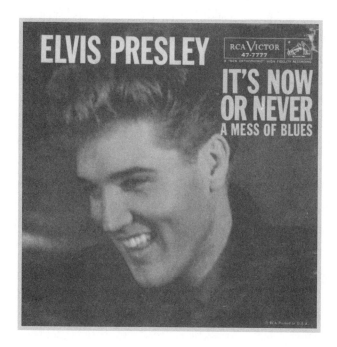

ELVIS PRESLEY
RCA VICTOR
47-7777
A "NEW ORTHOPHONIC" HIGH FIDELITY RECORDING
IT'S NOW OR NEVER
A MESS OF BLUES

W ith his #1 hit "Stuck on You," Elvis Presley proved that he could again rule the charts. But, even though it ran up millions in sales, many felt that his first post-military release was rather tame. Elvis's fans had expected the King to "put the rock back into rock 'n' roll" and bring a new edge to pop music. When they heard "Stuck on You" and saw the formally dressed Elvis singing on TV with Frank Sinatra, a host of teens questioned where the tough Elvis—the one who strutted onstage; the surly rebel whom their parents despised; the man who was blamed for the fall of the morality of American youth—had gone. Sadly for the fans who hoped to see a return to the "Hound Dog" days, Elvis's second post-service single would offer nothing but disillusionment and disappointment. But to the rest of the world, "It's Now or Never" would cast Elvis in a new light and spotlight a talent that exceeded almost everyone's expectations.

Elvis had been exposed to a wealth of musical genres and influences while he was in Germany. He heard songs sung in ways that literally sent chills up his spine, by voices that seemed to climb to the skies. Though he still listened to R&B and the blues, his musical tastes were growing and maturing. This came as no surprise to his close associates, as the singer had always embraced a wide variety of influences and styles. But Elvis's expanding tastes would soon shock his critics and the world.

One of the European songs that lingered in Elvis's mind and that often was heard on his lips was the Italian classic, "O Sole Mio." Written in 1901 by G. Capurro and Eduardo di Capua, this light aria was one of the best-known and most-loved operatic numbers in the world. In the 1940s "O Sole Mio" was given wide exposure in America by Mario Lanza. Yet, even though Lanza sang the song often in concerts, the famed vocalist who had scored a #1 hit in 1950 with "Be My Love," never placed the number on the popular charts. Elvis, who was just a child in the 1940s, obviously did not frequent Lanza's concerts, so Europe might well have been the first place that Elvis heard the song. Language was no matter: Elvis loved it, and he could not get it out of his head.

As the end of Elvis's time in the service drew closer, Hill and Range Music Company sent Freddie Bienstock, one of its representatives to Germany to meet with the singer-turned-soldier. RCA Victor needed Elvis back in the studio as soon as he returned to civilian life. Bienstock's job was to find out what music Elvis wanted to use in these upcoming sessions. Armed with demos and ideas, Freddie and Elvis spoke of scores of possible candidates for his next few singles and albums. One of them, suggested by Elvis, was "O Sole Mio."

Bienstock knew Elvis well enough not to be shocked by the strange request. The singer liked all kinds of music. After all, his first hit had been a straightforward hillbilly song. Unlike many rockers, Elvis also placed singers such as Bing Crosby, Frank Sinatra, and Tony Bennett at the same level as he did Big Mama Thornton, Fats Domino, and Hank Williams. Elvis was even a huge fan of Dean Martin, and he played his LPs frequently. Though he could not use them on his early recordings, the singer loved lush orchestration and soaring vocals. Many of the gospel songs that Elvis and the Jordanaires played around with before their recording sessions challenged the singer's vocal range much like the soaring pop ballads did. So there was a direct, though difficult-to-spot, tie to the singer's varying musical taste. Still, Bienstock found it hard to picture the rock star wowing the teenage girls back home with this operatic tune. Nevertheless, Bienstock promised Elvis that he would study the situation, even visiting with those at the publishing house about the possibility of putting down a new cut of "O Sole Mio" for a future record. As they parted, the singer added one more detail to his request: Elvis wanted new lyrics, written in English, for the Old World favorite.

Elvis may not have been aware that English words had already been written to go with the tune of "O Sole Mio." Pop singer Tony Martin's version had hit #2 on the American charts in 1949. In fact, "There's No Tomorrow" was Martin's signature piece. Even if Elvis did know about this version, Hill and Range probably would have still demanded that new lyrics be penned for Elvis. The publisher did not own the rights to "There's No Tomorrow," and it most likely would have refused to pay another company for rights to a tune that, set to new words, they could use for free.

Bienstock returned to New York with a list of songs he needed to prepare for Elvis's next session. As he walked into Hill and Range's New York offices, he was greeted by songwriters Wally Gold and Aaron Schroeder, who inquired about his meeting with Elvis. In a matter of minutes, the fast-talking agent updated the composers on the singer's changing taste in music. Bienstock then asked the duo if they would like to write new lyrics for "O Sole Mio." Once the writers got over the shock of learning that Elvis wanted to record the number, they asked, "Why not use the Tony Martin lyrics?" Freddie replied, "Elvis does not like them." Was this really the case, or did Hill and Range simply want a new effort for its own publishing house? The latter seems more likely. The publisher would not have earned royalties off the Martin song, but with new lyrics could cash in on another Elvis hit. With Hill and Range pushing them on, Gold and Schroeder hurried out the door, grabbed a taxi, and headed to Schroeder's studio in the Irving Berlin Building to pen the words before anyone else had the opportunity to cash in on what seemed like an incredibly easy job.

By the time their taxi pulled up at 1650 Broadway, the writers had already come up with the song's title, and it took the men just half an hour to complete the lyrics. A few hours later, Gold and Schroeder walked back into Hill and Range with their completed piece. An impressed Bienstock listened to the new lyrics just one time, then ordered the men to do a demo.

Schroeder had written for Elvis in the past, and he had a feel for the kind of things the singer liked. As he arranged the demo, he combined his knowledge of Elvis's work with the climate of the pop charts of the time. With additional input and direction from

Gold, the demo took on a Latin cha-cha flavor. For lack of a better description, when Schroeder finished his arrangement, this new version of "O Sole Mio" was "salsa meets opera." When the piece was fully orchestrated, the writers called an actor, David Hess, who would later appear in such films as *Swamp Thing* and *Valley of the Dolls*, to provided the vocal work for the demo. Schroeder and Gold handed over the final version of the demo to Hill and Range, hoping that Elvis liked their efforts.

Weeks passed, and Schroeder became concerned about the song. He was not troubled by the words—he believed that he and Gold had nailed the lyrics—but he wondered if Tony Martin would be upset that his signature number had been reworked and given to the most famous singer in the world. Schroeder liked Martin's style, and he did not want to upset the pop crooner. As Bienstock and Gold explained, however, it was too late to worry about that now.

One thing that Schroeder did not have to be worried about was Elvis's opinion of the new lyrics. The singer loved this Americanized "O Sole Mio," and he was eager to record it during his first trip to the studio in March. But RCA Victor had other plans. They didn't want to come out of the blocks with an "internationally flavored Elvis." The label scheduled the recording of the pop opera piece for the singer's second trip to the studio on April 3. Joining Elvis for this session were Scotty Moore on guitar, Hank Garland on bass, D. J. Fontana on drums, and Floyd Cramer on piano. Added to the cast of regulars was famed saxophone player Boots Randolph. As always, the Jordanaires provided the backup vocals.

RCA Victor's goal for the two-day session was the completion of all the tracks needed for a new Elvis album that was to be titled *Elvis Is Back*. Elvis's personal goal was to tackle those cuts and also to do justice to his new favorite song, "It's Now or Never." Relaxed, fit, and in fine vocal form, he was more than ready for the task.

Even with its soaring melody, demanding range, and seemingly endless vocal holds, Elvis completed a perfect recording of "It's Now or Never" after just four takes. Never had the singer's styling been more precise, his vocal inflections so tight. His interpretation of the song was so inspired that the musicians were even awed with the performance. In fact, everyone in the studio, from the board manager to the janitor, was blown away by Elvis's voice. Some wondered where all of that power came from and how they had not noticed it before. This was an Elvis they did not know, but nevertheless fully appreciated. But, they wondered, while this style might fly in Europe, would America like "the Pelvis" as an opera singer?

RCA Victor decided to package "It's Now or Never" with a B side of "A Mess of Blues." The company figured that the flip side, with its very R&B feel, might appease radio stations and fans who didn't want to hear a "Mario Lanza" Elvis. As it turned out, very few stations ever played the B side. In fact the power of "It's Now or Never" was so strong that not only pop stations, but also easy listening and R&B stations featured the Elvis cut on their playlists. The only chart it did not hit hard was the country playlist.

"It's Now or Never" had a twenty-week run on *Billboard's* pop list, entering the charts at #44 on July 18. On August 15 the song knocked Brian Hyland's "Itsy Bitsy Teenie Weenie Yellow Polka-dot Bikini" out of the #1 spot. Elvis's single held the top spot for five weeks before being replaced by Chubby Checker's "The Twist." Even then the tune stayed in heavy rotation for months.

Copyright problems prevented the single from being released in England until later in the fall. There, anticipation was so great for the new Elvis song that in the first week of its release in the

United Kingdom it hit #1. Record stores were overwhelmed by the demand for the single. Some outlets closed rather than fight the crowds. Others simply opened up special lines just for the sale of "It's Now or Never." Many stores took advantage of the single's popularity by tripling its regular price—and the single still sold out within hours. Try as they might, RCA Victor simply could not keep up with demand in England or around the world. Before it was finished, "It's Now or Never" sold more than twenty million copies worldwide. Even today it remains one of the five most-played songs in radio history. The *Guinness Book of World Records* lists it as the top-selling pop single of all time. More important than its sales, "It's Now or Never" made Elvis a worldwide star. The singer seemed to be loved by everyone, no matter their race, nationality, or religion. Yet, even as the royalty checks rolled in, Aaron Schroeder still wondered what rewriting the lyrics had meant to Tony Martin.

"We traveled a lot," recalls Schroeder's wife, Abby. "We were in Beverly Hills eating and we saw Tony Martin and his beautiful wife Cyd Charisse come into the same restaurant. Aaron was known as being outspoken in business, but in reality was very shy. I knew that he would love to meet Tony Martin—he had long admired his work—so I encouraged him to go over to his table. He wouldn't go. I finally told him that I would go with him and convinced him to walk over the two tables to meet Tony.

"Well, Tony knew who Aaron was, and Aaron, still a bit embarrassed said, 'I hope you don't hate me for what I did with "There's No Tomorrow."'

"Tony smiled at Aaron, shook his head and laughed. 'No, I had my run, it was great. The fact that it came back with Elvis showed how strong the melody was.'" Never were truer words ever spoken.

A weight was lifted from Schroeder's shoulders that day, and he finally began to enjoy the real power and influence of his work helping to create the now legendary "It's Now or Never." Thanks in no small part to Schroeder, the song, so far removed from the type of songs that Elvis had sung in the past, remains a musical icon a century after the melody was penned. Although some blame this tune for "destroying the world's greatest rock star," "It's Now or Never" actually positioned Elvis high above all other popular singers of the time. No longer could his fiercest detractors label the entertainer "lucky" or "talentless"; Elvis's voice and sense of style could no longer be argued. As soon as the song was issued, critics were forced to consider the rock giant as being on the same plane as Sinatra and Crosby. While a host of young Elvis fans didn't want to see him so accepted by the masses, this recognition allowed Elvis to achieve a personal goal and escape some of the insecurities of his youth. No longer was he the kid from the wrong side of the tracks, the boy with the worn-out clothes who lived in the projects. Now he was the living symbol of the American Dream to the whole world.

ARE YOU LONESOME TONIGHT?

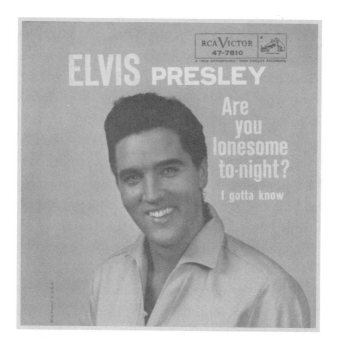

The King of Rock 'n' Roll sounded more like a future star of the New York Metropolitan Opera in the fall of 1960. The melodic aria "It's Now or Never" was the biggest hit he'd had in three years, and many of his longtime fans started to wonder whether Elvis had completely sold out to the country club set. His next single would do little to dissuade this concern.

Colonel Tom Parker's interest in Elvis's records had always revolved around money. He didn't care if he liked them; the manager just wanted them to sell in large numbers, and to double-dip into the profits by controlling a portion of the publishing rights. So it was indeed strange when the Colonel asked Elvis to record a specific song during the early April recording session that produced "It's Now or Never" and the LP *Elvis Is Back*. Always accommodating to his manager, Elvis naturally fulfilled Parker's request.

The Colonel's wife had a favorite song that dated back to the 1920s. It seemed more suited it vaudeville than to rock, but Elvis and RCA Victor believed that, with a bit of updating, "Are You Lonesome Tonight?" could find a niche in the modern marketplace. Little did they realize that this number would become one of the most beloved Elvis songs of all time, or that the old ballad would also earn Elvis a new level of respect from his peers in the entertainment world.

A very simple song about heartbreak and loss, "Are You Lonesome Tonight?" was written by Roy Turk and Lou Handman in the 1920s. Turk had been a vaudeville performer who worked with the likes of Sophie Tucker before becoming a Tin Pan Alley songwriter during the flapper era. As a composer, Turk worked with some of the era's great tunesmiths, including George Meyer, Charles Tobias, and Arthur Johnston. His best-known songs include "Walkin' My Baby Back Home," "I Don't Know Why (I Love You Like I Do)," the Billie Holiday classic "Mean to Me," and the great Bing Crosby hit "Where the Blue of the Night Meets the Gold of the Day."

In 1927 sound came to motion pictures. The "World's Greatest Entertainer," Al Jolson, ushered in the talking-picture craze with the words, "You ain't heard nothing yet." Jolson, whose black-faced minstrel music is now considered as outdated, distasteful, and as bizarre as separate water fountains for blacks and whites, was one of the first to latch onto a song that Turk had written with another ex-vaudvillian, Lou Handman. Yet, even though Jolson would sing the duo's "Are You Lonesome Tonight?" onstage and record the tune, the performer who, during his lifetime, placed ninety-one songs on the charts did not score a hit with the ballad. Perhaps the number just didn't work with his over-the-top minstrel style.

Vaugh Deleath, who claimed to be the first woman to sing on radio (the Academy-Award winning African American actress Hattie McDaniel also made this claim), recorded "Are You Lonesome Tonight?" for Edison Records. Deleath's rendition of the song hit #4 on the charts in November 1927. Then the great Henry Burr, who was often called the "Number-One Ballad Singer of American Music," recorded the song. This single, the 116th of his to chart and next-to-last release of his more than four-decade career, peaked at #10. After that, the song was forgotten for more than twenty years.

In 1950 the Blue Barron Orchestra, with Bobby Beers on lead vocal, cut a big-band version of "Are You Lonesome Tonight?" The single barely crawled into the Top 20, peaking at #19. Again the song was quickly forgotten. Yet it is probably the Blue Barron version of "Are You Lonesome Tonight?" that the Colonel shared with Elvis.

Elvis, who had obviously mellowed a great deal since his pre-service days, liked the song. He immediately sensed what he wanted to do with it. Using the same musicians he had employed on "It's Now or Never," the singer laid down a very simple and plaintive track. Adding a spoken soliloquy after the first verse, a paraphrasing of Shakespeare's act 2, scene 7 of *As You Like It*, Elvis gave the song a dramatic flavor that echoed the work of singers like Sinatra. Though many listeners would be shocked by the solemn and sincere words inserted into the ballad, this was not the first time that Elvis had used this technique. He had also spoken lines in "That's When Your Heartaches Begin" in 1956. But the fact that Elvis was now using the words of the great English bard, made this new effort sound much more sophisticated.

Unlike "It's Now or Never," the song did not test Elvis's vocal range, nor did it offer impressive long notes to hold. In fact, this song comes across as something like an intimate parlor piece. It is that intimacy that makes it so very strong and timeless. And Elvis's performance of the song radiated sincerity; his rendition seemed completely heartfelt. RCA Victor was overwhelmed by the final product, and the Colonel's wife was moved to tears.

Elvis's voice was just one aspect of the recording, however. In order to blend with with the singer's voice and presentation, the orchestration had to be more subdued than that found on any Elvis record since "Love Me Tender." In the final version, the musical accompaniment is so understated it seems almost inconsequential. The Jordanaires stand out more than the musicians.

If RCA Victor had any problem with "Are You Lonesome Tonight?" it concerned that song's tone. Given that Elvis's most recent hit had been the ballad "It's Now or Never," it seemed time to release a rocker. But Elvis and Parker both wanted "Lonesome" as the next single. Rather than hold it for later release, the label slapped a mild rocker, "I Gotta Know," on the B side and shipped the single to stations on November 1.

The response was overwhelming. "Are You Lonesome Tonight?" became the first American single to debut in the Top 40, at #35 on November 14. A week later it hit #2. On November 28, the single knocked Maurice Williams and the Zodiacs' "Stay" off the top spot. The Elvis ballad held the #1 position for the rest of the year, finally relinquishing the #1 spot on January 9, 1961. Incredibly, the ballad also enjoyed a ten-week run on the R&B

charts, peaking at #3. In Britain "Are You Lonesome Tonight?" topped the charts for four weeks. The single even made waves on the U.S. country charts.

In addition to its enormous international success, the song received three Grammy nominations. "Are You Lonesome Tonight?" was nominated for Record of the Year; Best Vocal Performance, Male; and Best Vocal Performance by a Pop Singles Artist. While Elvis did not win in any of the three categories, he believed that the nominations signaled that the entertainment world now considered him more than just a passing fad—in other words, that he had been accepted by the establishment and had become respectable.

Only in the crazy world of show business could a song that had first been recorded by "World's Greatest Entertainer" Al Jolson, become a vehicle of transformation for an entertainer who, almost three decades after his death, still reigns as the world's greatest. But "Are You Lonesome Tonight?" did just that. The song probably took Elvis farther down the road to becoming a respected star in the entertainment world than anything he had previously recorded. This was the goal that Colonel Parker had set for his star even as Elvis entered the service, and it now appeared that it would easily and quickly become a reality. The "Elvis for everyone" model was paying huge dividends for Parker and RCA Victor. Yet, for those who were just discovering that Elvis had real talent and a dynamic voice, the words of Al Jolson's jazz singer would prove true: "You ain't heard nothing yet."

SURRENDER

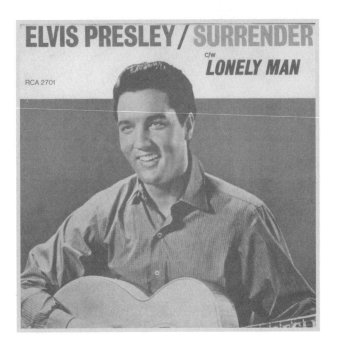

ELVIS PRESLEY / SURRENDER
c/w
LONELY MAN

RCA 2701

lvis Presley did not return to RCA Studio B in Nashville until October 30, 1960. During the previous months the singer spent most of his productive hours filming *G. I. Blues* and *Flaming Star*, and he'd recorded the movies' songs in Hollywood.

At the time, RCA did not pick out songs from movies for major singles. Although there were a dozen solid cuts on the *G. I. Blues* soundtrack, none was thought of as a candidate for the hit parade. At the time, for unknown reasons, the label held the view that the movies sold complete soundtrack albums, while other studio recording sessions produced hits that sold non–movie-related

LPs. It was a philosophy that would be maintained until the success of the *Blue Hawaii* soundtrack.

With work on *Flaming Star* just finished and Elvis's third post-service feature, *Wild in the Country*, to begin in November, RCA Victor booked Elvis into a recording studio for two of his few free days in October. The session, which occurred at the end of the month, would prove very rewarding. Not only would it produce a #1 hit, but the LP that was completed on Halloween Day would ultimately bring the singer his first Grammy Award.

Though Elvis's record label had been concerned about releasing two ballads in row, these songs had both been so well received that RCA Victor decided to continue with them. After witnessing the worldwide success of "It's Now or Never," the best-selling single ever for the label, it was decided to dip back into the classical well for Elvis's next single. Another turn-of-the-century Italian number was uncovered, and Hill and Range Music Company set about securing new lyrics for the old operatic standard. This time the publisher turned to the creative talents of Jerome "Doc" Pomus and Mort Shuman. At first glance, the team seemed an unlikely pair for this rather classical task. Nevertheless, the two would give the music publisher exactly what it needed.

In 1991 *Rolling Stone* declared Doc Pomus "one of music's most gifted and prolific songwriters." The magazine further stated that "Doc Pomus helped invent rock 'n' roll." But before he "invented" rock 'n' roll, this former blues shouter, a crippled polio survivor, opened the door for other white artists in R&B and led one of the greatest blues bands in history.

Initially, Pomus wrote only for his band. By the early 1950s, however, his songs had grown so popular in the African American clubs where he played that he actually cut back on performing to pen hits for the likes of Laverne Baker and Ray Charles. It was during this period that Doc met two other Caucasian blues composers, Jerry Lieber and Mike Stoller. Together, the three men generated a number of classic tunes for the new youth-oriented pop market, including the Coasters' "Young Blood" and a future Elvis hit, "She's Not You."

Influenced by Lieber and Stoller, Pomus began to stray from the blues, and he composed more rock and pop standards. His success in this area was guaranteed when he met a fledgling teen songwriter.

Mort Shuman was full of ideas and energy, but short on contacts. If he hadn't happened to take Pomus's cousin on a date, the young man might never have been given a break. Pomus liked Mort, and, despite their more-than-fifteen-year age difference, the two began to write together. Employing Pomus's honed skills and the sixteen-year-old Shuman's understanding of the youth market, the pair composed such classics as "This Magic Moment," "Teenager in Love," and "Turn Me Loose." The Elvis camp knew the team from their hits with other artists, but became much more fully aware of the team's talent when Elvis cut Pomus's and Shuman's "Mess of Blues," the song that would become the flip side of "It's Now or Never."

Had it been given a chance, "Mess of Blues" probably would have been a major hit on its own. Even in the shadow of "It's Now or Never," the tune earned some chart time, peaking at #32. Perhaps Hill and Range and RCA Victor thought that, because of the gigantic hit with which it had been paired, Pomus's and Shuman's song received the short end of the stick. Maybe that is why the companies asked the duo, rather than Aaron Schroeder and Wally Gold, to pen new words for the next Elvis single.

In the late summer of 1960 Hill and Range executives called Pomus and Shuman into its New York office and gave them a copy of "Torna a Sorrento" ("Come Back to Sorrento"). Though it had never appeared on any American bestseller playlist, Pomus at least must have been familiar with the song: Frank Sinatra had included it in a 1950 LP, and Dean Martin had recorded it two years later. The tune had also been used in various musicals and movies. Probably half the people in America, and almost everyone in Europe, could hum at least a part of the melody.

The Italian song's history dates back to just after the turn of the century. Written in 1911 by Ernesto and G. D. de Curtis, "Torna a Sorrento" was a well-known light-opera vehicle. Over the years, it was recorded by scores of Europeans, and Elvis had probably first heard the song while he was stationed in Germany. Because "Torna a Sorrento" commanded the same type of range and power as "It's Now or Never," Elvis and his label sensed that the melody would again show off the singer's dynamic voice. All the song needed, they reasoned, was new lyrics.

Pomus and Shuman must have considered this gig a walk in the park. Composing this number was probably the easiest paycheck the writing team ever earned. The tune was in place—all they had to do was provide a set of words to accompany it. Sensing that Elvis and RCA Victor would want something similar to the theme that had been employed in "It's Now or Never," the songwriters worked up a pleading love song. While it was, perhaps, a bit more demanding in tone, "Surrender" was really just "It's Now or Never," part two.

An October recording session had already been scheduled for the recording of a gospel album. Elvis loved the demo of "Surrender," however, and he wanted the tune for his next single, so the song was added to the session. The Pomus-Shuman rework of the popular Italian ballad would be the only secular title cut on either October 30 or Halloween Day.

Assembled in Studio B to back up Elvis were Scotty Moore on guitar, Hank Garland on bass, Buddy Harman on drums, Boots Randolph on saxophone, and Floyd Cramer (who might have been feeling some bitterness, as his recording of "Last Date" had been stopped at #2 behind Elvis's last hit) on piano. The Jordanaires were there for vocals, and, for the first time since Elvis's return from the service, Millie Kirkham provided a female voice. When needed, Elvis supplied some rhythm guitar fills.

Though most now feel that "It's Now or Never" is a vastly superior piece of music, "Surrender" was the more difficult one to perform, and it proved quite a challenge to Elvis and the other musicians. The song demanded not only fast pacing, but also precise tone. If Elvis undercut or overcut a note by just a hair, the mistake was obvious. He also had to bleed a wide variety of emotions into his vocal inflections, and it was no easy task to decide how to hit each phrase. Elvis found that it was not easy to sound as if he were begging for love while simultaneously pushing his voice to the limits of its power and range. Under the gun to cut a full gospel album as well during that session, and not wanting to fully drain the star's voice, the musicians eventually gave up on their attempt to cut a perfect take, and they handed over the tapes of all of their takes to RCA Victor's technicians in the hopes that a winner could be spliced together.

In early 1961 the record label finally produced an acceptable mix of several different cuts of the new song and sent this final master to the pressing plant. "Surrender" would be mated to another ballad, "Lonely Man." This marriage of two non-rockers seemed to indicate that RCA Victor no longer felt the need to push up-tempo Elvis music in the marketplace. In fact, the label had not shipped an Elvis rock single since "A Big Hunk o' Love," which had been released some two years before the release of "Surrender." To many fans, this seemed to further confirm that RCA Victor and the Colonel were killing the old Elvis altogether. Because of "Surrender" and other Elvis songs like it, millions of teens would begin to look elsewhere for a new rock idol.

Nevertheless, "Surrender" surpassed the initial success of "Are You Lonesome Tonight?" entering the charts at #24. A week later "Surrender" jumped to #4. It climbed two more places the next week, hitting #2 on March 13, and it topped the charts the following week. "Surrender" held the top spot for two weeks, but it was in the Top 20 for a total of just twelve weeks. Though initially it had seemed likely to surpass the success of "It's Now or Never," the song did not come close. Perhaps radio stations and the public were growing tired of classical Elvis.

Doc Pomus and Mort Shuman would write several more Elvis hits, including "Little Sister," which hit #5 in 1961, the great theme song from *Viva Las Vegas*, which remains one of the King's most-remembered tunes, and "Suspicion," one of the singer's greatest album cuts. The team's biggest Elvis hit, "(Marie's the Name) His Latest Flame," a mild rocker about lost love, hit #4 in the United States and topped the British charts in 1961. Pomus and Shuman's music would prove to be an important part of redefining Elvis in his post-military years.

After scores of hits and a decade of collaboration, Pomus and Shuman parted ways in the mid-1960s. Shuman moved to France, and Pomus returned to his blues roots on the East Coast.

The only white man ever to win the Rhythm and Blues Foundation's Pioneer Award, Doc Pomus was a writer who never surrendered his talent and never forgot how to give: Pomus would spend his last three decades seeking out R&B artists who had fallen on hard times and giving them a second chance at life and a career. Because of his compassion, Mike Stoller once called Pomus "the archangel of rhythm and blues." In fact, Pomus used most of the royalties that he received from his biggest Elvis hit to feed and clothe the people who had first given him breaks in the music business.

As "Surrender" ruled the *Billboard* chart, Elvis performed live for what would be the final time until his famed televised comeback special in 1968. As the headline act, Elvis took his magic to a Hawaiian stage on March 25 to raise money for the memorial of the USS *Arizona*. Singing seventeen songs that day, he proved to the crowd that his hips still moved and that he could still sing hard rockers. He tore up the place with "Hound Dog." Then, per part of the Colonel's master plan, he walked out of the public eye. But this time Parker's judgment was wrong. The Colonel had thought that, by taking Elvis out of the public eye for a time, the singer would be even more in demand. As record sales would soon prove, however, the public needed to see Elvis in person, not just hear him on the radio or catch him on a movie screen. And, if Elvis wanted to continue to score hits, he'd need to rock.

CAN'T HELP FALLING IN LOVE

n hindsight, one of the worst things that happened to the career of Elvis Presley was the success of *G.I. Blues*. This formula musical was a much larger box office draw than either of the singer/actor's straightforward dramas, *Flaming Star* and *Wild in the Country*, that followed. Not only did the musical enjoy solid box-office numbers, but the soundtrack flew off the shelves, as well. It didn't take Colonel Tom Parker long to figure out that B movies filled with Elvis, pretty girls, and a dozen songs made a great deal more money than those whose plots had intrinsic value. When the manager compared the time required to film a top-flight film versus a motion picture like G.I. *Blues*, he decided that, in the future, Elvis would avoid major drama work. Instead, the Colonel opted to toss his star into a series of sometimes entertaining but always lightweight movies that amounted to little more than ninety-minute commercials for the film's soundtrack album.

The first in this long string of films was *Blue Hawaii*. Though it is now considered one of the best of the Elvis post-service film efforts, it was never going to be confused with a major studio feature. The formula for this release was very simple: Elvis, as the movie's star, would sing a song about every eight minutes; have at least one cute scene with some little kids; save a damsel in distress; have a fight or two; and get the girl at the end of the flick.

Their lame plots aside, the early Elvis scripts looked pretty much like all Hollywood scripts—just thinner. Songwriters were given these scripts and asked to read them and find a place to insert a tune. The more places they found, the better. The writers would then submit their demos to the song screeners, who would judge the merits of each number and pick the ones that best served the film's needs. Occasionally a musical gem would find its way into one of these films, but usually the soundtrack was filled with the likes of "Ito Eats," one of the fourteen cuts from *Blue Hawaii*.

It was up to Jean and Julian Aberbach, at Hill and Range Music Company, to find the songs needed for this Hawaii-based, Hal Wallis produced film. To help in their search, the Aberbach brothers contacted record producers Hugo Peretti and Luigi Creatore. After reading the script, the two, who were not overly inspired by the movie's plot line, began to work on creating several songs for the flick. They decided to seek the assistance of a third writer, and they asked one of entertainment's most respected song scribes to join them in the endeavor.

George David Weiss was all but a music legend by the time he began working on songs for *Blue Hawaii* (which, at that point, was still blessed with a working title of *Hawaii Beach Boy*). While still a student at the Julliard School of Music in the 1940s, he wrote and arranged hits for Stan Kenton, Vincent Lopez, and Johnny Richards. Because of these efforts, the biggest names in the music business were soon lined up at his door looking for hits. And Weiss accommodated them: Perry Como, Patti Page, the Ames Brothers, Ella Fitzgerald, Jo Stafford, Nat King Cole and Sarah Vaughan were just a few of the hundreds who recorded Weiss's tunes. Most came back to him time and time again.

One of the composer's greatest strengths was his versatility. He penned "What a Wonderful World" as well as "The Lion Sleeps Tonight." He wrote the music for the dark drama *Murder, Inc.*, as well as for *Gidget Goes to Rome*. He even composed three success-ful Broadway musicals. So Weiss seemed like a natural choice for input into the new Elvis film. But the tunesmith doubted that even he could do anything with the script he was handed. "They [Peretti and Creatore] gave me the script to take home to read," Weiss recalls. "I read it, and it wasn't *Gone with the Wind*. In fact, the script was so bad I took it back to them and said I couldn't find any-thing that inspired me."

Weiss informed Peretti and Creatore that he was not inter-ested in the project, and that he would therefore pass on working with the producers. Before the writer was able to leave their office, Peretti argued, "You're crazy. This is an Elvis movie. Take the script home and read it again!"

Weiss hadn't known the movie was a Elvis vehicle. He had worked with Elvis on *Wild in the Country*, but that film had a real script. This paled in comparison. Nevertheless, he picked up the script and returned home to restudy it. After hours of searching, he still found little that spoke to him. He was ready to give up again when he came across one small part of the script that seemed to contain a bit of promise.

"I finally found a scene that moved me," the writer explains. "Elvis comes home to Hawaii from being in the service in Germany. He brings a gift of a music box to his girlfriend's grandmother. To me this was a sweet moment. I always loved the warm, tender quality of Elvis's voice."

Weiss went back to Peretti's and Creatore's office to show them what he had found. After discussing it, the three sat down and worked up a number that each felt would bring out the best qualities of Elvis's voice. When they had finished, they took the their songs to the publisher.

"With the five of us in the room," Weiss recalls, "I sang 'Can't Help Falling in Love.' When I finished singing there was a deafening silence."

Weiss, Peretti, and Creatore waited in that awkward silence for several seconds before Jean Aberbach finally spoke.

"That was very pretty, but we would prefer something with a beat like 'Hound Dog.'"

For the next ten minutes, the parties went back and forth arguing the merits of the new number. Weiss was not going to give an inch. He felt that they had composed a perfect song for Elvis and that it should be in the movie, in the spot he had found. The publishing executives saw things differently, and they demanded a rocker. Finally the Aberbachs agreed to allow a demo of "Can't Help Falling in Love" to be made if Peretti and Creatore would find more music for the film. The publishers also promised to for-

ward the "Can't Help Falling in Love" demo to the movie's producers. Weiss ultimately supplied the vocal for that demo.

A few weeks later a team was assigned to preview demos for the
soundtrack. As they placed the Weiss-Peretti-Creatore tune on the
record player, Elvis happened to walk by.

"Elvis heard part of the song," Weiss was later told, "stopped,
and said, 'I want to hear that again.' The demo screeners replied,
'Oh, that's just some dumb little ballad.'"

Elvis was not dissuaded. Rather than pass on the number, he
demanded to hear it in its entirety. When the number finished,
Elvis flatly stated, "I want to do that in my movie." When the King
commanded that the tune be included, the discussion ended.

Elvis recorded "Can't Help Falling in Love" on March 23,
1961, at Radio Recorders studio in Hollywood. Scotty Moore and
Hank Garland were there on guitars, Bob Moore was on bass, and
Floyd Cramer had been flown in from Music City to play keyboard.
Dudley Brooks was also in the studio, handling both piano and
celeste. Boots Randolph had flown in to play saxophone, George
Fields was blowing the harmonica, and the session had three drum-
mers—D. J. Fontana, Hal Blaine, and Bernie Mattinson. To capture the sound of Hawaiian music, Alvino Ray was brought to play
the Hawaiian, or steel, guitar, and Fred Tavares and Bernie Lewis
played ukuleles. As always, The Jordanaires were on hand, and this
time they were joined by a group known as the Surfers. Most of the
songs were not very challenging, and the fourteen-tune session was
completed without problems. Elvis's work was solid throughout the
session, but his touching presentation of "Can't Help Falling in
Love" seemed the most inspired. On this number, Elvis gave his
heart. In each carefully crafted word, the singer's sincere love of the

ballad could be heard and even felt. Though incredibly simple in its arrangement, because of Elvis's work, the little love song had a power that few ballads possessed. While "It's Now or Never" demands that it be listened to, "Can't Help Falling in Love" sneaks in the back door and gently finds a place in the heart. In that sense, the song seems to reveal not as much the deep talents of the singer as the essence of his soul.

Production on *Blue Hawaii* ended in late spring. Almost immediately, Elvis began work on his next film, *Follow That Dream*. While the star was busy in Hollywood, a confident RCA Victor released three non-movie-related new singles as follow-ups to "Surrender."

The first record was a cover of "I Feel So Bad," an old R&B classic. This number peaked at #5 on the U.S. charts. An up-tempo pop ballad, "(Marie's the Name) His Latest Flame," was next, and it climbed to one step higher. The final cut, the strongest rocker since "A Big Hunk o' Love," was called "Little Sister." Though it was catchy, this single peaked at #5. While the latter two singles would hit #1 in the UK, they were still disappointments for the label. RCA Victor was just beginning to realize that Colonel Parker's transformation of their singer into "Elvis Lite" was not translating into good news at the cash registers.

Elvis needed a #1 hit in his homeland. Dance-craze songs were hot at the time, so RCA Victor turned to a number from the *Blue Hawaii* soundtrack. After all, the number moved, it was up-tempo, and it might appeal to those who liked to try new dances. But the label quickly discovered that banking on "Rock-a-Hula Baby" was not a sound investment. George David Weiss remembers the release very well.

"In those days, a single released from an album had an A side and a B side. No one ever heard or played the B side. The Aberbachs [and RCA Victor] put 'Rock-a-Hula-Baby' on the A side, which they assumed would be the hit single, and buried 'Can't Help Falling in Love' on the B side." Needless to say, Weiss was disappointed.

"Rock-a-Hula Baby" was shipped on November 21, 1961, the same day that *Blue Hawaii* premiered in theaters nationwide. Although the movie showcasing the tune was doing well, the single died on the vine. Even with RCA Victor's heavy promotion, the dance number never made it higher than #23 on the charts.

"The movie came out," Weiss recalls, "and 'Rock-a-Hula-Baby' was released. Nothing happened. It was a flop. However, astoundingly, listeners started calling in to their local radio stations requesting the DJs to play the B side. Gradually there was a groundswell, and 'Can't Help Falling in Love' took off."

The groundswell was probably created by the movie itself. After seeing *Blue Hawaii*, moviegoers left theaters talking about "Can't Help Falling in Love." The number immediately became the favorite Elvis tune of hundreds of thousands of fans. Most were unaware that it had been designated the lesser of the two songs on Elvis's latest record. They simply wanted to hear it, and they called radio stations to request the song. Within a week, "Can't Help Falling in Love" was in heavy rotation.

This B side hit the chart at #57 on December 4. As more fans saw the film, and more radio stations fielded more requests for "Can't Help Falling in Love," "Rock-a-Hula-Baby" was forgotten in a wave of excitement that slowly crossed the country. On Christmas day "Can't Help Falling in Love" crept into the Top 10. On February 3 the song would climb to #2 on the *Billboard* pop charts, and it remained in the Top 10 until the end of the month. Though the dance single "Peppermint Twist" kept the single from reaching the top of the *Billboard* list, "Can't Help Falling in Love" did hit #1 both in Britain and on the U.S. Easy Listening chart.

When Elvis returned to live performance work in 1969, "Can't Help Falling in Love" became his signature closer. It would therefore become the very last song he ever sang in public. Perhaps no B side has ever had as much success or made as great a mark on the world of music. During Elvis's lifetime, the soundtrack from *Blue Hawaii* was his best-selling album. Most agree that the huge sales racked up by the song "Blue Hawaii" were due to the power and beauty of "Can't Help Falling in Love," a song that, initially, only Elvis and the ballad's writers had any faith in at all.

GOOD LUCK CHARM

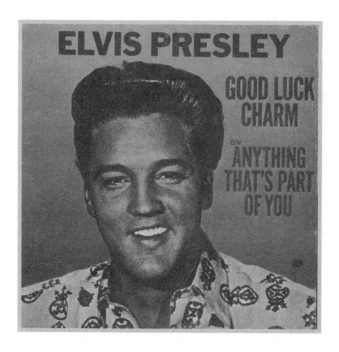

"Can't Help Falling in Love" was a genuine Elvis hit, both on the charts and in terms of boosting Elvis's career. The song was so popular that it had erased some of the concern that many listeners felt about the singer's apparent musical slide. These doubts had surfaced when other recent Elvis records had struggled to make it into the top five. On October 15, 1961, when RCA Victor brought Elvis back to Nashville for a non–movie-related recording session, they did not know that a throwaway number from *Blue Hawaii* was going to come out of nowhere to temporarily rejuvenate their star's career. At the time of the session, the only thing on RCA Victor executives' minds was that a song had to be found to reestablish Elvis as the top artist in rock 'n' roll music. In order to guarantee the best possible material for the session, RCA Victor and Hill and Range Music Company decided to contact proven songwriters, including one man who had been responsible for four other Elvis hit records, three of which had hit #1 on *Billboard's* pop charts.

In the weeks before the fall recording session, Aaron Schroeder received a call from the Aberbach brothers at Hill and Range. They asked Schroeder for his help. The composer knew that Elvis's chart numbers had not been as strong as they had been during his first four years with RCA Victor, and he was not surprised to hear from Elvis's people. What must have shocked him, however, was how little time he had, between the date of that phone call and that of the upcoming studio session, to write a hit song.

At the time, Schroeder was writing a great deal with Wally Gold. It was Gold who had helped Schroeder rework "O Sole Mio" into "It's Now or Never." When Schroeder tried to find Gold to tell him about this new challenge, he got some bad news. Gold was in the hospital.

"I was with him," remembers Schroeder's wife, Abby, "and he had this idea. He wanted to write a song around that idea, but only with Wally. He didn't want to work with anyone else."

The Aberbachs had already explained to a select number of writers that they needed a strong single, not an album cut or a movie song. They were looking for a major hit—something that would refocus radio play on Elvis. It needed to be a rocker that harkened back to the best songs of Elvis's early career, but still fit into today's "softer" musical playlist. It needed to have a hook or a gimmick like "All Shook Up," and it had to bounce like "Don't

Be Cruel." Most of all, it had to sell. This time, nothing but the very best would be accepted.

Schroeder was an experienced writer; he knew that even a great song would need a bit of luck to reclaim the kind of magic that Elvis had known in the 1950s. Back then, Elvis had defined music; now the singer was just a part of it. That was a deep hole from which to climb. As the writer fiddled with ideas, he kept coming back to the concept of the luck that was needed to get a break in life, fall in love, or score a #1 song. As he played with this theme, he started to grin. It was easy for his wife to see that Schroeder was excited about the potential of a song that embraced luck. What he needed was a hook to flesh out the concept.

Schroeder almost always worked with other composers. A team player, he liked to share ideas with and get input from trusted associates. But, although there were a host of other writers within minutes of Schroeder, as he played around with the Elvis tune, he realized that this song had to be written with Gold. Initially Schroeder vowed to wait until his cowriter was released from the doctors' care. As the session date grew closer, however, he grew a bit antsy. Finally, just days before Elvis was due to record, the writer decided he had to visit his sick friend.

"Aaron went to the hospital," Abby explains, "and he took along what he had already done on the song. Together, Wally and Aaron polished the song in the hospital room during the visit."

The starkly clean hospital setting was a much different scene than the songwriter's normal atmosphere. Schroeder was used to writing in smoky rooms, with cigarettes spilling over ashtrays and an old piano serving as both an instrument of creation and a platform to hold scores of coffee cups and soft-drink bottles. But, even though their environment was all wrong, the team plowed ahead.

Gold was tired of being cooped up, and ideas spilled out of his brain. Schroeder was so excited to be working again with his good friend that the inspiration needed to pad his original idea came easily. While the doctors and nurses might not have been too wild about the tunesmiths using their health facility as a studio, within just a few minutes of being locked in this sterile environment the writers had created a pretty solid little rocker. They had also added some color to Gold's cheeks.

Schroeder and Gold built their song around the themes of fate and luck. Not wanting to miss a single element, they incorporated horseshoes, four-leaf clovers, a rabbit's foot, silver dollars, and lucky pennies into the song's three verses. The duo shunned the dark side of fate and focused on good fortune and hope in their up-tempo love piece. Simply put, the song was the story of a guy who couldn't lose as long as he had the woman he loved on his arm. As that was exactly how Schroeder felt about his own life with his wife, Abby, the concept seemed a natural to the writer.

Schroeder immediately went into the studio and cut the demo for his latest tune. He then put it in the mail for Elvis. The singer received the single the day before his session. As he listened to the Schroeder-Gold number, his instincts told him that "Good Luck Charm" would be a hit. The following morning he brought the demo into the studio with him.

Waiting for Elvis in RCA Studio B were Scotty Moore and Jerry Kennedy on guitar, Bob Moore on bass, D. J. Fontana and Buddy Harman on drums, Boots Randolph on saxophone, and Floyd Cramer on keyboard. The Jordanaires and Millie Kirkham, who were now used in all of Elvis's sessions, were there as well.

Unlike the early days, when Elvis had to struggle to find himself in each new song, the singer was now comfortable with who he was and how he wanted to sound. As a result, sessions were much easier. Adding to the ease of this particular session was the way in which Aaron Schroeder had prepared the demo. The writer knew the artist's style so well, the demo already sounded just like Elvis. The singer simply played the record, and the musicians figured out what they needed to do to duplicate its sound. Elvis just eased through each take. His phrasing was precise, but the mood was fun. The melody moved, but it was never in a hurry. It had a beat, but a light one that begged to have the listener sing along, not to move out to the dance floor. For lack of a better word, it was cute—and, after just four takes, "Good Luck Charm" was in the can.

To promote Elvis's film *Blue Hawaii*, RCA Victor needed to release a song from that movie before it could release "Good Luck Charm," and the new tune would be held for several months before it was issued. During this time "Can't Help Falling in Love," a song from *Blue Hawaii* that hadn't been considered a potential hit, surprisingly worked its way up the charts. A week after that song peaked, "Good Luck Charm" was shipped. On the record's B side was a very strong and mournful ballad, "Anything That's Part of You." The latter would receive some airplay on easy listening stations, but it was "Charm" that made the big splash on the pop charts.

"Good Luck Charm" hit the Top 100 on March 17, debuting at #51. It would take a huge leap to #14 the next week and land in the Top 10, at #9, on March 31. The first week in April saw the new Elvis hit move to the third spot, and by April 14 it was at #2. The only thing keeping "Good Luck Charm" out of the #1 spot was Shelley Fabares's "Johnny Angel." (Ironically, Fabares's song was one of Elvis's favorites at that time.) Seven days later, however, "Angel" dropped to #2, and "Good Luck Charm" took over the top spot. The song remained at #1 for two weeks.

RCA Victor, which felt pressure to continue Elvis's string of having at least one #1 hit on the *Billboard* charts each year, breathed a sigh of relief that "Good Luck Charm" had turned out to be a chart-topping success. "Can't Help Falling in Love" had fallen just short of this goal. With "Good Luck Charm" ruling the playlist, Elvis had earned a #1 hit on the *Billboard* charts every year since 1956. Today, the Beatles are the only act that can match a string of hits that long.

"Good Luck Charm" did even better in England than it did in the States. The single rode the charts for seventeen weeks, five of them at #1. Meanwhile, even the B side of this single made it into both the American and the British Top 40 lists.

Thanks to an outstanding made-to-order song provided by Aaron Schroeder and Wally Gold, Elvis was back on top. He again seemed ready to reassert his power on the charts, but the Colonel's management style would get in the way. Tired of dealing with Parker and his demands over publishing rights, Aaron Schroeder stopped composing songs for Elvis.

"Aaron would not give up rights as publisher," Abby Schroeder explains. "We had our own publishing company now, and we wanted to hold onto the rights of our own songs. So 'Good Luck Charm' represented the end of the era. Aaron loved Elvis, but did not like the Colonel at all. The soured relationship with the business people around him [Parker] caused Aaron to go to war with them. He wanted to make sure all writers, not just us, got a fair shake."

Having already lost Leiber and Stoller over the same issue of shared publishing rights, Elvis could not afford to lose the likes of composers such as Schroeder and Gold. But the duo quit sending their demos to Elvis, as would another incredible writing team,

Doc Pomus and Mort Shuman. None of the writers ever blamed Elvis for these splits, but the quality of the material sent to the singer would soon show that the old carnival barker who took 50 percent of every dollar Elvis made was no "Good Luck Charm." Over the next few years, as more bad Elvis movies were released and, per Parker's instructions, the King shunned concerts and television appearances, some began to wonder whether the Colonel was even a good manager.

RETURN TO SENDER

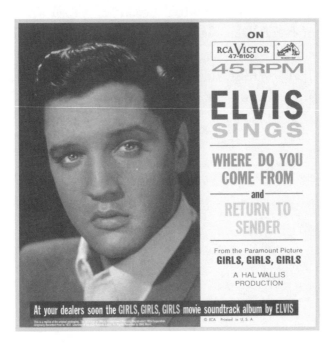

A fter "Good Luck Charm," RCA Victor shipped the wonderful ballad "She's Not You." Elvis nailed the recording, but, while the song was beautiful and its lyrics were haunting, it was not unique. "She's Not You" was a pop tune, not a rock song. It was a number that anyone from pop's Frank Sinatra to country's Jim Reeves could have performed just about as well as did the rock star. Though Elvis loved it, many of his fans looked elsewhere for their music favorites. They wanted songs that had catchy tunes, and artists who exhibited a lot of energy.

Sensing a need to get back to rock 'n' roll basics, Hill and Range Music Company and RCA Victor contacted a man who had penned two of Elvis's biggest early hits. It had been almost six years since Otis Blackwell had written "Don't Be Cruel" and "All Shook Up." The first was still the most popular single of all time, and the title of the latter had evolved into an important part of the American language. Each hit had a bounce and rhythm that were largely missing from Elvis's post-service crop of records. Publishing and label executives didn't want to stun fans who had grown used to Elvis the crooner, but they did want some music that would remind audiences that Elvis had really brought rock 'n' roll to the world. Blackwell, therefore, must have been stunned to learn that the label was not looking for a new single that had that kind of energy; they simply wanted songs to fill out the score for his upcoming movie, *Girls! Girls! Girls!*

After receiving the call from Hill and Range, Blackwell got together with his friend and cowriter, Winfield Scott. He had met Scott in the late 1950s, and had written with him off and on for three years. Winfield had also penned songs for Elvis, so the teaming of the two men for this project seemed a natural marriage. After looking through the film's rather anemic script, the men set to work. They penned several tunes to fit scenes where the script's writers had placed, in bold type, "ELVIS SINGS," but ultimately, only one of their compositions seemed to fit the script. The winner was a fishing ditty that the duo called "Coming in Loaded."

As much as any songwriter, Blackwell worked off hooks. His second big hit for Elvis had been inspired by a bottle of Pepsi-Cola. But he found nothing in this script that jumped out as offering a place for a gimmick or a hook. How many songs could be written about walking on a beach, kissing a pretty girl, having a fight, or being tossed into jail? After a while, each number seemed indistinguishable from the next, and Blackwell and Scott pretty much gave up after several hours of writing nothing of which they were proud. But, even though they struck out at coming up with anything remarkable for Girls! Girls! Girls!, inspiration for another song did strike the two. This time it would be in the form of a returned piece of mail.

Songwriters often deal with returned mail. Demos are constantly returned; record labels move or go out of business, managers or artists quit show business, and producers switch record labels or lose their jobs entirely. In each case, there is rarely a forwarding address. Sent out with hopes of making money and maybe earning a Grammy, these returned packages offered little but depression and dashed dreams. Yet on this day, they brought forth one of Scott and Blackwell's best ideas.

Undeliverable mail was returned bearing the U.S. Post Office stamp "Return to sender! No such person! No such zone!" The postal service saw a piece of mail such as this as a failed parcel, but to Blackwell and Scott, the words that were stamped onto the envelopes were lyrics about the failing love of a spiteful woman and a heartbroken man. Most writers would have penned a song based on this concept as a slow, mournful ballad. But Blackwell's mind worked differently. He did not see music through one genre of expression, and it was his ability to see past the obvious that made him such a unique talent.

Blackwell had fallen in love with cowboy songs at about the same time as he had R&B when he was a young man. As a result, his music influences ranged from Bob Wills to Chuck Willis. This allowed the writer to pen songs for every possible record market. His creative spark knew no bounds—he could not be pigeonholed. His hits ranged from Peggy Lee's "Fever" to Jerry Lee Lewis's "Breathless," and his style influenced everyone from Elvis to Stevie Wonder. Before he died in 2002, Blackwell was hailed by critics of rock, R&B, blues, and country as one of the greatest songwriters of all time. Almost two hundred million records have been sold with his name written on the label as songwriter. Yet it is doubtful that he ever wrote anything quite as innovative as "Return to Sender."

The song's lyrics were laid out to capture the emotion behind rejection; Blackwell didn't care whether they adhered to the literal meaning of the postal service's words. If the heartbroken man knew where the woman lived, then the letter would not have been returned with the words "No Such Person, No Such Zone." Obviously the person and the zone would have been correct in this case. But the fact that the lady receiving the mail despises the man so much that she claims not to live at her own address makes the sender's plight that much sadder. It was a brilliant concept—everyone has gotten a letter marked "Return to Sender" at some point in their lives, and everyone can identify with liking someone who does not return those feelings. In two verses, a chorus, and a bridge, Blackwell and Scott penned one of the tightest songs of heartbreak ever written. But the real genius was their combination of the song's sad lyrics with a bouncy melody that seemed to embrace life with a puppy-like zeal. Had anyone else written a song in this way, its lyrics and its melody probably would not have worked together. In these songwriters' creative hands, however, it was a perfect marriage.

A few weeks later Blackwell met with Colonel Parker, representatives from Hill and Range, and movie song screeners. He played them the few numbers that he and Scott had produced for the movie. The response of those in the room was hardly inspiring. Before everyone left, however, Blackwell took a chance and played his demo of "Return to Sender." Most agreed that it was a nice song, but they pointed out that it didn't fit into the plot of *Girls! Girls! Girls!* Nevertheless, they took the demo with them and promised to consider using the song down the road. A few weeks later the writers were shocked to learn a portion of the script had been rewritten so that "Return to Sender" could be included in the final version of the new film.

On March 27, 1962, Elvis resurfaced at Radio Recorders studio in Hollywood. His task that day was to cut the thirteen largely forgettable songs that filled out the soundtrack for *Girls! Girls! Girls!* Scotty Moore, D. J. Fontana, Boots Randolph, Dudley Brooks, and the Jordanaires were in the studio, as were Barney Kessel and Tiny Timbrell on guitar, Ray Siegel on bass, and Hal Blaine and Bernie Mattinson on specialty drums. Elvis, by now almost as unexcited by his songs as were his fans, no longer conducted his sessions as the ultimate perfectionist; instead, the singer quickly pushed through the bulk of the songs that were on the day's agenda. Though his voice remained strong on each new track, he seemed to be simply going through the motions. Then came "Return to Sender." Using the very same styling that Blackwell had employed on the demo, Elvis's energy level went up, and the singer cut the number in just two takes. Like "Don't Be Cruel" and "All Shook Up," this was a fun, commercial song. It gently rocked, its lyrics brought smiles, and its melody stuck in the head. "Return to Sender" was an easy song for Elvis to learn to perform. Maybe that is why, as they watched Elvis work his way through "Return to Sender," Scotty and D. J thought that the old magic had returned.

Few realized it at that time, but "Return to Sender" has a certain something that makes it musically timeless. Part of it is the melody; once heard, it sticks in people's minds. Another bit of genius was Elvis's decision to lead the chorus with Boots Randolph's saxophone rather than with the usual guitar. But perhaps the song's greatest attribute is its rather up-tempo, "happy tune" framework, something not usually paired with what is essentially a woeful ballad. Everyone at both Hill and Range and RCA Victor thought that "Return to Sender" was not just the best song on the *Girls! Girls! Girls!* soundtrack, but also the perfect follow-up to "Don't Be Cruel" and "All Shook Up." The number so recaptured the happy enthusiasm and unbridled joy that were a part of rock 'n' roll in the mid-1950s, many wished that it had been recorded and released in 1957.

"Return to Sender" was pressed with another *Girls! Girls! Girls!* soundtrack number, which served as its B side. No one was going to mistake "Where Do You Come From" as a hit, and it was not surprising that, unlike most Elvis singles of the period, this B side would earn no chart time at all.

This new Elvis single was shipped on October 2, 1962, with little fanfare, and the Blackwell-Scott number did not make much noise on the charts until *Girls! Girls! Girls!* appeared in theaters at the end of the month. Then it exploded.

On November 3 "Return to Sender" hit #10. A week later it moved to #4. It then spent the next five weeks at #2, behind the Four Seasons' monster hit, "Big Girls Don't Cry." In England, however, Elvis was hotter than ever, and the "Return to Sender" single rocked the BBC, hitting the top spot on the British charts just before Christmas and holding that position for three weeks. Considering that the movie was the song's only vehicle of exposure (in accordance with the Colonel's wishes, Elvis continued to avoid the public eye; there were no concerts or TV shows in which to sing, and promote, the song), its success in both the United States and the United Kingdom showed just how incredible the Black-well-Scott tune really was. After all, had Elvis not pumped "Don't Be Cruel" and "All Shook Up" in hundreds of concert appearances and several national TV spots, it's almost certain that they would not have remained in the Top 10 as long as they did. Exposure was the key to promotion, and Elvis was now nothing more than a cel-luloid image.

Elvis would score a minor hit with another Blackwell number in 1963. "One Broken Heart for Sale" also benefited from the unique bond between the two men—a bond made even more remarkable by the fact that the two never met in person. Yet "One Broken Heart for Sale" marked the end of Blackwell's working rela-tionship with the singer. The brilliant song scribe continued to pen hits for other artists, but he never again wrote for Elvis. In addition, it would be seven years before any writer scored another #1 Elvis hit on the American pop charts. After "(You're the) Devil in Disguise" and "Bossa Nova Baby," both released in 1963, it would also be two years before an Elvis song even made it into the Top 10. In spite of the fact he was making millions of dollars, it was obvious that the wheels were coming off the singer's career.

The new generation of record buyers knew Elvis only from his movies. Most teens of the 1960s had never seen him in concert or on television. Ricky Nelson used TV to pitch a new song each week. *American Bandstand* exposed new acts weekly. Every major pop star and group used the tube to hawk their new songs and con-certs and to make new fans. But, thanks to Colonel Tom Parker, Elvis had all but disappeared. This made the singer a much more difficult product for RCA Victor to sell. For this reason, although it did achieve success, "Return to Sender"—one of the best songs Elvis ever cut—was not the hit it could have been.

CRYING IN THE CHAPEL

n 1964 the Beatles had arrived and, for all practical purposes, buried Elvis. One has only to only look at the fact that none of the nine Elvis singles released in 1964 and the first half of 1965 climbed higher than the #12 spot on the charts. The singer who had once defined cool now seemed as out of step with the times as a Model T in the era of space travel. And, though they still made money, Elvis's movies resulted in no new fans of the King. Those who actually watched these flicks were not inspired by the singer's talent. In addition, by this time Elvis's original fans were approaching thirty; most were married and had kids of their own. Rock 'n' roll was the last thing on their minds. Yet the Colonel would not yet change his tune. He was still keeping Elvis out of sight and, as a result, out of the minds of the new generation. While John, Paul, George, and Ringo seemed to be everywhere, the King of Rock 'n' Roll was nowhere to be found.

RCA Victor was starting to get desperate. The label foresaw a time when no one would be buying Elvis records in large enough numbers to warrant their continued release. The singles from Elvis's movie soundtracks were now making little more noise at the cash register than was Dean Martin's most recent album. To kids, even Bob Hope or Phyllis Diller seemed more hip than Elvis. The Colonel's misguided control over Elvis was no longer a laughing matter. The powers at RCA Victor realized that something had to be done. But what could they release that would revitalize what once had been their most successful property?

In a move that seemed to reek of panic, the record label decided to dig back into its vaults for something the singer had cut just after his return from the service. It was not a rocker or a ballad, but a gospel song. As the original cut of this inspirational number had been deemed unfit for Elvis's incredibly successful gospel album of five years before, the number seemed a strange vehicle for RCA Victor to drive into a hit parade dominated by the Beatles, the Rolling Stones, and the Supremes. It also seemed bizarre to make an attempt to update Elvis's sound by going back five years in time and releasing a once-rejected session cut. But that is just what RCA Victor was going to do.

The song had not been composed for Elvis. In fact, it had not even been penned by a professional songwriter. "Crying in the Chapel" had been written in 1953 by Artie Glenn. Glenn was working as a Fort Worth, Texas, factory worker at an aircraft plant when he was stricken with a serious back problem. A retired guitar player who had once toured with Bob Wills and the Texas Play-boys, this man knew more about smoky honky-tonks than all-day gospel sessions and Sunday school picnics. Yet when he became gravely ill, Glenn looked for answers in church, not in the more familiar bars.

In the hours before he was to undergo spinal surgery, the young man prayed long and hard. If God would allow him to walk out of the hospital, he promised he would change his wild ways. When the surgery proved successful, Glenn remembered that vow. As soon as he was released from Harris Hospital, even before he went home to be with his wife and children, he found a church and offered himself to God. The chapel he visited, a modest structure known as the Loving Avenue Baptist Church, had been con-structed of wood removed from an ancient mule barn. In this hum-ble structure Glenn fell to his knees and wept.

Walking out of the chapel, the now-healed man reflected on the miracle of his life. By the time he got home, Glenn had already written a simple tune and a chorus. That evening he finished his very personal ode of faith and sang it to his family and friends.

The first person to record Glenn's "Crying in the Chapel" was his brother Darrell. Released by a local Texas label in the summer of 1953, Darrell's recording miraculously landed on the national charts and climbed into *Billboard's* Top 10. Fueled by the single's suc-cess, a host of other artists, including June Valli, Ella Fitzgerald, Art Lund, and the R&B group Sonny Til and the Orioles, raced to cover the song. Sonny Til and the Orioles' version of "Crying in the Chapel" became a bestseller and was certified as pure gold. It was this version that would be hailed as one of rock 'n' roll's first major hits.

For the next seven years, "Crying in the Chapel" was viewed as an R&B standard, and it was dismissed in both black and white gospel circles. Artie Glenn's song about answered prayer and redemption might have remained buried in rock 'n' roll history had Elvis not decided to cut it as a straight gospel effort in 1960. Elvis, who had been raised with both black and white gospel influences, had fallen in love with "Crying in the Chapel," thanks to Sonny Til and the Orioles' rendition of the song. Using their styling, he recorded the gospel/rock number during an October 30, 1960, session devoted to religious standards.

In the studio with Elvis that day were Scotty Moore and Hank Garland on guitar; Bob Moore on bass, D. J. Fontana and Buddy Harman on drums, and Floyd Cramer on piano. The Jordanaires and Millie Kirkham provided the backup vocals. Carefully and tenderly, Elvis crafted his version of "Crying in the Chapel." He sang it just as he would have in a church service; he converted the old R&B classic to pure gospel, with sincerity leaping from every phrase. It was slow, it was prayerful, and it embraced a message the singer believed. Elvis's version of the song was both moving and beautiful. It had the feeling and pacing of "Are You Lonesome Tonight?" combined with the heartfelt faith of the singer's youth. This was a performance that would have brought tears to Gladys Presley's eyes. After just a few takes, Elvis thought he had nailed it. But when the Colonel could not get the publisher and Glenn to give up a share of the song's rights, Elvis knew that its chances of ever being released were all but dead. In addition, RCA producers chimed in with less-than-favorable reviews of the song, and Elvis's "Crying in the Chapel" quietly disappeared. Fortunately, even without this classic, Elvis's gospel LP *His Hand in Mine* became a huge hit.

Five years later, even the Colonel was beginning to wonder what was going wrong with his plans for Elvis. He could not believe that British groups were erasing his singer's influence. When the record label asked him if he would agree to allow RCA Victor to revisit the old recording of "Crying in the Chapel," the manager gave his permission. In the face of a bunch of seemingly wild and heathen rock groups who were now dominating the airwaves, Parker and the label reasoned that, with this gospel classic, perhaps Elvis could resurface as the alternative—a God-fearing, all-American hero. This was a far cry from the Elvis image the Colonel had nurtured a decade before.

Using the third take from the 1960 session, "Crying in the Chapel" was shipped to pop, country, rock, and religious radio outlets on April 6, 1965. On the B side was "I Believe in the Man in the Sky," another song from the 1960 session. No one really expected any more than mild play on the rock side; this release was meant for easy-listening and gospel stations. When the song suddenly appeared on the Top 40 playlist, there was jubilation on Music Row. As it turned out, "Crying in the Chapel" was just getting warmed up.

After an almost two-year absence, Elvis appeared Top 10 on May 22. "Crying in the Chapel" lept to #6 the following week, and it jumped another two places on June 5. The song peaked on the rock charts at #3, beneath "Wooly Bully" and "Back in My Arms Again." Though it did not make #1, this gospel single remained in Top 10 for seven weeks. During this same period, the Beatles stayed in the Top 10 for only four weeks with their #1 hit "Ticket to Ride."

On most gospel lists "Crying in the Chapel" held the #1 spot for more than a month. RCA Victor had expected this kind of power from the religious charts. But the real shock came from the across the pond. In Merry Ole England, the home of the Beatles, Elvis's "Crying in the Chapel" became his fifteenth #1 single. It was with more than a bit of pride that the singer enjoyed his sudden domination over the rival Beatles on their home turf.

Sadly, "Crying in the Chapel" would prove to be no more than a bizarre blip on the rock charts. Its success would not open the door for more hit rock singles for Elvis. "Crying in the Chapel" worked simply because it was so different, and because listeners and DJs believed that Elvis had put his heart into the number. Most had not felt much heart in Elvis's work for some time. When the next movie single was shipped and revealed as another uninspired formula song sporting an unemotional Elvis vocal, radio stations largely ignored it. More and more, this was the pattern for all new Elvis releases. For the next two years, Elvis landing in even the Top 20 was reason to celebrate.

As rock grew heavier and music completely detached itself from anything that Parker understood, it was rumored that the Colonel was considering trying to reinvent his singer as a gospel act. RCA Victor was not about to let that happen. With his films still making money and the soundtracks from each feature generating some profits, the label would leave Elvis alone for now. But, almost a decade since his last TV appearance, Elvis was considered by most kids to be little more than an icon from a black-and-white age. Television had brought Elvis to the world; it would take TV to bring him back.

IN THE GHETTO

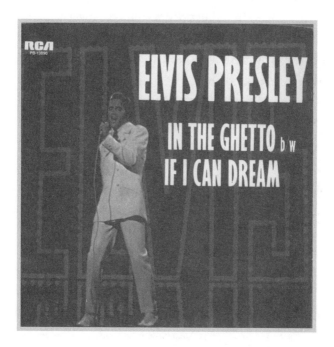

O ne of the first pioneering rock 'n' roll stars with whom Elvis developed a friendship was Lubbock, Texas, native Buddy Holly. During his years with Sun Records, the Memphis singer often ran into the West Texas teen while he was working Texas clubs. The two budding musicians drank Cokes together and visited backstage before and after shows, and they even had their picture taken together from time to time. Over the next few years, they both kept up with each other's career and songs. When Elvis was stationed in Germany, a plane crash dashed Holly's career just as it seemed ready to jump into high gear. Friends said at the time that Buddy's death hit Elvis hard, and the singer had to figure that no one from that West Texas city would ever mean as much to him as Buddy had. Elvis could not have guessed that, a decade later, another young man from Lubbock would play a very important role in redefining the King's own career and musical direction.

Scott Davis was born on January 21, 1942, on the flat Texas plains that surrounded the city of Lubbock. Davis always loved music, and, growing up in an area where Western swing met rock 'n' roll, he heard a lot of different types of songs. Inspired by both Holly and Elvis, Scott—who was known as "Mac" to his friends—began his own rock 'n' roll band. By the early 1960s, Davis had moved to Atlanta and expanded his musical outreach. Not only was he fronting his own group, but he was also the regional manager for Vee-Jay, a Chicago-based record label. His success at Vee-Jay opened up new doors of opportunity for the young man. In 1967 Mac moved to Los Angeles and took over Liberty Records' publishing outlet, Metric Music. Here the creative Davis ran into not only a host of songwriters, but some of the hottest West Coast recording acts, as well. One day, in his role as Metric's manager of operations, Davis received a call inquiring if any of the company's writers would be interested in submitting some compositions for Elvis Presley's next movie, *Live a Little, Love a Little*. Mac didn't know about anyone else, but he was sure he wanted to be included in this group.

"I had written a couple of things for the movies," Davis recalls, "and Billy Strange told me that Elvis was looking for new writers and new materials. In the script there was this situation where Elvis's character was leaving this swimming pool and going home with a girl. At that point they had inserted the words, 'Elvis sings.' I submitted a song I had already written and they used it. It was kind of a lucky fluke." More than three decades later, this composition would sweep the world, but at that moment, it was simply the song that got Elvis interested in Mac's work.

A few months later Davis got another call. Elvis was in need of new music, as well as some type of positive exposure. Movies like *Live a Little, Love a Little* were no longer doing enough to sell the singer or his songs. The Colonel finally sensed that he was going to have to do something on a much grander scale. In early 1968 the manager dialed up the networks and told them that Elvis wanted to do a Christmas special. NBC-TV bought the idea, and the Singer Company signed up as the lone sponsor for the one-hour special. In Parker's mind, this program would be nothing more than Elvis's version of what Bing Crosby did every year: sing a few carols, have a skit with a couple of well-known guests, and go home. Producer/director Steve Binder had other things in mind. He wanted to reintroduce the real Elvis to a new generation. To make this a reality, he needed creative writers like Mac Davis to provide original material.

Binder dreamed up a show that was half Broadway-style production numbers and half live concert. The showcase portion would have Elvis dressed in black leather and singing his old hits to a crowd filled with pretty girls. Filmed in late June 1968, the concert was pure magic. The production portion, also filmed that week, would tell the Elvis story in song. Because Elvis so liked his work, Mac Davis was called, then brought in to arrange the scores and pen original music to bookend various segments of the program. One of these Davis numbers, the beautiful ballad "Memories," gave Elvis a chance to review his life and career. Elvis loved it and declared it to be one of the best things he had cut in years.

Airing on December 3, 1968, the Elvis special was not just a ratings winner; it was also one of the most riveting pieces of television ever broadcast. It was Elvis at his rocking best, interacting with an audience as he never had on film or on programs such as *The Ed Sullivan Show*. This hour-long musical special, simply titled "Elvis" but now referred to as the "1968 Comeback Special," proved that the singer was still the most powerful live entertainer in the world. Millions who had never before listened to Elvis found themselves caught under the singer's spell. Binder had the singer conclude the special with an incredible topical protest song, "If I Can Dream," which was staged in front of a twenty-foot-high wall of lights that spelled "Elvis." Even the harshest of critics stated that chills raced up their spines. "Elvis," declared magazines and newspapers the next day, "is back!"

Over the next few months, "If I Can Dream," the inspired and hopeful show-ending protest song, sold well enough to hit #12 on *Billboard's* Hot 100 chart, Elvis's highest spot on the rock charts in two years. But executives at RCA Victor thought that Elvis could still do much better. They started looking for a heavy, powerful number to take the singer in a new direction. Little did they know that Elvis had already found the song that could accomplish this mission, and that it was anything but a rocker.

Mac Davis had been invited to Elvis's Los Angeles home one evening for a small party. As was usually the case, it was a tame affair filled with conversation, a little gospel singing, and story swapping. As Davis and Elvis talked, Elvis asked the songwriter if he had anything special that could be used in his upcoming recording session. Davis answered by picking up his guitar and playing a song that had been inspired by a boyhood experience in Lubbock.

"I grew up with a young kid whose dad worked for my father," Davis explains, recalling the history of the song he sang to Elvis that night. "My father's employee was a black man, and his son was about my age. My dad had a warehouse in the area where they lived. After we would play together, we would often take Smitty home. Basically, their home was on a dirt street lined with houses that had broken windows, leaking roofs, and peeling paint. The area was called Queen City. I always wanted to know why did this little black kid have to live where he did, and why he couldn't live in the nice part of town, like I did. As a kid, it was something that bothered me a great deal."

No one could give Davis any answers about Smitty's plight. Mac was simply told again and again, "That's just the way things are." Though long separated from the situation and the childhood friend, Davis again thought back to that time as he watched the world come crashing down around him during the race riots of the 1960s.

"On the news I kept hearing the term 'ghetto' being used to describe the slums in Los Angeles, Chicago, and New York," Mac recalls. "I had always thought of ghettos being associated with Europe during World War II. I had never thought of our slums as being ghettos."

Davis watched the news and saw the faces of the children in these areas, their homes on fire and violence everywhere. The hopelessness of the kids' plight and their mothers' sadness all but overwhelmed him. It also took him back almost twenty years.

"It was like the world my friend had lived in at Queen City," says the songwriter. "It was a vicious cycle. A kid is born into a situation like that and never gets out. And when he dies, another kid takes his place."

Davis knew that, coupled with recollections of his own childhood experiences, his thoughts on the plight of the poor had the makings of a powerful song. Still, he didn't immediately try to pen the number. First, he had to figure out how to tell the story of a hopeless, horrid situation and somehow capture the life of a family in Watts or the south side of Chicago in three minutes. The solution was not something that came to him overnight. But, as weeks became months, he continued to come back to the idea.

"One night I was with Freddie Weller," Davis continues. "He is a country singer now, but then was playing with Paul Revere and the Raiders. Freddie showed me a guitar lick and it stuck in my mind. I went home that evening and wrote the song about my childhood friend who had been born on the wrong side of the tracks in a world where he could not get a break. I wrote it around Freddie's guitar lick."

Mac changed the location of the story from Lubbock to Chicago, and he moved the setting from Queen City's dirt streets to the concrete world of the slums. But the guts of the number were still locked in the unanswered questions and experiences of his youth. He called his finished piece "The Vicious Circle." But because the subject was both serious and depressing, he hadn't pushed it to any recording artist until he played it for Elvis. Having grown up poor on the wrong side of the tracks, Elvis immediately identified with the number. The singer told friends that he felt a "calling" to share Davis's emotional and important song with the world. Elvis assured his friend that this song would be on his next album.

Elvis brought "The Vicious Circle" with him when he returned to Memphis to record what some would consider one of the most dynamic and impressive sessions in music history. In addition to the song about life in the slums, Davis's "Don't Cry, Daddy" would join a long list of other powerful numbers, and it would even become a Top 10 hit in 1970.

Though Elvis pushed to record "The Vicious Circle," RCA Victor and the Colonel were not sold on Davis's protest song. In the Colonel's mind, this was a political hot potato that was better suited to the likes of George Harrison or Peter, Paul, and Mary. Yet Elvis, who in the past had usually given in to the Colonel, would not back down. Elvis now felt a need to make a difference in the world, and he was convinced that this song could do just that. In spite of the dangers that others perceived in its message, Elvis demanded that the tune be included in the Memphis session.

"When I got the word he was cutting it," Mac remembers, "I was as shocked as anyone. Elvis had always stayed away from the protest thing. It had to be pretty scary for him and must have taken a lot of courage to risk a part of his career with that song."

On January 20, 1969, just six weeks after Elvis's triumphant television special, the singer walked into American Sound Studios in Memphis. Al Pachucki served as engineer for these recordings, and Chip Moman took the helm as producer of what for Elvis was a homecoming. As the singer relished recording so close to the spot where his musical career had begun at Sun Records, a new group of musicians surrounded him. Reggie Young played guitar on this eight-track recording session. Tommy Cogbill and Mike Leech were on bass. Gene Chrisman beat the drums. The piano was manned by Bobby Wood, while Bobby Emmons created magic on the organ. Though the final version of the single would contain strings, horns, and backing vocals, all of these were added later. It would be just this small core group creating the powerful sound that brought to life Mac's story of grief and despair.

Elvis, who in the past few years had hurried through most of his soundtrack recording sessions, took great pains to get Davis's song right. Harkening back to his first RCA Victor sessions, he forced the musicians to record "The Vicious Circle" over and over again. The singer fought to present the message of this song in a powerful and almost sermon-like fashion. The song was, in a sense, a ballad, but Elvis demanded that its message be more than that. He wanted the number to be a musical version of what Martin Luther

King's "I Have a Dream" speech had become. This was a vehicle for change, and the singer did not want the message to be lost in vocal theatrics or too much orchestration. Therefore, he kept it simple. But a simple arrangement did not mean that the session was easy. Elvis kept going and going and going, always looking for perfection. This was a song that he felt would define him for years to come. Though almost thirty takes were rumored to have been cut, it would be the twenty-third that was picked for pressing. RCA Victor used a ballad, "Any Day Now," as the B side. Then, with great reservations, the label shipped the song, now retitled "In the Ghetto," to radio stations and record outlets on April 14.

On May 10, the new Elvis single became the fastest moving record on the *Billboard* rock charts, jumping thirty-eight places, from #79 to #41. On Memorial Day weekend "In the Ghetto" hit #9. It would hit #3 on the rock playlist a week later, and would remain in the Top 10 until July 5. The Beatles' "Get Back" and Henry Mancini's "Love Theme from *Romeo and Juliet*" would prevent Elvis from taking #1 on the American rock lists, but it would be the American singer who would overtake the Liverpool group and rule the British charts with his song about the tragedy of life on the south side of Chicago. Elvis would also top all other American pop and easy-listening charts at the time. More important than just sales and playlist numbers, however, it was the song's impact on the social movement of the era that would be most lasting.

"In the Ghetto" was a song that captured a snapshot of the plight of millions trapped in American poverty. This song, inspired by a boy from Queen City, Texas, and written by a young man from the flat plains of West Texas, made people think and feel. At least a portion of the reforms passed by Congress to combat poverty and create programs designed to reach out and improve the lives of poor children caught in American ghettos can be traced to the sincere, prayer-like manner with which Elvis sang Davis's song. Elvis's voice and determination brought a problem into a context that anyone could understand. It woke people up, and it forced many to look beyond long-held prejudices. Elvis and "In the Ghetto" proved again that music could change the world.

"Elvis recording 'In the Ghetto' turned my life around," Davis remembers. "In fact, Elvis was the first major artist to cut anything I had written. His cutting those songs put me on the map. And when 'In the Ghetto' went #1, I was suddenly the fair-haired boy of the songwriting world. Everyone wanted to cut my songs. Thanks to the success of that record, I had a bullet in the charts every week for a year and half."

Mac Davis would go on to write numerous pop, rock, and country hits, eventually landing his own recording contract and becoming one of the most important players in both the pop and country fields. His success would then extend to television, movies, and finally, Broadway. And Mac owed it all to an unanswered question from his youth and a singer who once played Lubbock with hometown hero Buddy Holly.

"In the Ghetto" was Elvis's most important single since the double-sided single "Hound Dog/Don't Be Cruel." This protest number reestablished the singer as a major force in the music world. Within four months of releasing "In the Ghetto," Elvis would again claim a #1 record and rule the Las Vegas stage as the world's highest paid and greatest entertainment force. Few would have predicted it in 1968, but by the end of the next year, Elvis would be cool and on top again.

SUSPICIOUS MINDS

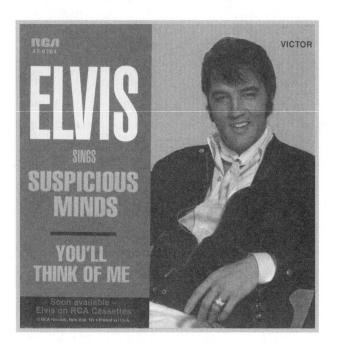

There is no doubt that, with his incredible voice, Elvis could have taken very mediocre songs to the top of the charts. On one occasion he did just that. Fortunately, over a career that spanned less than twenty-five years, Elvis was blessed by the talents of many of the country's most incredible songwriters. These men provided unforgettable musical vehicles for the singer's many rides up the charts. Almost every popular music fan knows the names of Jerry Lieber, Mike Stoller, Otis Blackwell, and Mac Davis. Yet Aaron Schroeder, Doc Pomus, Mort Shuman, and Mark James deserve to be lionized as well. Each of these song scribes provided Elvis with not just hit singles, but some of the very best songs of the rock 'n' roll era, as well.

Mark James might well be the youngest of this group, but it is one of his Elvis tunes that stands apart from all the rest of the Elvis chart toppers in terms of popularity, longevity, and uniqueness. It is not a rock 'n' roll song, ballad, or blues standard; certainly it's not country or gospel. But, though it can't be classified as a part of any musical genre, this Grammy Hall of Fame song is one of the most unforgettable Elvis numbers ever written.

"Suspicious Minds" was hatched in the fertile brain of Francis Zambon. Born in Houston, Texas, this son of an Italian immigrant grew up with music all around him. Zambon played the violin before he learned how to read. By the time he entered junior high he had already mastered the piano and the guitar. In 1959, with his group the Naturals, the high schooler found a bit of regional fame with a self-produced single titled "Jive Note." Changing his name to Mark James and forming a trio, in the early 1960s he penned and recorded two more minor hits: "Running Back" and "She's Gone Away." Determined to make it in the music business, James jumped from gig to gig, all the while honing his writing skills. The only time the young man was not directly involved in show business was during a mid-1960s stint in Vietnam.

In 1968 James ended up in Memphis working for producer Chip Moman and his American Sound Studios. Producer Moman hooked Mark up with hot new pop singer B. J. Thomas. It would be Thomas who would really launch James's career by recording the writer's "Eyes of a New York Woman" and "Hooked on a Feeling." As it turned out, a local Memphite was deeply impressed with both tunes and decided to take a closer look at Mark and his music. This interest lead Elvis, the Memphite, to request demos from the young man. A year later Elvis cut James's "It's Only Love." While it was not a hit for the King, the song paved the way for another James demo to find its way into Elvis's hands. A new version of that record would soon become the singer's biggest song in the second half of his career.

The "1968 Comeback Special" put Elvis back on the entertainment map, and Elvis's recording of Mac Davis's "In the Ghetto" made the singer a real force on the charts again. Wanting a follow-up to this socially conscious hit, Elvis and RCA Victor found the song in one that had been recorded during the same session. This number came from Mark James's hand.

At first glance, "Suspicious Minds," seems to be a tale of two lovers who do not trust one another. This lack of trust naturally leads to discourse and heartbreaking arguments. But in the late 1960s, with the growing generation gap and social unrest due to the civil rights movement and the war in Vietnam, trust at every level was in very short supply. There were now millions who felt they had been cheated by the events of the time. At this moment in U.S. history, dialogue was needed to bring peace and harmony, but it couldn't get started because everyone was shouting too loud for a single voice of reason to be heard. Suspicious minds were, literally, everywhere.

James brilliantly caught this national mood and carved it down to a single relationship. He made it personal. In doing so, he took a musical snapshot of history and showed the world's pain through the eyes of a man who simply wanted to reunite with a lover who no longer trusted him.

While Elvis had once relished his status as the King of Rock 'n' Roll, he now wanted his voice to be relevant. He had a desire to be more than a singer; he wanted to be a person who made a difference in the world. Elvis had recently been honored by several different groups for his work with charities. "In the Ghetto" was being hailed as a song that put a new spin on the plight of America's poor. To Elvis, who had spent most of the 1960s seemingly wasting his great talents in meaningless films and on some rather lame songs, this adult recognition and respect brought a new sense of pride. He finally felt as if he were on the same plane as stars such as Frank Sinatra and Bing Crosby. As a result, Elvis believed that he now needed a song that reflected his personal passion, the national mood, and a more grown-up sound. James's "Suspicious Minds" provided all of that and more.

Elvis was blown away by the demo of "Suspicious Minds." He loved everything about the song, from its message to its arrangement. Elvis believed that "Suspicious Minds" would be a natural continuation of the more adult themes he had embraced with his two recent hits, "If I Can Dream" and "In the Ghetto."

The version of the song that Elvis first heard was one that James had released the year before. The writer had not been able to chart with his own single. Yet Elvis was so impressed with James's arrangement that he did not change anything about the song.

On January 22, 1969, during his third day of work at the American Sound Studios in Memphis, Elvis checked in with James's boss Chip Moman. Moman acted as producer on this session, with Reggie Young on guitar, Tommy Cogbill and Mike Leech on bass, Gene Chrisman on drums, and Bobby Wood and Bobby Emmons on keyboards. All Moman wanted to do with this core group was capture a solid foundation on his eight-track recording unit. The strings and horns heard in the final cut were added after Elvis had finished. Finally, Moman brought in Jeannie Greene and future Country Music Association's Entertainer of the Year Ronnie Milsap to sing the backup vocals.

It was a huge thrill for Elvis to record in his hometown for the first time since 1955. In a rare interview with *Billboard* on February 1, 1969, he spoke of his three days in the studio there. He summed up the experience with the simple observation, "This is where it all started for me. It feels good to be back." As would first be proven by "In the Ghetto," then again with the release of "Suspicious Minds," Elvis's career not only began in Memphis—it was also reborn there.

In that historic session, Elvis didn't sing "Suspicious Minds" so much as he emotionally attacked it. In certain parts his voice seemed to be pleading; in other spots he sounds angry. At the end of the song, Elvis comes close to voicing his pain through tears. Through take after take, Elvis lived and relived the number, squeezing out his soul on each note. Perhaps for this reason, his voice does not sound smooth like it had on his many hit ballads. Instead, this vocal performance has a raw edge to it, somewhat smoky with a hard rock mix. It was like nothing he had ever done before. In the end "Suspicious Minds" brought forth an Elvis no one in the studio had ever heard.

There was no set ending for the song, so it was decided during the session to simply fade it out. Yet, when Elvis kept singing, the producer brought the levels back up and continued to record. This unique effect was kept in the released version. The thinking for this "double ending" approach was that stations could choose to end it with the first fade, or they could make the single a bit longer by using the added repeating of the chorus. Most opted for the latter.

Elvis introduced "Suspicious Minds" before RCA Victor had even pressed it. On July 26, at the International Hotel in Las Vegas, in his first live show in eight years, Elvis brought a who's who of celebrities and high rollers to their feet with his gutsy presentation of the James tune. This song was one of the capstones in what has been called the most incredible night in Vegas entertainment history. The show began with Elvis walking out to the center of the stage, only to find that he could not perform: the audience simply would not stop screaming and applauding. Before he could sing a note, the crowd was standing, at least half of them on top of their chairs. Cary Grant, Ann-Margret, Nancy Sinatra, Sammy Davis Jr., and hundreds more of the greatest names in show business were greeting a man they thought of as their King. It took more than five minutes for the crowd to calm down enough to allow the show to begin. Then, more than two dozen times that night, the show was again stopped with this type of adulation. The comeback that had started on NBC and continued in a spectacular recording session in Memphis had now been fully recognized in Las Vegas. Elvis was back.

With demands coming from Vegas crowds for copies of the new song, RCA Victor shipped "Suspicious Minds" to radio stations on August 26, 1969. The label opted to pair the James tune with "You'll Think of Me." The new Elvis single entered the charts on September 13. It was the fastest moving number in the Top 100 the next week, jumping from #77 to #36. It rocketed into the Top 10 on October 18 at #6. It moved only one spot the next week, but it leapfrogged hits by the Archies, Sly and the Family Stone, and The Temptations to take the top of the chart on November 1. Though it was knocked down a spot on November 8, by the Fifth Dimension's "Wedding Bell Blues," "Suspicious Minds" remained in the Top 10 for the rest of the month.

"Suspicious Minds" was Elvis's first American rock-chart topper since "Good Luck Charm" in 1962. It would also be the last time he ruled the *Billboard* pop playlist during his lifetime. Although some of his songs would hit #1 on other major American playlists and on the British charts, none climbed higher in the

Billboard pop charts than #2. In that sense, Elvis's glory days were behind him. But the King's reign as the greatest concert performer in the world was just beginning.

Mark James would continued to play a part in Elvis's recordings. Elvis would record the Houston-born writer's "Always on My Mind," "Raised on Rock," and the #1 country hit, "Moody Blue." James would go on to write songs for other performers, as well, including "Sunday Sunrise," "One Hell of a Woman," "Disco Ryder," "Everybody Loves a Rain Song," as well as the complete score for the award-winning movie *Kramer vs. Kramer*. To this day, James continues to score films.

"Suspicious Minds" was recently picked as the thirty-first most programmed song in the history of popular music. Amid the huge body of Elvis Presley recordings, this composition stands apart; nothing like had ever been, or would ever be, recorded by the King. The song's lyrics capture a moment in history, and its theme provides a snapshot of the mood of the nation in the late 1960s. "Suspicious Minds" was exactly the song that the King of Rock 'n' Roll needed to bring his real power and influence back to American music. Perhaps it is appropriate that, within months of Elvis's return to the top of the *Billboard* chart, the Beatles would break up, leaving Elvis alone as the most recognized performer in rock music.

THE WONDER OF YOU

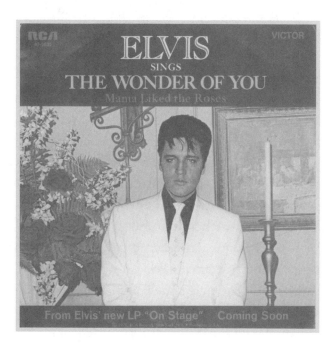

"In the Ghetto" reopened the rock-chart door for Elvis Presley. The now thirty-four-year-old legend had followed the successful protest song with "Clean Up Your Own Backyard," another message song. This time, few responded to the musical preaching. Elvis switched gears, and he struck magic with the dynamic "Suspicious Minds." He then scored another solid hit with the Mac Davis–penned ballad "Don't Cry, Daddy." In early 1970, Elvis recorded Eddie Rabbitt's and Dick Heard's answer to "Rainy Night in Georgia." Though "Kentucky Rain" was not a huge hit, it was a successful song. As Elvis entered 1970 he once again enjoyed vast amounts of airtime on music stations across the country, winning over a new legion of fans who had not even been born when he cut his first tune at Sun Records. Even more important than his recording success, however, might have been his concert appeal. From coast to coast and border to border, Elvis was selling out the largest venues in the country. He even filled the Astrodome. Once again it appeared that Elvis owned the enter-tainment world, and his swagger was back to prove it.

While many performers had released live "albums" that cap-tured the power of their showmanship, Elvis had yet to release such an effort, due to his almost decade-long absence from the concert scene. Now, with the live Elvis winning stellar reviews everywhere he appeared, RCA Victor decided that a concert album could gen-erate significant sales figures at the cash register. The International Hotel in Las Vegas was chosen for Elvis's first life recording ses-sion, largely because of its controlled atmosphere and the fact that engagements in the city lasted weeks rather than a single day. As every new LP needed a single to help push sales, several non-Elvis hits were added to these Vegas shows. One of these songs had been a minor hit on the rock 'n' roll charts a decade before. That num-ber had been written by one of the most dynamic composers of the teen-idol era, Baker Knight.

Knight grew up in Birmingham, Alabama, spent the early 1950s in the service, and formed a country band when he returned home from overseas. For a couple of years, he juggled working in a factory by day and playing clubs by night. When he felt his band had hit its stride, he took the group to Nashville in hopes of finding a label to spotlight their work. They were rejected at every corner, and except for one young lady who worked in publishing on the West Coast, no one was interested in any of Knight's original compositions.

It was a disappointing blow to Knight and his band, and the band broke up as a result of it. Not long after that, the factory where Knight worked shut down. Behind on his rent and car payments, Knight was almost ready to pawn his guitar when he got a call from an old service buddy. "There's work for movie extras in Los Angeles," the struggling songwriter was told. "Come on out and live in the sunshine!"

Knight sold everything he had except his car and guitar and headed west, but there was more rain than sunshine. His work as a movie extra lasted just one day, and a month later Baker was down to his last thirty-eight cents. He knew that, within days, he would lose his apartment and be forced out onto the streets. The displaced Southerner took some small comfort in knowing that he'd probably starve to death before he became homeless.

Since his arrival in Los Angeles, Knight had been knocking on doors, trying to find a publisher for his original songs. The only glimmer of hope he had been given during the daily rejections was when he ran into the same woman who had liked his stuff in Nashville. She took down his address and said that she would tell a friend about Knight's work. The songwriter was busy counting his last thirty-eight cents for the fifth time when someone knocked at his door.

"I was surprised to see Ricky Nelson," Knight recalls. "He told me that he had heard I had some songs he might like. So I picked up my guitar and went to work."

Baker played the teen idol a couple of what he thought were his best numbers. Nelson offered no response. A few minutes later, the singer thanked him and left. Thinking he had blown his final chance at success, a depressed Knight sat on his couch and stared at the walls. Then, a couple of hours later, he heard another knock at the door. This time it was the Nelson family attorney, carrying a two-thousand-dollar advance check and a publishing contract. A few months later, Nelson scored a major hit with Knight's

"Lonesome Town." Within a year, the singer had placed several more of Knight's tunes on the charts, and a host of other performers were coming to him for songs. The writer's success paid for cars, food, and lodging, but it came so fast it all but overwhelmed the country boy. Fears and insecurities caused him to drink more and more each day. In early 1959 the writer found himself in an Alabama hospital trying to sort out if he wanted to live or die.

"I had an ulcer," Knight recalls, "and was very disillusioned about things. I guess I was on a spiritual search, and while I was laying in my hospital bed, I just started writing a song, trying to sort out my relationship with God. In truth, the song was really very poorly put together at that point, but it was a prayer of thanks for God not giving up on me. I finished it when I went back to L.A."

The writer felt that the song, which had evolved from being a gospel number to being a love song rather, had a "Perry Como feel" to it. Yet the first person to cut Knight's "The Wonder of You," was one of TV's favorite doctors, Vince Edwards. Edwards played the lead in the TV show *Ben Casey*. Though the actor did not have a hit with the song, his version caught the ear of another singer, Ray Peterson. This Denton, Texas, native had just landed a contract with RCA Victor, and he needed a hit. "The Wonder of You" put Peterson on the charts. His next single, "Tell Laura I Love Her," became a rock classic.

"Elvis really liked 'The Wonder of You,'" Knight explains. "In fact, Presley liked Ray Peterson's version so much that he asked Ray to visit a movie set and meet with him. Elvis took Ray out to lunch, almost asking permission to cut the number."

Elvis, who at the time was spinning hits with songs like "It's Now or Never," did not record the song then. But he never forgot it, either. A decade later, Knight got a call that sent him into the clouds.

"I had just gotten a divorce, was living in an apartment in Ventura. I was always a night person and slept during the day. Anyway, the phone rang at 7:30 in morning. I couldn't imagine who would be calling me at that time. On the line was one of the folks in Elvis's band, Glen Hardin. He asked me if I could give him the words to 'The Wonder of You.' Elvis needed them because he had decided to cut the song on stage that very night.

"I was thrilled. I had been a Elvis fan since 'That's All Right (Mama).' I couldn't believe that he was going to record one of my songs."

The lyrics were quickly transcribed over the phone and rushed back to Elvis. The singer spent the day learning them. That evening, in front of a sold-out crowd at the International Hotel in Las Vegas, Elvis sang "The Wonder of You" for the very first time. For Baker Knight, hundreds of miles away in Ventura, this February 18, 1970, was one of the most wonderful evenings of his life. The biggest name in the business had just cut his song.

Elvis was accompanied onstage that night by his regular touring band, which included Rick Nelson's first guitar player, James Burton. Filling out the band was John Wilkinson on rhythm guitar, Jerry Scheff on bass, Bob Lanning on drums, and Glen Hardin on piano. Bobby Morris and His Orchestra accompanied Elvis's band, and Elvis's close friend Charlie Hodge, the Sweet Inspirations, and the Imperials all provided backup vocals. (The familiar soprano voice that would be heard on the actual release was not recorded that evening; Millie Kirkham added her vocals later in the studio.) This version of Baker Knight's song was arranged by pianist Glen Hardin, with a great deal of input by Elvis himself. Like so many of the songs that Elvis covered, he made "The Wonder of You" his own from the very first note on. Elvis sang the song with great power. In retrospect, "The Wonder of You" might seem somewhat schmaltzy, but, for a live recording, it was very solid. Captured live, the performance seemed sincere, as if Elvis believed the message of the song. If there is a real weak point, it is Elvis's final long, high note. That night at the International Hotel, however, no one seemed to care. The number worked so well that many in the crowd gave the singer a standing ovation when he hit the last note.

Elvis felt very strongly about his February 18 performance of "The Wonder of You," and he asked RCA Victor to release it as a single. A plaintive country music standard, "Mama Liked the Roses" was pressed as the B side of the record, and the single was shipped on April 20. Before summer, "The Wonder of You" was the #1 song on the new Adult Contemporary chart. To the surprise of many, the ballad also climbed into the Top 10 on the rock charts, and it even made it into the Top 40 in country music. The song did even better in England. This old rock 'n' roll cover topped the British charts for six weeks, becoming one of England's best-selling and most successful records of 1970.

"The Wonder of You" continued to illustrate the wide variety of songs and styles that Elvis could spin into hits. But many of the fans who had gotten turned on to Elvis by his "1968 Comeback Special" yearned for the singer to really rock. As it turned out, the King would rock again, although fans had to wait two more years for him to do so. When he finally went back to his roots, millions of his old fans and a legion of new ones turned out to cheer this return. In the meantime, the Elvis road show continued, and hundreds of thousands purchased tickets to catch Elvis perform the songs that had made him a star in the 1950s.

BURNING LOVE

Elvis hit the top of the Adult Contemporary chart again in late 1970 with "You Don't Have to Say You Love Me." The singer enjoyed performing ballads, and he loved having them score with older audiences, but RCA Victor wanted Elvis to produce another rock hit for teens and young adults. In 1972, during a break from his seemingly endless tour schedule, producer Felton Jarvis brought Elvis into a Los Angeles studio with the goal of proving to the world that the King could still rock. It would be a West Texas native who would provide the musical vehicle for Elvis's final trip to the top of the rock playlists.

Dennis Linde had left San Angelo, Texas, and moved to St. Louis, Missouri, with the hope of making it in the music business. For a while he played in a local band at night and drove a dry-cleaning truck during the day. Always in a hurry, Linde lost his driver's license after having received several tickets for speeding. With no way to get around St. Louis, Linde stayed home and wrote songs. He gave them to music insider Bob Cuban. Cuban liked them, and he got Linde a songwriting gig in Nashville. In 1970 Roger Miller and Kris Kristofferson would become the first two artists to record Dennis's work.

"Everything I was writing at the time was Texas based," Linde explains. "Songs like 'Tom Greene County Fair' and 'Where Have All the Average People Gone.' I was getting some things cut, but not making much money."

Linde met his future wife, Pam, in Music City, and the two were married in 1971. Pam Linde believed in her husband's dreams and talents, and she helped him set up a studio in their Gallatin, Tennessee, home.

Probably because he was a newlywed, Linde began writing songs that embraced love as their central theme. Strangely enough, one of his new compositions was a rocker.

"It sounded like a Sam and Dave hit to me," Linde says. "I wrote all the words down, raced to my bedroom studio, and laid down the melody."

Linde spent the next three days filling out the demo by adding bass, drums, double-necked guitar licks, and backup vocals, all of which he performed himself. He also served as his own producer, capturing each new facet of his work on his four-track tape machine. The final result was not professional quality, but at least he had enough on tape for folks to listen to his "Burning Love."

"Sam and Dave weren't recording at the time," Linde laughs, "so I took it to Bob Beckham. He really liked it. I had done an album of my own stuff for Intrepid Records the year before, and Bob thought I should go into the studio and cut a new album for Electra."

Linde booked time at Cinderella Studios and recorded a cleaner version of "Burning Love." He hoped that the song would land him radio time as a singer. While it didn't advance his career as recording artist, his recording of "Burning Love" was about to create an incredible opportunity for the songwriter. But first it had to take a Southern detour.

"Bob got it cut by Arthur Alexander," Linde continues. "Alexander was a soul singer out of Alabama. The song went nowhere, and again nothing happened with it. Then I got a call telling me that RCA producer Felton Jarvis wanted Elvis to do some rock 'n' roll things again. I made an appointment with Felton and played him three of my songs. He took the demo of 'Burning Love' with him. That was one that he wanted to do."

A now hopeful Linde soon discovered that what Jarvis wanted Elvis to sing was one thing; what Elvis wanted Elvis to sing was another. The singer was not interested in getting back to his rock 'n' roll roots. Elvis liked crooning. He thought that the slow numbers with the soaring melodies drew the loudest applause. Besides, Elvis loved showing off his vocal range on ballads. Rockers did not present him a real opportunity to display the full range of voice. As far as Elvis was concerned, it was fine with him if he never cut another rock song. But Jarvis would not give up. He wanted to see a bit of the fire and soul of the original Elvis and, using his influence, he pressured Elvis to learn Linde's song.

Jarvis set up a West Coast recording session on March 28, 1972, at RCA's Hollywood studios. The producer brought in the core players from Elvis's show band: James Burton on lead guitar, John Wilkinson and Charlie Hodge on rhythm, Emory Gordy on bass, Ronnie Tutt on drums, and Glen Hardin on keyboards. Elvis's favorite bass singer, J. D. Sumner, was also in the studio, as was Sumner's Stamps Quartet.

Though he might have originally wanted to pass on the rock 'n' roll number, Elvis tossed himself into "Burning Love" with a passion. His vocal work was tight, precise, and gritty. Singing the song, he actually sounded a decade younger than he did on the ballads he recorded that day. With each new take of Linde's tune, every corner of the studio surged with energy. By the fourth take, the song was hot. By the sixth take, the studio was smoking, and everyone was in perfect form. It had been a long time since anyone had heard Elvis like this. With his great vocal work and a driving bass guitar line, this was a magical return to rock 'n' roll.

Jarvis was pleased with the way "Burning Love" had been cut that day, but he was not completely satisfied that the song was finished. The producer thought that it still needed some work. Back in Music City, he brought in Jerry Carrigan for some added percussion. Then he called Dennis Linde and inquired if the writer could work up some special licks on his double-necked guitar. "I was excited and nervous," Linde remembers. "Rumor had it that Elvis would be coming into the studio that day as well. I wanted to meet him. As it turned out, he didn't drop by, but I still loved working the session."

To complete "Burning Love," the producer added the final elements of some strings and orchestra riffs. Satisfied that the number finally represented a rock 'n' roll classic that would work in a 1970s market, Felton matched it with "It's a Matter of Time" and sent it to the presses. On August 1, 1972, "Burning Love"—Elvis's first real rocker since "Big Hunk o' Love"—was shipped. Longtime fans noted the similarity of these two rockers, though Linde himself had not even thought of the old Schroeder-Wyche classic when he penned his number. Nevertheless, it was these two musical "hunks" that connected the old and the new Elvis, and that brought rock 'n' roll alive again.

At end of October "Burning Love" hit #1 on *Cashbox Magazine's* pop lists, and it peaked at #2 on the *Billboard* rock charts. The irony of Elvis knocking rock 'n' roll icon Chuck Berry's novelty hit, "My Ding-a-Ling," off the top of the charts was lost on no one. With Rick Nelson's "Garden Party" also in the Top 10, it seemed as though the music world was caught in a time warp and had been sent back a full decade into the past.

As great as "Burning Love" was in the studio, it was even better live. Crowds were worked into a frenzy when Elvis swung his hips and screamed "a hunk a hunk of burning love" over and over again. This was the Elvis that millions had been wanting to see— the force who had not only changed music, but had also literally brought rock 'n' roll to the whole world. Even Dennis Linde was blown away by Elvis's hit song.

"The first time I heard it on the radio, I almost wrecked my car. I kept writing country hits, but nothing in country music could compare to that. This hit came totally out of the blue. I never ever expected to have a pop hit, even though the music I loved the most was rock 'n' roll. The most I ever hoped for was for Sam and Dave to land another recording gig and cut 'Burning Love.' To have Elvis record the song was more than I could fathom."

Not long after "Burning Love" ruled the charts, the Lindes moved into a new home. They christened it "the House That Elvis Built." Without a doubt, a #1 hit by Elvis certainly earned enough in royalties to build a home, as well as lay the foundation for a very successful songwriting career.

Elvis Presley would cut a few more rockers during his final five years of life, but none would climb into the Top 10, nor would they have the fire and passion of Linde's "Burning Love." 1972 was a special moment in time: Elvis was at his vocal and performing peak, and he was once again the most important force in the music world. He had not yet begun to become a caricature of himself. Sadly, in the short time left in the King's life, there would never again be a song like "Burning Love."

MOODY BLUE

n the mid- to late 1970s, Elvis all but disappeared from the rock charts. In a sense, his new songs held little relevance for pop music fans. Yet as these doors shut, country music rediscovered the man who had first found fame on its playlist and on the stage of the genre's historic *Louisiana Hayride*. Beginning with "I've Got a Thing About You, Baby" in early 1974, Elvis became a consistent Top 10 hit producer in country music. Yet it would take three more years before Elvis landed a #1 hit on *Billboard*'s country playlist. Strangely enough, that song would be penned by the man who had given the singer his last #1 hit on *Billboard*'s rock chart—Mark James.

By 1976 James had become one of the industry's most promis-
ing songwriters. One of the most incredible things about his talent
was the variety of styles in which he could write. While most songwriters who worked by themselves tended to create a certain type
of music, James seemed able to compose anything, and his songs,
from "Disco Ryder" to "Always on My Mind" to "Hooked on a Feeling," were embraced by almost every major music audience. This
great success brought James numerous major awards, including several different "Song of the Year" honors from organizations that represented a host of different genres. Willie Nelson, B. J. Thomas,
and many other singers loved his work. So did Elvis, and the King
relished the chance to sink his teeth into any new James tune.

The Elvis who had cut "Suspicious Minds" in 1969 and the
one who decided to record James's "Moody Blue" in late 1976 were
two very different people. In 1969 Elvis was lean, sexy, and confident. He sang with authority, and he walked into any room as if he
owned it. Seven years later, the singer was heavy, middle-aged, and
almost lost. Sam Phillips, the legendary Sun Records producer who
had discovered and first recorded Elvis, would later tell reporters
that Elvis seemed to have reverted back to a self-image he had
exhibited when he first walked into the Sun studios. "He felt very
inferior," Phillips explained. Perhaps it was his weight. Perhaps it
was the fact that America's youth no longer responded to his
music. Maybe it was the effect of years of prescription drugs. What-
ever the reason or reasons, this was not the Elvis of the "1968
Comeback Special." The recordings that he made during this time
give an insight into the singer's insecurity, as well.

At first, just after he'd become the most celebrated star in the
world, Elvis had needed only Scotty, Bill, and D.J. onstage with
him. Elvis's early recording sessions were almost as sparsely popu-

lated. But now the singer had scores of musicians and as many as ten vocalists on stage with him each night. Sometimes even more people were used on records, some of which featured orchestration that was so heavily overproduced that Elvis's magnificent voice sometimes seemed all but lost. Between tours, Elvis retreated more and more into the self-sustaining environment of Graceland. It was no longer just his home: it was his whole world. RCA Victor found it difficult to get the singer into the studio. For some reason, Elvis no longer felt comfortable in an environment filled with state-of-the-art equipment and professional musicians.

Frustrated by their inability to get him to come to them, RCA Victor moved a portable studio to Elvis's den, which was nick-named "the Jungle Room." Here the label surrounded the singer with session players he knew and could feel comfortable around. Elvis had become a true night owl, and these sessions usually began at midnight and lasted until dawn. The last tracks that Elvis would record were laid down in February and October of 1976. These recording gigs were neither easy nor very fruitful. His voice was still incredible, but the singer no longer seemed to believe in his own talents. At times it was like pulling teeth to get Elvis to bring his full effort to each number.

Mark James must have thought of Elvis when he composed "Moody Blue." It is hard to imagine the song being done justice by any of the other singers that James wrote for. But the song, which mixes the themes of the thrill of gambling and the difficulty of understanding the whims of a woman, was perfect for Elvis's range, talent, and ability to generate energy in any number that rocked.

James had established himself as a writer who could weave unconnected ideas together in a fashion that made sense. On the surface, the spin of a roulette wheel and the moods of a woman seemed unrelated. James understood, however, that the urge to gamble against the odds was much like falling in love. Neither was logical, and both usually offered little but pain and loss—but, if the numbers, or emotions, did come together in the right way, the rewards were substantial. Most important, in both cases there was a thrill in these games that made the risks worth taking. A woman who was moody might well bring about heartache, but she also might provide life's ultimate high.

Elvis had risked his heart and lost on several occasions, but no loss was as emotionally profound or publicly humiliating as that of his dissolved marriage. The women who followed Priscilla were beautiful, and they offered some solace, but Elvis's gamble on love never paid off. "Moody Blue" was therefore not just something that Elvis could sing—it was something that he had lived.

Elvis cut "Moody Blue" on the final day of a three-day session at Graceland. This February 4, 1976, session would be the next-to-last time that RCA Victor would get to record the voice of its greatest act. Sitting in the Jungle Room were James Burton, John Wilkinson, Chip Young, Charlie Hodge, Jerry Scheff, Ronnie Tutt, Tony Brown, and David Briggs, as well as vocalists Myra Smith and J. D. Sumner and the Stamps. As winter winds blew outside, Elvis attempted to get through James's challenging song.

"Moody Blue" was lyric-heavy. The writer had loaded the beginning of the song with long, descriptive phrases that jumped along on a very fast lead melody line. Elvis's enunciation had to be quick and precise. It would have been difficult for Elvis to accomplish this a decade earlier, when he was on top of his game. At this point, it sometimes seemed impossible for him to meet "Moody Blue"'s timing. Finally, after having fully learned the words by heart, he was able to spit them out in a rapid but casual manner, and the song came together in very special way. Executives from RCA Victor felt sure that the song would be a hit.

Paired with the classic country standard "She Thinks I Still Care," "Moody Blue" was shipped at the beginning of 1977. The single found its way onto the country charts on January 17, just a week after Elvis's forty-second birthday. On the nineteenth day of the next month, Elvis earned his first #1 country song since December 2, 1957, when "Jailhouse Rock" had replaced the Everly Brothers' "Wake Up Little Susie" atop the charts.

Though Elvis's "Moody Blue" had actually knocked a George Jones–Tammy Wynette single out of the #1 spot, Elvis had to note that many of the entertainers who were now creating waves in country music could be tied to his own influence in rock 'n' roll. Ronnie Milsap had been on top of the charts the last week in January, and Conway Twitty had been the chart king the week of January 22. Tom Jones would follow Elvis with a #1 country hit. All three men idolized and emulated the King during the initial days of their careers. Now each could claim to be a country music king.

RCA Victor was hardly surprised when "Moody Blue" hit the top of the country charts. The label knew it was a very solid cut. To promote the album of the same name, the company pressed it in blue vinyl. This gimmick would prove to be successful for two reasons. One was obvious—its color was unique. The second reason the gimmick worked, however, was actually due to an unexpected turn of events. Just as the blue album took off, Elvis died. The mood of Elvis's fans fit the color of the King's final album.

Although "Moody Blue" barely cracked the Top 40 on the pop charts, its #1 status in country music should have pumped up Elvis's faltering ego. It also created a foundation on which RCA Victor could refashion Elvis into an award-winning country star. The genre was exploding, and new generations of fans were pouring into the marketplace; the role of country-music star now carried a great deal of status. Country fans were generous in their admiration of performers. Neither Elvis's advancing age nor his expanding waistline would hinder his ability to relate to these fans. RCA Victor envisioned that, within three years, their biggest star would be named country music's Entertainer of the Year. "Way Down," a midsummer follow-up single to "Moody Blue," brought another #1 hit on the British charts and seemed to support RCA Victor's ideas for the King. But the plans for Elvis's country music superstardom would be buried before they really had a chance to take hold. "Moody Blue" was not Elvis's final curtain call on the charts, but it would be the last #1 hit that Elvis would see during his lifetime. While the life was no more, however, the hits would keep coming.

WAY DOWN

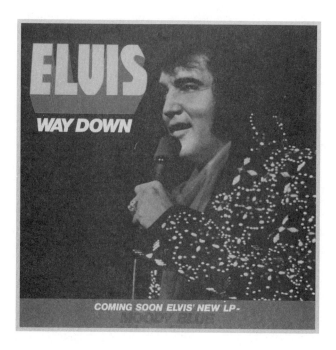

By the summer of 1977, Elvis was heavy, middle-aged, and no longer an important factor in rock music. He had not hit the Top 10 on the pop charts since "Burning Love" in 1972. Though he seemed to tour constantly, the life and energy that had once lit up the stage now seemed to be little more than a shadow of what they had once been. Worst of all, he appeared bloated and sick. Still, no one dreamed that this would be the King's final summer. Certainly Layng Martine Jr., did not realize that his song would be the last Elvis single to climb the charts during Elvis's lifetime.

"I grew up loving Elvis," Martine recalls. "I taped myself singing 'Heartbreak Hotel' as a kid. I actually lived for the guy. I even brought his albums to my seventh- and eigth-grade music classes. I thought he was the coolest man who ever lived."

In the early 1970s, soon after he had arrived in Nashville seeking fame and fortune as a songwriter, Martine began to send songs to Elvis's producer. He was rejected time and time again. But Martine knew that Elvis was now focusing strictly on country music—the same genre in which the tunesmith was writing—so he continued to pitch his songs to Elvis's people. In truth, his goal was not so much to get an Elvis cut as it was to simply get his idol to listen to one of his tunes. That was his simple prayer.

"One day I was out on the street and ran into Bob Beckham," Martine explains. "Bob asked me if I had anything for Elvis. Elvis's producer, Felton Jarvis, was going to pick up some stuff from Bob that day. I had four songs I wanted to pitch, but Elvis liked to listen to demos on a disk. All of mine were on tape, and I didn't have the money to pay to get all four put on two different demo records. So I was going to have to choose which ones I thought had the best chance to be cut and go with those two."

The fact that Elvis didn't like to deal with cassette tapes put Martine between a rock and a hard place. He didn't know which way to turn. He thought that all four of his songs had potential, but which was right for Elvis? The songwriter decided to get some input from his publisher, the gifted Ray Stevens.

Stevens, one of the industry's most talented musicians, performers, producers, and songwriters, had given Martine his first break, and had even set him up with an office. The fact that the office was actually a closet didn't bother the hungry writer at all. He would have written outside on the porch in the dead of winter as long as Stevens continued to believe in his talent. Martine raced into the producer's office, only to discover that his boss was not there. With only a couple of hours to get two of the four cuts pressed into a demo record, Martine didn't have time to wait for Stevens. The song scribe asked Shirley Welch, Stevens's secretary, which of the quartet of songs had the best chance to impress Elvis.

"I asked her, 'Which do you think, Shirley?'" Martine recalls. "She didn't hesitate; she told me 'Rub It In' and 'Way Down.'"

"Rub It In" was a song that was built around old rock 'n' roll sounds. Martine figured that it might remind Jarvis and Elvis of the Otis Blackwell hits from the 1950s. But the writer couldn't really see a middle-aged Elvis cutting anything that sounded this silly. Ultimately, Elvis would pass on the number, but Billy "Crash" Craddock would later land a #1 on the country charts with the tune.

"Way Down" was a much different song. It was not really country or rock. It wasn't a true ballad or an up-tempo classic, either. In some ways, it was a gimmick number—Martine had written the tune with a bass tag line that literally dropped off the scale at the end of each verse. But "Way Down" was also a song about the power of passion, and it had a melody that varied in tempo. The song was part blues, part R&B, and a little bit contemporary country, and the songwriter thought that it might appeal to Elvis.

"I wrote it in the closet at the office," Martine laughs. "I would just think of things, lines and stuff, and write them down. I was just trying to write as much as I could in those days. The song came from one of the lines I scratched on the paper and grew from that. I knew I had something when Ray liked it too.

"Ray sang the bass lines on the demo. He did a great job. When we cut it, Ray's voice lit up the room. I think his part was one of the things that made the song so very special. Ray also brought in some of the best studio musicians in town to work the session. It was great. When we finished, I fell in love with the song and decided I was going to take it to the best people I knew. Now, with Felton looking for material, I had a chance to get it to a man I had always dreamed of having record my stuff. I was both excited and nervous. After all, in my mind Elvis always had been the best."

Taking the last bit of money he had in his pocket—funds he had been saving to spend on lunch—Martine hurried to get a demo record pressed from his tape. Once he got a copy, he rushed back to Beckham's office and dropped it off. Then came weeks of waiting.

"Felton called Ray," Martine remembers. "I was not in the office. Felton told Ray that he thought Elvis would really like 'Way Down.' That was in the early fall. By January 1977 I had still not heard anything."

Martine all but gave up on "Way Down." In fact, the song-writer heard that Elvis was again looking for songs for his next ses-sion, and Martine was working on new material to submit. It was Ray Stevens who checked back with Felton Jarvis on the status of Martine's original demo. What Ray found out shocked Martine. Elvis had not only liked the song, he had recorded it in October.

"I completely lost it when I found out," the songwriter explains. "I would have been satisfied if I had found that Elvis had just heard the song, but to have recorded it—wow!"

As the struggling songwriter dealt with his emotional high, Ray Stevens must have been laughing. Martine's mentor had to have known that "Way Down" was perfect for Elvis for a number of different reasons. For starters, it had very catchy lyrics. Ever since the beginning of his career, Elvis had liked this facet of songs. "Way Down" also had a challenging melody and an ever-changing rhythm, which would allow Elvis to exhibit his great vocal range and song styling abilities. But the song's most important hook was that it allowed the King to show off the vocal work of his own mentor and hero, J. D. Sumner.

Sumner was singing in Memphis back when Elvis was a truck driver there, and it was Sumner who had encouraged the young man to go into gospel music and join a quartet. He had even been there when Elvis auditioned for a spot in a local group. Over the years the two men had stayed in touch, and Elvis almost always attended the National Quartet Convention to watch Sumner and the Blackwood Brothers Quartet, as well as all the other great gospel acts of the era. On many occasions, scores of these performers would come back to Graceland for all-night gospel singings. But, even in a room full of legends, it was usually Sumner who found the spotlight. After all, the man had the lowest human voice ever recorded. He could literally drop his bass notes an octave below the lowest key on the piano. "Way Down" would give him a chance to do just that. Naturally, Elvis would want to share the spotlight with his buddy.

It was very difficult to get Elvis out of Graceland when he was not on tour. By this time he had all but withdrawn from the real world. Rather than force the singer to leave his home, RCA Victor had brought the studio to him. For the October 29, 1969, session that captured "Way Down," Elvis's den was transformed into a recording studio. There were microphones, mixing boards, amplifiers, pieces of recording equipment, and musical instruments everywhere. Fitting in wherever they could find a place was the band, which was made up of James Burton, John Wilkinson, Chip Young, Charlie Hodge, Jerry Scheff, Ronnie Tutt, Tony Brown, and David Briggs. Sitting or standing around wherever they could locate a spot and a microphone were vocalists Myra Smith, Kathy Westmoreland, Sherrill Nielsen, and of course, J. D. Sumner and the Stamps Quartet. It was a crowded affair, but no one seemed to mind. As was the custom at Graceland, the session began late at night and ran until dawn.

From the beginning, the sound this group produced on "Way Down" was simply incredible. The song fell into place on the first take. This was a driving rocker, but the pace was easy. Elvis didn't try to be smooth; instead, he pushed his vocals to a raw edge. Sumner's voice, falling an octave below the line Stevens had sung on the demo, brought both laughter and applause. Elvis's grin when the bass singer bottomed out at the end of the number was said to have been huge. After the second take, Elvis thought their recording of "Way Down" was perfect, and the group moved on to other numbers.

During the winter, RCA Nashville began to work on some overdubbing that was needed to complete "Way Down." While they were finishing up the single, the studio executives called Martine and asked if he wanted to hear what Elvis had done with his song.

"The day I went to RCA was dizzying," Martine recalls. "I can't begin to explain to you how it made me feel or what it meant to me to hear Elvis's voice singing my song."

RCA Victor opted to release "Way Down" in the middle of the summer. It was shipped to country, pop, and rock radio outlets on July 6. The flip side of the single was a cover of the old Johnny Ace R&B classic "Pledging My Love."

"Way Down" started strong on the country markets, and it earned an immediate bullet. Fans so loved Sumner's bass work that the single was in heavy rotation by the third week of July. Bouncing into the country Top 10 in early August, "Way Down" then began to make some waves on the rock side. On the British pop charts, it was racing toward the top of the pop list. The numbers on "Way Down" were so strong that Elvis was looking forward to featuring J. D. Sumner and the new hit during his upcoming August and September tour dates. He knew that, with Sumner providing the song's final bass line, it would be a phenomenal live number.

On August 16, 1977, just as *Billboard* magazine released its chart numbers for the week, Elvis Presley died of a heart attack at Graceland. Contributing factors in his death were his excess weight and his heavy use of prescription drugs. Elvis had passed away just as his "Way Down" hit the top of the country charts and was nearing the top spot in England.

"Way Down" ruled the country list for only a week, and it peaked at #18 on the rock charts. The song lost its footing in the charts not because it fell out of favor with fans, but because stations across the country pulled the new single in order to play Elvis's classic hits instead. Suddenly everyone wanted to hear "Hound Dog," "All Shook Up," "It's Now or Never," and "Don't Be Cruel" again. In England, however, "Way Down" held the #1 spot for five weeks, and it became one of the most successful Elvis cuts ever released in the United Kingdom. Unlike the Americans, the Brits seemed to want to hear both the new and the old Elvis material.

Colonel Tom Parker was in Maine preparing for Elvis's next tour when word came to him that his singer had died. Before he flew back to Memphis, the manager met with RCA Victor executives. Over the next two days, Parker burned up the phone lines. He realized that there would now be a rush on all things Elvis, so the manager made sure that RCA Victor had all of its plants available to press Elvis records twenty-four hours a day. He also issued a number of new licenses for Elvis products. Elvis might have been dead, but, thanks to Parker the *business* of Elvis was kicking into high gear, with new merchandise appearing on shelves even before the funeral.

One of the people who was most shocked to hear of Elvis's death was Layng Martine Jr. At the time it did not occur to him that having the last #1 issued during Elvis's lifetime would mean so much to the writer or his career. Scores of other song scribes would have given everything they had to trade places with Martine. But on August 16, the only thing the songwriter felt was a real sense of sadness. Martine, like millions of people around the world, felt as though he had lost a friend.

"I felt so incredibly lucky when I found out that Elvis had cut 'Way Down,'" the writer explains, some twenty-seven years later. "I still feel the same way, maybe even more so today. I can never thank Bob Beckham enough. And I still tell Ray Stevens thank you at least once a year for believing in me and that song. It was a dream come true for me."

On the day that Elvis died, another struggling songwriter, R. C. Bannon, was inside a Kroger grocery store, buying a steak to celebrate some very good news. That morning he had been told that the King of Rock 'n' Roll was going to record one of his songs, and that it would be released as Elvis's next RCA Victor single. As a result, Bannon knew that his career was about to take off. The royalties he'd earn from record sales and publishing would pull him out of poverty. Once Elvis recorded his song, he'd be on the map as a songwriter. As Bannon checked out of the grocery store, the lady at the cash register looked up and said, sadly, "It's too bad about Elvis, isn't it?"

"What do you mean?" Bannon inquired.

"He died today," came her reply.

"He can't die," Bannon whispered. "He hasn't cut my song yet."

It would take R. C. Bannon a few more years to land a big hit with another artist. The songwriter never again tried to sell the number he had penned just for Elvis. The song that could have been Elvis's last record has now been buried just as long as Elvis. Instead of Bannon, it was Martine who penned Elvis's final call.

GUITAR MAN

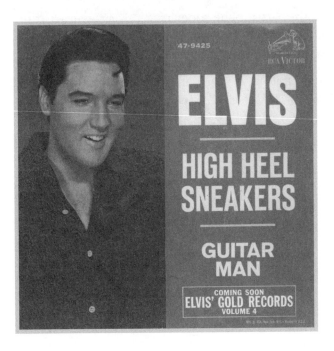

Beginning with "My Way" in late 1977, RCA continued to release Elvis Presley singles to country music and pop outlets after the King's death. Over the next three years "Unchained Melody," "Are You Sincere," and "There's a Honky Tonk Angel (Who Will Take Me Back In)" found their way onto the country chart and into the list's Top 10. But by 1980 it appeared that the label had either run out of new Elvis material or that it had quit plugging what once had been RCA Victor's premier act. In reality, the record label had not given up. At that time, Felton Jarvis was busy trying to find a recording with hit potential in the company's vaults. The Elvis pickings were now very slim.

Over the last seventeen years of Elvis's life, RCA Victor had pretty much released Elvis records as they were cut. If they didn't come out as singles, they were placed on albums. There was nothing extra that had been simply filed away for future consideration. About all that was left in the vaults were alternate takes, unfinished tracks, and movie-soundtrack rejects. Though new albums could be pasted together using alternate takes and other second-rate material, then sold to rabid fans as "historically important" albums, the only unreleased songs that had any merit had been recorded during concerts. In many of these cases, the sound quality was simply not up to modern standards. Some of the recordings featured performances that contained mistakes, by either the band or Elvis. In addition, almost all of these numbers were covers of very well known hits that had been recorded by well-established artists. It must have been very frustrating for Jarvis to try to mine gold from this material. Yet there was a gem waiting to be rediscovered and reworked.

The same year that Elvis recorded his famed comeback special on NBC, the singer had come in contact with a song that intrigued him. Elvis was fascinated not just by the lyrics and the tune, but also by the performer's carefree vocal style and unique guitar work. Though few heard it when it was first released in 1967, "Guitar Man" had been thirty-year-old Jerry Reed's first charting single for RCA Victor. The tune stayed in the Top 100 on *Billboard's* country charts for nine weeks, but it never climbed higher than #53. It would be Reed's next single, "Tupelo Mississippi Flash," (which was something of an ode to the King) that did find airplay, and that song would crawl into the Top 20.

Though he was only entering his third decade of life, Reed had been a professional musician for almost fifteen years by the time

"Flash" hit the charts. Having been signed to a record and pub-lishing deal as a teen, Reed had penned the Brenda Lee bestseller "That's All You Got to Do," and scored with Richie Valens and "Crazy Legs." In 1962, after Reed had spent two years in the serv-ice, Porter Wagoner took one of Reed's songs, "Misery Loves Com-pany," to the #1 spot on the country charts. After the demise of his original recording gig with Capitol, Reed made his living penning songs and working sessions as a picker. For the most part, his live performances were limited to local clubs.

Chet Atkins was one of the first in Music City to fully grasp Reed's incredible talent. The man known as "Mr. Guitar" signed Reed to RCA in 1965. While using him for session work, Atkins also tried to groom Reed into a star. The first indication that Jerry Reed might have what it takes was his recording of "Guitar Man."

"Guitar Man" was really little more than Jerry's autobiography in song. The lyrics told the story of a young man coming up through years of one-night stands and false starts to finally become an "overnight" sensation and headline in a top club. The song's sub-ject's claim to fame was the way he picked his guitar. The single, which was produced by Atkins, allowed Reed to show off his play-ing as much as his singing. In format, tone, and style, "Guitar Man" was a snapshot of things that would follow when Reed would take the music world by storm, writing and recording "Amos Moses," "When You're Hot You're Hot" and "East Bound and Down."

Elvis was deeply impressed with Reed and his music—so much so that he asked for some of the young man's demos. Elvis found one he liked in late 1967. A few months later RCA Victor released Elvis's version of Reed's "U.S. Male." "U.S. Male" was more than a song; it played like a Mark Twain tale set to music. The song fooled around with the various meanings of its lyrics, used humor to deliver its message, had a bit of talking on each of the verses, and featured a guitar-driven accompaniment so distinctive that every session player in Music City knew it was Reed's work. Elvis's recording of the song made it to #28 on the pop charts during the months leading up to the airing of the "1968 Comeback Special." Had the song been released after the top-rated TV program had aired and Elvis fever had fully resurfaced, it probably would have gone much higher.

"U.S. Male" did not make the NBC program, but "Guitar Man" was featured throughout the television special's main production number. The only real difference between this version and Reed's original cut was that Elvis was now singing the lead, and a set of special lyrics had been added for the production number's big closing. It was a catchy tune that seemed to have "hit" written all over it, and Elvis sang the number with energy. His voice again sounded vital and strong. But the arrangement, which almost duplicated that of Reed's recording, was probably too country and not enough rock 'n' roll.

RCA Victor had Elvis cut "Guitar Man" from the special's soundtrack album. The label also released the song on the B side of a throwaway movie tune, "High Heel Sneakers." As the single did not make any of the major American charts, few heard "Guitar Man" then. The number would remain largely forgotten until Felton Jarvis discovered it while searching for new Elvis material.

Because he was one of the most powerful forces at RCA Nashville, Jarvis knew all the label's acts very well. He was well aware of "Guitar Man," its writer, and its history. But Jarvis believed that few outside the music business would realize that the song was its writer's life story. The producer knew that, if they heard Elvis sing the song, people would probably think that he was referring to his own experiences. In fact, during the 1950s many critics had labeled Elvis "just another guitar man." While the number seemed perfect for rerelease, however, there were problems.

The "Guitar Man" tracks the producer uncovered in the vault sounded dated. They also did not have the drive and energy needed to gain airplay on 1980s radio. Jarvis also thought that the arrangement was uninspired. Still, rather than give up on the number's potential, the producer took the master recordings from the original sessions and headed back to the studios.

After much study, Jarvis ultimately decided he liked just one thing about Elvis's original cut of "Guitar Man," and that was the lead vocal work. In the producer's view, nothing else measured up to Elvis's performance. None of the other facets of the record had the singer's energy or enthusiasm. Rather than try to massage it by tweaking levels in different ways or overdubbing, Felton stripped the recording clean of everything but Elvis's voice. Then he called Jerry Reed.

Reed had matured into a huge star by 1980. He and Atkins had released a series of critically acclaimed guitar duet albums, and the singer had charted more than forty records on country music playlist, scored two #1 hits, and was a recognized character actor in major motion pictures. Nevertheless, Reed, who still felt indebted to Elvis, was more than happy to come into the studio and lay down some hot licks for an updated version of "Guitar Man."

Jerry's new studio work matched all the energy and drive that could be heard in Elvis's voice. Using his incredible timing and dynamic skill on the strings, Reed brought life to the fabric of the song in a way that made it seem fresh and new. It was a perfect meshing of vocal work and instrumental performance. As Jarvis listened to the final take, the producer found it hard to believe that almost fifteen years separated the original session and this one. Judging by the recording, anyone would think that Reed and Elvis had been in the studio together on this day late in 1980. Using other Nashville session players, Jarvis finished what he believed to be a perfect single. He put the project to bed just before the Christmas holidays. A few days later the producer suffered a stroke. He died on January 3. Felton Jarvis never heard his final production played on the radio.

RCA Victor pushed on with the project, and shipped the reworked "Guitar Man" to radio stations in mid-January. The label hoped the single would earn enough airplay to sell its latest Elvis LP release, which was also titled *Guitar Man*. As it turned out, it would accomplish much more than that.

"Guitar Man" hit the Top 40 on country playlists in February and raced up the charts as no Elvis record had done since "Way Down." Jarvis had been right. Few fans had heard this old cut in its original form, and millions seemed to believe that it was a new Elvis record. And it sounded fresh and new; because of reworking the arrangement and the new production techniques that had been employed in putting the recording together, the single sounded like it had just been cut. Requests for the song poured into stations from coast to coast. Country music was exploding in popularity—and riding the crest of its wave was the late King of Rock 'n' Roll.

On March 14, Elvis Presley earned his eleventh #1 record in country music. The single also surprised the pop world by hitting #28 on the rock charts. For a man who had been dead almost four years, this was a remarkable comeback.

It seemed appropriate that Felton Jarvis found a way to bring Elvis back to the top of the same playlist where the singer had earned his initial hit. Elvis had scored his first #1 hit on the country charts in January 1955 by knocking Red Sovine and Webb Pierce's duet "Why, Baby, Why" from the top of the chart. That Elvis cut was called "I Forgot to Remember to Forget." Twenty-six years and three months later, "Guitar Man" shoved the Bellamy Brothers' "Do You Love As Good As You Look" from the peak of the country-hit mountain and put Elvis back on top one more time.

Elvis Presley first found acceptance and success in country music, and this #1 hit seemed a fitting way to close out a remarkable recording career. In reality, however, the story was not over. Almost two decades after "Guitar Man" hit #1, another producer would use the Jarvis formula to bring Elvis back to the top of pop charts all over the world.

A LITTLE LESS CONVERSATION

O f all the stories of Elvis Presley's #1 hit records, the tale of "A Little Less Conversation" is beyond a doubt the strangest. This number's history, from its rejection by America's greatest soul singer to its inclusion in one of the worst of the Elvis films to its becoming the soundtrack for a shoe-company commercial in Europe to its sudden rise as a monster cult hit in 2002, has taken so many different turns that even its writer finds its pedigree, and its recent success, bizarre. But "A Little Less Conversation"—a single that was so overlooked during its initial release that it failed to crack either the American or the British Top 40— introduced Elvis to new generations of fans who had never heard "Hound Dog" or "Can't Help Falling in Love."

In 1968 Billy Strange had been chosen to find music for what would be one of Elvis's last Hollywood motion picture. *Live A Little, Love A Little* contained less substance than even *Clambake* or *Tickle Me*. After reviewing the plot, Strange called budding song scribe Mac Davis.

"Elvis scripts were written with 'Elvis does this and this and this,' then there was a note that said something like 'Elvis sings,'" Mac recalls. "There was one scene where the script called for a song as Elvis was leaving a swimming pool. That is the spot I filled with 'A Little Less Conversation.'"

Most songwriters would have drawn a complete blank when considering the swimming pool scene, in which Elvis's character tries to get a beautiful girl to leave the pool with him. But Davis had just the song concept for the moment. In fact, he had already penned the song.

"I had already written 'A Little Less Conversation,'" the songwriter explains, "hoping that Aretha Franklin would hear it and want to record it. I thought it fit in so well with what she was doing at the time."

In retrospect, Davis was right. The message in "A Little Less Conversation" is a great deal like the themes of Franklin's then-current hits "Respect" and "Think." It is easy to imagine the soul singer's dynamic voice wrapping itself around the lyrics of "A Little Less Conversation." It is also easy to see how Mac imagined such a number while thinking of the great soul singer. But with Franklin showing no interest in the song, Davis passed it on to Billy Strange to consider for the Elvis flick. The movie was forgettable then, and even fewer folks remember it today. But *Live a Little, Love a Little* did open the door for Davis to compose more material for Elvis, as well as to become an important contributor in scoring the production numbers for the famed "1968 Comeback Special."

RCA Victor released a single from each of Elvis's movies in order to sell the movie's soundtrack album. *Live a Little, Love a Little* was no exception. In the fall of 1968, "A Little Less Conversation" was released as the B side of "Almost in Love." The record was not right for the times. Elvis's work was solid, and his vocal was driven and filled with energy, but the song simply did not fit onto the playlists of the time, which embraced hard rock standards. The A side peaked at #98. A few stations flipped the record, and "A Little Less Conversation" managed to make a four-week run on the charts before topping out at #69. *Live A Little, Love A Little* was a box-office disaster, but Davis's song did have at least a short stint in a rather dim spotlight.

Later, Elvis would record the Davis-penned "Memories," "In the Ghetto," and "Don't Cry, Daddy," paving the way for Davis's success as a songwriter, performer, television personality, and actor. In that light, "A Little Less Conversation" deserves credit as having brought one of entertainment's great talents into the spotlight. One of the most bizarre aspects of "A Little Less Conversation" was that it was recorded a second time by Elvis. Much thought was given to using the tune in the "1968 Comeback Special." In a June 23 session used to record music for the special's production segments, another version of the Mac Davis composition was put on tape. This version was included on the special's soundtrack album, but nothing else was done with it. It was not used on the special itself. It was almost as if it had never existed.

For the next thirty-four years "A Little Less Conversation" saw no action at all. No oldies stations programmed it; it was not covered by other artists; and it was never discussed in retrospectives of Elvis Presley. Then a shoe company decided that to "just do it" right for a World Cup soccer television promotional ad blitz, it needed a special song to go with its televised spots. Someone at Nike uncovered "A Little Less Conversation" and thought that the song's call for "less talk and more action" was perfect for a sports campaign. Nike contacted RCA/BMG and Elvis Presley Enterprises and shared its desire to use the old song. The two companies that controlled Elvis's musical empire struck a deal with Nike, and the alternate version of "A Little Less Conversation" was pulled from the vault containing the master recording of the "1968 Comeback Special."

Nike loved Davis's lyrics and Elvis's vocal work, but it felt that the original arrangement was too dated and not exciting enough for the techno age. A producer from Holland was contracted to bring the number up-to-date.

Tom Holkenburg was born the year before Elvis recorded "A Little Less Conversation." Growing up in the Netherlands, Tom mastered piano, drums, and bass as a child, and as a teen he joined *Weekend at Waikiki* as a musician and producer. After splitting from Waikiki, Holkenburg formed the industrial rock band Nerve and performed alongside vocalist Phill Mills. Striking out on his own in 1995, Tom became one of Europe's hottest producers, and he worked with rock bands, video game companies, motion picture studios, and television commercial outlets. Everyone seemed to want his services. Holkenburg became such a workaholic that he burned out in his mid-twenties. At the age of twenty-seven, a serious heart condition brought on by stress almost killed him.

After he regained his health, Holkenburg reinvented himself as Junkie XL. The "XL" stood for "expanding the limits" of his talents and musical influence. Describing himself as a "master alchemist, electronic daredevil, and breaker of sound barriers," JXL (as he was now billed) toured both Europe and America with some of the hottest groups in rock music. By 2000 he had helped to create some of the most exciting recordings in the pop field.

As an ad producer, Holkenburg constantly worked with a wide variety of companies, including Nike in Europe. So when the shoe giant brought Elvis's "A Little Less Conversation" to Holkenburg to rework into a vehicle to promote the World Cup, it had no doubt that the producer would deliver solid results. But even Nike could not have predicted what the JXL mix would mean to the campaign—and to the song.

Using his own techno ideas and musicians, Holkenburg reinvented the Mac Davis number. Basing all the updates around the original vocals and accompaniment, Tom stirred it all up into a mix that sounded unlike anything normally played on American radio. In a true techno style, Holkenburg did all the final production work using an Apple Macintosh G4 computer. The resulting sound and mix was truly incredible.

In the spring of 2002 the Nike ad that featured "A Little Less Conversation" began to air on television all across Europe. The music used on the spots was so popular that thousands called radio and TV stations and asked to "hear the ad again." Many wanted to know where they could purchase the CD as well. RCA/BMG had not planned on putting together a single of the JXL remix. But as demand for replays of the ad came in, plans were quickly put into motion for a new Elvis cut. In June 2002 the label shipped three versions of "A Little Less Conversation" on a CD single. One was a three-minute, thirty-second recording that was geared for radio play. The second was a six-minute, seven-second version for use in special promotions or as a dance track. The third was the one-minute, thirty-nine-second 1968 original. The CDs immediately flew off the shelves in England and across Europe; RCA/BMG simply could not keep up with demand for the product. In the Americas, the Middle East, Asia, and Africa, radio stations began playing the new version even before the label could print enough to ship the CD to those areas.

"A Little Less Conversation" first topped the singles airplay and sales charts in Britain. This marked Elvis's eighteenth #1 U.K. single, breaking a tie with the Beatles and making Elvis the most successful recording artist ever to release music in England. By the end of the summer, "A Little Less Conversation" had topped the charts in more than thirty other countries, including the United States. No Elvis single had ever before been so universally received.

Elvis's label had a problem on its hands. "A Little Less Conversation" needed to be on an album, but there was no time to produce a special project and get it shipped while demand was still peaking for the single. At the time, RCA/BMG was set to release an album titled *Elvis's 30 #1 Hits*. Without bothering to change the title or the artwork, the company tacked on the new #1 hit to the CD. Today, both the album and "A Little Less Conversation" have gone multi-platinum. In addition, the single has resurfaced in several major Hollywood films, in the music of a host of different commercials, and as the theme for the television show *Las Vegas*.

Asked about "A Little Less Conversation," Mac Davis laughs, "It was a lucky fluke." But, thanks to the JXL arrangement, the real power of Davis's lyrics and Elvis's vocal was revealed for the very first time. It turned out that the song's potential was always there; it just took a new perspective to bring it out.

Will this song be the last Elvis #1 hit, or are there other hidden gems waiting to be uncovered and polished for a new world? Only time will answer this question, but one thing seems certain: as was proved by "A Little Less Conversation," the King may be dead, but his music, and his influence, live on.

Index

"When You're Hot You're Hot," 248

"Where Do You Come From," 195

"Where Have All the Average People Gone," 226

"Where the Blue of the Night Meets the Gold of the Day," 164

White, Barry, 139

"White Christmas," 44, 95

"Why, Baby, Why," 8, 252

Wilburn Brothers, the, 14

Wilburn, Doyle, 14

Wilburn, Teddy, 14

Wild in the Country (movie), 175, 177

Wilkinson, John, 223, 228, 234, 241

Williams, Claiborne, 124

Williams, Hank, 6–7, 133, 157

Williams, Maurice, 166

Willis, Chuck, 192

Wills, Bob, 192, 199

Winterhalter, Hugo, 96

Wise, Fred, 118

"Witch Doctor," 112

"Witchcraft," 154

Witherspoon, Jimmy, 28

Wizard of Oz, The (movie), 44

"Wonder of You, The," 219–224

Wonder, Stevie, 193

Wood, Bobby, 209, 215

"Wooly Bully," 201

Wyche, Sid, 142–143, 145–146, 229

Wynette, Tammy, 235

"Yakety Yak," 105

"You Don't Have to Say You Love Me," 225

"You Send Me," 92

"You'll Think of Me," 217

"Young and Beautiful," 91

"Young Blood," 170

Young, Chip, 234, 241

"Young Dreams," 119

"Young Love," 66

Young, Reggie, 209, 215

Young, Vicki, 71

"(You're the) Devil in Disguise," 196

Zambon, Francis. *See* Mark James